W9-BCL-201

No Innocent Deposits

Forming Archives by Rethinking Appraisal

Richard J. Cox

The Scarecrow Press, Inc.
Lanham, Maryland, and Oxford
2004

SCARECROW PRESS, INC.

Published in the United States of America
by Scarecrow Press, Inc.
A wholly owned subsidiary of
The Rowman & Littlefield Publishing Group, Inc.
4501 Forbes Boulevard, Suite 200, Lanham, Maryland 20706
www.scarecrowpress.com

PO Box 317
Oxford
OX2 9RU, UK

Copyright © 2004 by Richard J. Cox

All rights reserved. No part of this publication may be reproduced,
stored in a retrieval system, or transmitted in any form or by any
means, electronic, mechanical, photocopying, recording, or otherwise,
without the prior permission of the publisher.

British Library Cataloguing in Publication Information Available

Library of Congress Cataloging-in-Publication Data

Cox, Richard J.
  No innocent deposits : forming archives by rethinking appraisal /
Richard J. Cox.
    p.   cm.
  Includes bibliographical references and index.
  ISBN 0–8108–4896–1 (alk. paper)
    1. Appraisal of archival materials.   I. Title.
CD973.A77 C69 2004
025.2'1—dc22   2003015231

Manufactured in the United States of America.

*For all of my students
who have participated since 1989
in my course on archival appraisal;
they will recognize
what they have contributed.*

Contents

Acknowledgments

These reflections on the daunting task of archival appraisal undoubtedly will produce different reactions from different archivists, users of archives, and others just seeking to gain an understanding of archives. My thoughts about appraisal have been influenced, to varying degrees, by discussions with many colleagues, some of whom I have known a long time and others I have met much more recently. Whatever value these chapters might have is due to my discussions (sometimes arguments) with individuals like Nicholson Baker, Jeannette Bastian, Frank Boles, Terry Cook, Barbara Craig, Bruce Dearstyne, Luciana Duranti, Terry Eastwood, Tim Ericson, Mark Greene, Elisabeth Kaplan, Kate Manning, Tom Nesmith, Jim O'Toole, Helen Samuels, Joan Schwartz, Patricia Sleeman, David Wallace, and Beth Yakel (and many others I am forgetting).

1

Introduction: Treasures Everywhere

TRASH AND TREASURES

Much has been written about America as a "throwaway society." We do not need to read to confirm that we regularly toss away immense quantities of unwanted materials. The weekly trash day suggests that we are still tossing out lots of stuff, amazing quantities of discarded and spoiled food remains, paper and plastic products, and old containers of every shape and former purpose. Where I live, we recycle every two weeks, and the bright blue plastic or paper bags holding metal, plastic, and old newspapers pile up like modernistic sculptures in a trendy art boutique. Bulk trash day is even more dramatic, leading to scenes that suggest the aftermath of a tornado striking a department store. I note that we have four chairs in various places in our home retrieved from the curbside on those mornings. My next-door neighbor wanders through the neighborhood on these days, and her front porch is a perennial storage site for furniture, art, ceramics, old signs, architectural elements, and other objects that she has rescued from the street. On those bulk pickup mornings, you can also see secondhand and antique store owners prowling about, looking for materials they can recycle, for a price, to individuals who decline the adventures of the curbside hunts.

Those who are especially concerned about the environment, public health, and the economy emphasize the paradoxes of the wealthiest nation on earth and its wasteful use of natural and other resources. Millions of Americans are members of organizations lobbying for us to clean up our act and for the government to pass stricter or fairer laws supporting everything from recycling to renewal of basic resources. We are constantly reminded of the need to rethink what we use and what we throw away. Teeming landfills, toxic wastes, polluted water supplies, and other such challenges have not disappeared as we have moved from a reliance on heavy industry to the promises (or dreams) of the lighter manufacturing of an information or service economy.

Yet, as with everything in a culture, there is a counterpoint. It also would be easy to characterize us as the "save it all culture." Noted American historian Michael Kammen wrote a book about the paradoxes of American life, and I guess we have here just one more of those seeming contradictions. Kammen's observations plunge right into the heart of what I am reflecting on here. He notes that we have tended to focus scholarship and other scrutiny on "politics and public institutions," an emphasis that, because of a "certain underlying consistency to the ways men compete for power and distribute it," forces us to ignore some of the contradictions of our society. Kammen urges us to look elsewhere:

> If, on the other hand, we think about the uses and abuses of human energies in America—what we create and what we destroy—our emphasis may alter. For we have shifted from being a conquest culture to being a consumer culture, from a culture of exploitation to a culture of exhibition, from a culture of self-sufficiency to a culture of self-indulgence, from a culture that would maximize its labor to one that would maximize its leisure, from provincial powerlessness to paralyzed omnipotence.[1]

We can see some of what Kammen is ruminating on right under our very noses.

We are not merely dumping; rather, as if at an archaeological dig, we are sifting through the debris as we go. While we clean out our garages and basements, we market these items in yard sales or replace them with new purchases made at flea markets and second-hand shops. Recycled architectural remnants have become a big business, and those nineteenth-century cornices or art deco tiles that once could be plucked from the garbage now bring trendy prices at antique galleries. In my house, you can find old tin ceiling tiles, wrought iron remnants, recycled tile, old windows, and old window pediments. Glance out my dining room window into my backyard, and you find more architectural elements, tile, and antique garden items. While we have always reused building materials (on one excavation, we found an early nineteenth century house that had reused bricks from a structure of an earlier century, and *that* structure had used bricks salvaged from the seventeenth century), now it is both big business and fashionable. The local bookstore is filled with books heralding garden junk, shabby chic, and the flea market look. Old and rusty is good, while new and shiny seems passé.

While many wring their hands over our tendencies to toss out home appliances, to give up on automobiles after a couple of years, and to purchase disposable eating utensils and dinnerware, we are also busily filling our homes with old stuff. Thousands of transactions occur daily on the online auction house eBay. We watch the *Antiques Roadshow* in rapt attention, perhaps hoping that a hidden treasure will appear that is also sitting on a shelf in our own living room. The Bombay Company, Pottery Barn, and other chain stores market furniture, bric-a-brac, and other items that look like the desired collectibles. Even the guru of American merchandizing, Martha Stewart, is selling pottery, kitchenware, dinnerware, and linens that are reproductions of items that have become pricier or harder to find. If you can't find the desired old stuff in a flea market or antique store, you can probably find a reasonable substitute in the mall or a discount store like T. J. Maxx or Marshall's. Although the present ease of finding old materials with decorative possibilities or reasonable reproductions of them might diminish the thrill of the hunt for some or lessen the sense of possessing unique stuff, the growing business catering to such interests is evidence of a need for us to connect with the past or to comment on the sterility of the present.

The past is both ever present and important to us inhabitants of the twenty-first century. Most of us fill our houses with old photographs of family members as a means of connecting ourselves to the stream of time that has moved before us. If we lack such reminders of our own lineage, we may buy old photographs of someone else's family and frame and mount them on the wall. This is a kind of visual genealogy, and genealogical research has long since moved from being a process whereby we prove our right to join a social elite to a function intended to place ourselves both within the present and past, to give us meaning, to sketch out a context for who we are and what we represent. Historians and social commentators have debated in recent years just how we Americans feel about the past. Although some have argued that most of us know far too little about it, others have seen our penchant for collecting and museum going, our taste for historical documentaries and docudramas, our appetite for historical best sellers (fiction and nonfiction), and our pursuit of genealogy, among other activities, as examples of our vital relationship with the past.[2] Indeed, even these debates about how we relate to the past are indicators that we cannot function without some understanding of history. And more to the point, testing ourselves about who the fifth president was or the years the Civil War started and ended is a very different matter from having a sense that the past is important to our present. The nuances between public memory, historical knowledge, and mythology are real and substantial, but the crucial connection might be that *all* attest to a modern feel for the past.

MUSEUMS, LIBRARIES, AND ARCHIVES
AND TREASURE HUNTS

There are some basic challenges to that understanding, however, that extend beyond the connection with the past and its meaning to citizens in the modern world. The public seems to believe that museums, libraries, and archives save *everything* because everything has value for understanding the past. All that stuff at yard sales and flea markets is more than junk. It makes us feel good about ourselves, it places us into a larger existence than the mere present, and that stuff has often been the nucleus of collections that wind up at cultural institutions. But these cultural institutions can't save everything; in fact, their professional staffs can't even examine all the candidates for their collections. Recent studies of the financial and managerial troubles of the New-York Historical Society and the Historical Society of Pennsylvania[3] have pinpointed the source of their troubles as being the propensities of these pioneering historical societies to acquire far beyond their financial means to care for historical manuscripts, rare books, decorative arts, prints, furniture, paintings, and other artifacts. For the founders of these historical societies, everything had value, and their successors discovered that it was both difficult to divest themselves of what they had and to stop collecting.

As it turns out, many of the troubles of such institutions stem from public perceptions about what they were doing or what they should be doing. In this regard, the Historical Society of Pennsylvania in Philadelphia is instructive. The theme of the history of the Historical Society of Pennsylvania (HSP) authored recently by Sally Griffith is that the Society possesses a public persona that suggests such organizations are affluent, acquire and preserve everything, and possess limitless space, funding, and staff resources, allowing them to do pretty much as they want. The reality is that these organizations are often strapped for cash and beset by other problems and, most importantly, that institutions like the HSP must make hard decisions about their mission and activities. Griffith notes that the Historical Society seemed to be "possessed" by its collections rather than "possessing" its various "treasures." She perceives a kind of "connoisseurship of relics" that makes it hard for the institution to divest itself of any of its holdings, no matter their relevance to the HSP or the means by which they were acquired, even though growing collections and proportionally declining financial resources threaten the care of the very holdings that have been so prized.[4] As Griffith describes the more contentious debates about the Society in the late twentieth century, she shows us that places like the HSP are seen as a link to the past, and any efforts to modify their methods can be viewed with suspicion. The HSP originally thought that "achieving the truth of the past seemed a fairly simple process of assembling and arranging its surviving relics."[5] But this point of view led to rampant collecting, especially of things far outside the scope of the HSP's mission, often not so much to avoid offending someone as because acquiring things was what the institution was about. Even as the HSP struggled to grapple with these problems in a careful and professional manner in the last decade, a public furor ensued. The HSP's main constituency was its scholarly researchers, but they were the least able to contribute to the solution of the Society's financial problems and generally the least willing to see the HSP make more dramatic changes or refocus its mission. In one of the book's most telling assessments, Griffith notes how Susan Stitt, HSP head in the 1990s and leader of its most profound changes, was really at odds with how the public saw the HSP:

Ironically, the professional training and experience that had given Stitt
a heightened sense of her obligation to the collection had not prepared
her to appreciate that for many ordinary Philadelphians the possession
of historical objects was a matter of emotion and identity, not simply
professional responsibility.[6]

The emotional connection to objects of the past, from documents
to books to artifacts from the decorative to the industrial, can be
powerful. We visit the National Archives rotunda to view the original documents even though we have the words in civics textbooks,
on the World Wide Web, and in other easily accessible places. We
travel to see Plymouth Rock ensconced under its neoclassical portico
even while we wonder how anyone could know that this is the very
rock the Pilgrims disembarked on (and, in fact, we know that this
particular rock was not identified until long after the English colonists first set foot on it). Still, we sense something special about even
a rock, and we draw on its symbolic attributes for an ever-changing
variety of political, commercial, and social purposes.[7] We long to
preserve a semblance of the genuine landscape of the battlefields of
the wars fought on our soil as a remembrance. We neatly stack large
segments of the Twin Towers of the destroyed World Trade Center
in New York City for "future exhibitions" and "memorials" (and so
soon after its destruction that it is impossible to distinguish between
educational and remembrance activities).[8] The passage of time
between a particular event and the present may enhance and transform our understanding of it, but many events remain in the public
consciousness and serve as links between past and present.
    There is a poignant dilemma in such thoughts. Most of our insti-
tutions charged with preserving the objects of our past—the documents, books, printed ephemera, furniture, architecture, decorative
arts, and mechanical implements—are sorely pressed to accomplish
this end. And it is not just because of financial and expertise
resources. There is simply too much stuff out there to deal with, and
the artifacts and documents are generally designed not to last forever. Once we get beyond the obstacle that a newspaper or poster
and many other things are created with short-term objectives by
their producers, no matter what other values we might assign to
them, it is clear that there are other challenges that are even more
daunting. The typical archives staff, for example, cannot hope to
examine all or even the majority of the physical documentation that

somehow falls within their repository's mandate. This was true before the advent of the computer. Now, we have billions of e-mails and other electronic records to deal with, ranging over organizational and personal life, with very different maintenance needs that burden even more our expertise and other resources. What was once a difficult job has become an impossible one.

We can go a bit further with this, pressing perhaps our best hope to save as much of everything as we can. While the challenge of even viewing a portion of our documentary universe is nigh impossible, there is the other matter that *not* everything needs to be preserved in our libraries, archives, and museums. Some argue that we must save things because we cannot anticipate their use in the future (or the use of any historical source, for that matter). This kind of argument has two basic flaws, however. First, it is often based on older survivals that we have seen used. Second, it fails to take into account the creativity with which scholars and other researchers utilize historical sources. It is just as easy to argue that modern researchers have far too much documentation to try to shift through and that they face a task in many ways more daunting than researchers working with the limited documentation of the ancient world. When the historical societies like those in New York and Philadelphia were founded, the quantity of historical sources was much more limited, and collecting proceeded in order to preserve what had already survived; the notion of collecting contemporary materials, except for freak shows and circuses or natural history and other scientific museums and institutes, is a rather recent phenomenon. That some of these repositories of curiosities eventually were absorbed or replaced by what became the modern museum is somewhat beside the point. The motives of the older collections, usually with commercial profits as the main objective, are much different from those of most modern museums, archives, and libraries.

The strategy two hundred years ago was to get these documents and artifacts into repositories so that they would be protected. The strategy today is to have documentary objectives that conceptually limit the universe of sources. To be captivated by curiosities, unique collectibles, and mysterious artifacts might be fun, but we need to be more calculating and realistic than this. The good archivist is as good a destroyer as a preserver. If we do not allow some materials to deteriorate by inaction in favor of those that need action because of their documentary values and evidence, we will run the risk of losing much that is valuable and necessary for understanding the past and placing ourselves in the present. Filling every nook and cranny of our public repositories with the debris of the ages might seem responsible and well-intentioned, but it swamps the researchers charged with sorting through it all, taxes the ability of the custodians to establish intellectual control, and seems to send a message that everything is worth saving or, even more extreme, *must* be saved.

PUBLIC UNDERSTANDING
OF ARCHIVAL APPRAISAL

The selection/destruction framework is not well understood by those outside our museums, libraries, and archives. Even more problematic, it is often vigorously debated *within* these institutions and their supporting professions. Recently in one of my class sessions in my course on archival appraisal, one of my students related a conversation with a historian friend of hers that captured one aspect of the problem. As they talked about the historian's research into a local archives, the historian expressed outrage that someone, especially an archivist, had selected the records residing in the archives. We might ask, with incredulity, just how the historian thought the historical records had been accumulated. We might also wonder why the historian would be surprised, and we could speculate what graduate training teaches about the use of historical records. Can one really be prepared to be a historian, becoming efficient in historical research methods, without understanding something about the nature of records, record-keeping systems, and the formation of archives? I wouldn't think so, but apparently a gap persists, both in the preparation of historians and in the mutual understanding between historians and archivists.

If historians, the primary scholarly users of archives, do not understand such matters, can we expect much more from the public? Nothing has driven home the misunderstanding better than novelist and essayist Nicholson Baker's crusade, best exemplified by his scathing denunciation of library and archives preservation in his highly publicized book *Double Fold: Libraries and the Assault on Paper*.[9] In this book, named after a librarians' test for paper brittleness, Baker laments how perfectly good books and newspapers have been destroyed in favor of microfilming and other reformatting means such as digitization. Baker makes a compelling argument, one that will have all the eBay and *Antiques Roadshow* fans nodding in agreement (or, perhaps, licking their chops with eager anticipation of getting their hands on the discarded originals). But he ignores the reality of what librarians and archivists face. He does not want to hear about the recent struggles of the Historical Society of Pennsylvania. Baker believes that libraries and archives are little more than inexpensive warehouses for storage, that librarians and archivists are little more than stock clerks, and that every object has value demanding that the original be saved. He ignores the improved access that the microfilming of newspapers bestows. Baker declines to discuss the other challenges that libraries and archives face as part of their mandate.

The problem with Baker's book might rest more with its reception than with what its author believes is going on in libraries and archives. *Double Fold* seemed to have hit a nerve. Positive review after positive review appeared in newspapers, literary journals, and e-journals. One reviewer, historian Robert Darnton, who criticized Baker's methodology and narrative style, still bought his arguments that librarians and archivists are somehow implicated in a grand conspiracy and violation of a public trust.[10] Darnton's stand may reflect historians' reluctance to accept that others, that is, nonhistorians, might be determining what goes into archives. If professional scholars responsible for interpreting historical evidence have problems with this dilemma, what can we expect of the lay public? Baker, historians, and other parties to the arguments made in *Double Fold* could best turn their focus to the plight of libraries and archives: supporting basic operations that actually threaten their holdings because of modest resources, a huge documentary universe to contend with, and a lack of public appreciation for what these repositories face and how they function. The considerable space that Nicholson Baker devotes to the market value (financial worth) of some of the book and newspaper discards of libraries and archives shows how far off base his case is. The market is hardly rational, and financial worth does not equal historical worth. The fact that one can sell practically anything at eBay or a flea market does not convey true historical value to the goods. Furthermore, institutions such as the New-York Historical Society and the Historical Society of Pennsylvania have found that legal, ethical, and professional standards bar them from readily converting their collections into cash.

The practice of the Carnegie Institution in Pittsburgh in holding an annual Preservation Fair (an event for which the first part of this chapter was drafted as part of a public presentation), at which experts examine objects not to assess financial value but to ascertain what should be done to preserve them for the enjoyment of their owners and descendants, provides a clue for a new role for our libraries, archives, and museums. If in the past these repositories rushed to acquire, today they must be more cautious and strategic to ensure that the collections of extraordinary historical value are identified, cared for, and made available for use. In cases in which the physical encasing is of little or no research importance, these institutions might even negotiate the creation of surrogates (copies) to ensure that the information and evidence of particular items is preserved and accessible while the originals stay with their owners.

John Q. Public should enjoy his books, manuscripts, paintings, broadsides, photographs, and whatever else he might possess without the distraction of whether these objects deserve to be in a library, archives, or museum or even whether they have some financial value. Many librarians, archivists, and museum curators have long since thrown off their competitive impulses and now seek to cooperate with other repositories sharing their regional or documentary mandate. They have done this because they recognize that no one institution can claim or hope to possess or preserve all the sources relating to a particular topic, geographic region, or event. The Preservation Fair reminds us that another positive benefit, and another form of cooperation, of these repositories is to assist the members of the public to appreciate and care for their own private collections. Maybe someday one in a million of these sources or collections will come to reside within a library, archives, or museum, but that is not the point of this exercise. These artifacts and documents connect us to the past, and they play just as important a role when they rest in the possession of private individuals, especially descendants of the original owners or creators of the historical materials.

The sentimental, romantic, and nostalgic attachment to such sources that many, perhaps most, people feel can be nurtured by their care of their own family heirlooms, the interesting objects and documents they discover at antique shops and flea markets, or even their occasional scavenging along the curbs on trash day (not that we want to encourage or endorse the latter activity). Such attachment is a powerful and human impulse that is part of the very fabric that makes us human. Rather than denying that it exists, which one can be tempted to do if siding with Nicholson Baker and his suggestion that everything (or even one of everything) should be saved in its original state, we should enhance individuals' and families' appreciation of certain objects and, in the process, help them understand the societal and cultural roles of libraries, archives, and museums. Perhaps these institutions will hold the most important records or a mixture of the most important and representative historical sources, but if they cannot be responsible for everything, these repositories must at least determine their role and explain themselves so the public can distinguish them and their role from the televised spectacles of unarchived treasures being financially assessed and the collecting frenzy at auctions, flea markets, and yard sales.

Not only is this important to the public; it is crucial to the professionals staffing these institutions. While the public perceives an archivist as one who is covered in dust, salvaging historical records Indiana Jones fashion, the reality of the archivist's mission is much different. Yes, there are treasures everywhere, but how we identify, manage, and protect them is the most important aspect of this societal legacy. Archives are not merely vaults of historical documents in general; they also preserve records important to the public because they hold governments, corporations, and individuals accountable. Some archival treasures are not the kind you appraise on a television antiques show or look for on a dot.com site on the Web, but they are the kind that speak to what makes us both Americans and human. We cherish them for other reasons. Archivists and the other professionals working in our public repositories play a vital role in many facets of modern society. And, along the way, they are there to assist people protect their own treasures, ones that are just as important to them as the holdings of libraries, archives, and museums.

THE PLAN OF THIS BOOK

The swelling public interest in the past and its treasures has not necessarily brought greater understanding, by the public or scholars, of the way archives are formed. Postmodernist musings about archives wander so far over the landscape of society as to lose an idea of what archives are. We have had few serious examinations of how our

archival repositories and collections come to be. This book, borrowing its title from a provocative description of archives by an oral historian,[11] suggests that archives do not just happen but that they are
consciously shaped and sometimes distorted by archivists, the creators of records, and other individuals and institutions. This book
endeavors to examine how archives come into being from a variety
of perspectives so that archivists can muse over their function of
appraisal and historians and other users of archives can appreciate
what these institutions are about.

This is not a primer on archival appraisal, but it is a set of chapters
reflecting my own wrestling with the challenges and contradictions
(and there are both) of the archival function of appraisal. The chapters say more about thinking about appraisal than doing appraisal,
although I hope every archivist agrees you cannot have one without
the other. I leave it to others to try to write the basic, how-to manuals
on appraisal. I also leave it to others to try to squeeze from these
pages their own workable set of principles for archival appraisal,
partly because I have attempted this before[12] but primarily because
each type of archival repository and even each archivist may need
different guiding principles. Chapters 2 through 10 appear in the
order I wrote them (the publication dates suggest otherwise, but the
reader will have to take it at my word that the essays follow a chronological order in my writing of them), partly because they revolve
around many related themes (and this arrangement seemed to make
as much sense as any other) and partly because the structure might
reveal some of my own evolution in thinking about archival
appraisal over the past six or seven years.

The first part of this chapter considers how society seems to see
treasures everywhere, spurred on by such popular activities as bidding on eBay, watching the financial evaluations on the popular
television show *Antiques Roadshow,* and dredging through the tables
at fair markets and secondhand stores. Yet archives, libraries, and
museums can't collect or save everything, although the general public does not understand this. In this chapter, originally presented at
a Preservation Fair for individuals seeking advice about caring for
their own collections, I argue that a new role for museums and
archives might be to advise the public how to maintain and "treasure" their own treasures without a thought to whether they have
financial value or whether they should be in one of these public
repositories. The idea is a reflection of how functions such as archival appraisal might be changing, and for good reasons.

The next chapter continues the reexamination of archival appraisal. Given archivists' difficulties in mapping out systematic approaches to selecting items for their repositories, this chapter asks whether scholars in the future will study archives more for what they represent in society than for the specific records they hold. By asking these kinds of questions, we begin to see the problems associated with rampant, unfocused, and sometimes undisciplined acquisition. Moreover, this exercise forces us to ask what makes a record archival—some set of values, the process of appraisal, a decision by an archivist, or simply placement within something recognizable as an archives. This chapter was originally published in *Archival Science* in 2002.[13]

Chapter 3 tries to consider just whether archival appraisal is a method of collecting, and, if so, just how the psychology of collecting informs us about the process. Discourses on the history, psychology, and nature of collecting by individuals and institutions such as libraries and museums have many insights to offer about the nature of collecting by archivists and archival repositories. This chapter brings together two previously published book reviews[14] and suggests how others might examine archivists and their collecting, leading to some speculation about whether collecting is appraisal at all.

The traditional model of the archives or historical records repository has been that of an institution capable of collecting or documenting everything in a particular region or on a certain topic. The next chapter deconstructs this old paradigm, and it also considers the stresses and strains that such a model places on the institution, especially on its resources and public profile. The new archives must be cooperative in spirit and practice, and it must play a role whereby it seeks to nurture the development of other archival programs rather than participating in some sort of competitive process. This chapter was originally published in 2001.[15]

American archivists and their predecessors have been busily engaged in collecting for two centuries, and they have commented on it, debated it, proposed new approaches, and reflected on its success all along. Chapter 5, originally published in 2002,[16] summarizes the ongoing professional discussion about the role and nature of archival collecting and speculates on its future.

Surprisingly, one of the least understood connections with archival appraisal is that of the records manager's responsibility for records retention scheduling. Despite common historical origins, archival appraisal and records retention scheduling seem to have developed largely in a disconnected fashion, jeopardizing the ability of institutions such as governments and corporations to be able to deal realistically with their records. Chapter 6 seeks to bring the two approaches together in both a theoretical and a practical way, resolving many problems in the way archivists and records managers view each other in this function of assessing which records to maintain for the long haul. The chapter was published originally in 1999.[17]

Many archivists have begun to worry about the loss of their historic sense of a cultural mission as they must contend with new and emerging digital records and record-keeping systems. Chapter 7, previously published in November 2001,[18] argues that "evidence" may be the most critical approach necessary for archival work, but it also argues that the stress on evidence is not at all incompatible with other cultural and historical missions. Records possessing value for their evidence can also be valuable for their symbolic meaning or their information content.

Many wonder whether the growing use of digital technologies will leave us any documentary heritage at all. Drawing on thirty years of thinking about archives, the technologies of record-keeping, and the methods of appraising records, I view this question through the lens of equipping future archivists via education. Chapter 8 stresses that dealing with electronic records is not merely a matter of technical knowledge; it is rather a challenge we should address by giving archivists a full understanding of records and record-keeping systems that includes their political, economic, social, and historical dimensions. Archives may look different in the future, and they may be used in new ways, but there will be archives. This chapter was the keynote address to the Irish Committee for Historical Sciences in May 2002 in Limerick, Ireland.[19]

Over the past twenty years, scholarship on public memory has become one of the major aspects of historical research and writing. This scholarship, while diverse and wide ranging, has suggested that people connect to the past in remarkably diverse ways, including archives and museums. Many of the ways the public builds memory—through oral tradition, landscape, memorials and monuments, reenactments, movies, and documentaries—extend far beyond the traditional range of archives. Chapter 9 speculates on what this suggests, or does not suggest, about how archivists appraise and select records. Do traditional appraisal approaches have any connection to the public memory movement, or should they? Do archival appraisal methodologies, principles, and theories still make sense in light of what we have learned from the scholarship on public memory? This chapter was given as a paper at a conference held at the University of Salamanca, Spain, in October 2002.[20]

Many archival appraisal models floating about the archival profession are being used or at least pointed to as the authority for how archivists appraise and select records for their repositories. The appraisal task seems daunting, if not impossible, and includes preserving and protecting any aspect of the documentary heritage that is endangered; acquiring a systematic documentation of particular aspects of society; serving diverse constituencies with very different objectives; meeting the institutional needs of the creators of records; providing a cultural or public memory role; safeguarding records as both artifacts and information systems; sustaining identity, community, and collective memory of particular segments of society and important segments of society; ensuring the accountability of public officials and civic and corporate leaders; managing records of all media; and serving as a repository of last resort for records that have been stranded by their creators. While this swarm of approaches has produced a richer professional literature, it has not necessarily led to better success in archival appraisal, and it certainly has not resulted in better public understanding. Can archivists pull all these diverse approaches together to form a more coherent methodology, one more approachable by the public and policy makers? The final chapter was presented at a conference at the Henry Ford Museum in Dearborn, Michigan, in November 2002.

NOTES

1. Michael Kammen, *People of Paradox: An Inquiry Concerning the Origins of American Civilization* (New York: Alfred A. Knopf, 1972), 11.
2. Roy Rosenzweig and David Thelen, *The Presence of the Past: Popular Uses of History in American Life* (New York: Columbia University Press, 1998) is an excellent starting point for considering such matters.
3. Sally F. Griffith, *Serving History in a Changing World: The Historical*

Society of Pennsylvania in the Twentieth Century (Philadelphia: Historical Society of Pennsylvania, 2001) and Kevin M. Guthrie, *The New-York Historical Society: Lessons from One Nonprofit's Long Struggle for Survival* (San Francisco: Jossey-Bass Publishers, 1996).

4. Griffith, *Serving History*, 2, 47.

5. Griffith, *Serving History*, 14.

6. Griffith, *Serving History*, 456.

7. John Seelye, *Memory's Nation: The Place of Plymouth Rock* (Chapel Hill: University of North Carolina Press, 1998).

8. I have discussed the problem of thinking and teaching about current events in my "Current Events as Seminar Topics: A Case Study in the Relevance of LIS Education in the Modern World," *Reference Librarian*, forthcoming. This essay was also published as the concluding chapter in my *Flowers After the Funeral: Reflections on the Post 9/11 Digital Age* (Metuchen, New Jersey: Scarecrow Press, 2003).

9. Nicholson Baker, *Double Fold: Libraries and the Assault on Paper* (New York: Random House, 2001). My own views on Baker's book can be found in *Vandals in the Stacks? A Response to Nicholson Baker's Assault on Libraries* (Westport, Connecticut: Greenwood Press, 2002).

10. Robert Darnton, "The Great Book Massacre," *New York Review of Books* 48 (April 26, 2001): 16.

11. Paul Thompson, *The Voice of the Past: Oral History* (Oxford: Oxford University Press, 1978), 97.

12. See my article "The Documentation Strategy and Archival Appraisal Principles: A Different Perspective," *Archivaria* 38 (Fall 1994): 11–36. This essay also was reprinted in *American Archival Studies: Readings in Theory and Practice*, ed. Randall C. Jimerson (Chicago: Society of American Archivists, 2000): 211–241.

13. "The End of Collecting: Towards a New Purpose for Archival Appraisal," *Archival Science* 2 (2002): 287–309.

14. "The Archivist and Collecting: A Review Essay," *American Archivist* 59 (Fall 1996): 496–512 and "Making the Records Speak: Archival Appraisal, Memory, Preservation, and Collecting; A Review Essay," *American Archivist* 64 (Fall/Winter 2001): 394–404.

15. "The Traditional Archival and Historical Records Program in the Digital Age: A Cautionary Tale," *Records and Information Management Report* 17 (May 2001): 1–16.

16. "The Archivist and Collecting," *Encyclopedia of Library and Information Science* (New York: Marcel Dekker, Inc., 2002), 70 (supp. 33): 1–21.

17. "Archives and the Digital Future," *Journal of the Irish Society for Archives 8* (2001–2): 35–48.

18. "La valoracion como un acta de memoria," *Tabula: Revista De Archivos De Castilla Y Leon* no. 6 (2003): 51–73.

17. "Evidence and Archives," *Records and Information Management Report* 17 (November 2001): 1–14.

18. "Meta-Scheduling: Rethinking Archival Appraisal and Records Management Scheduling" in *Bridging Records, Information, and Knowledge: ARMA Proceedings* (Prairie Village, Kans.: ARMA, 1999), 59–66.

2

The End of Collecting: Toward a New Purpose for Archival Appraisal

It used to be so simple. Archivists and manuscript curators acquired records with historical or continuing value, and researchers came to the repository housing the records and used them there. Archives were gathered from individual, family, and institutional creators in both small and large volumes. Records were in traditional paper and eye-readable formats in reasonably stable recording media. Appraisal decisions could be delayed with confidence that, barring unforeseen natural and human-caused catastrophes, the records would be there for a later evaluation. Archivists could proceed cautiously and conservatively in making appraisal decisions and in getting the records prepared for use. Archivists knew good records when they saw them, based on an intimate understanding of the subjects represented by the records, an iterative learning process about appraisal gained by field experience, and a knowledge of those likely to want access to the records for research. Researchers were content to come to the repository and to use what records they

19

could find on their topics, even if doing so required lengthy days and weeks of meticulous and painstaking inspection. The mere presence of archives and historical manuscript repositories provided a symbolic reassurance that interest in the past existed and that an understanding of the history of any conceivable topic, event, place, institution, or individual and family could be obtained with some careful work. Records were routinely created by activities that were important and unassuming, analyzed for their value for historical and other research, and competently selected by experienced archivists and manuscripts curators. The past, through archives and historical manuscripts, could become a familiar country to anyone wanting to visit.[1]

Much of this comfortable landscape has been challenged in recent years. The accelerating development of information technologies has produced a growing demand for fast and ready access to the information found in records. The majority of researchers wanting to use the records found in archives are not content to settle in for a leisurely prowl through the boxes, bound volumes, folders, and bundled files, often reflecting the idiosyncrasies of both the creators and the past custodians of the records. The opportunity to wait until long after the records have fallen from current use by their creators before appraising them has also been transformed. In many cases, archivists will need to build appraisal decisions into records systems before they are put online, when both the scope of records being created and the risk of their being lost increase by many orders of magnitude. Whereas before, archivists could sometimes deal with records thirty or forty or more years after they had become obsolete, now they have only a few years before a system of creating records is deemed obsolete, upgraded, or replaced. Complicating this swirl of issues even more is the fact that some adherents to postmodernism and other contemporary sensibilities have called into question the veracity of traditional records or have revealed their limitations as sources of information for understanding the past. In addition, archivists can easily become wrapped up in acrimonious debates by competing societal groups who hold perspectives not drawn from traditional sources of historical evidence, such as represented by archives and historical manuscripts. (As just one example, the Afro-centrist view of Africa as the cradle of Western civilization rather than Greece and Rome has generated debates contrasting traditional evidence with oral tradition and public memory.)

The appraisal of records never did work like this ideal, of course. Thirty years ago, archivists already knew of both the power and the subjectivity of collecting and appraising (terms often used interchangeably), then disguised in an array of jargon and approaches representing archival appraisal as something more scientific.[2] H. G. Jones, the quintessential historian-archivist of his generation, had a number of pertinent things to say about these pitfalls in his 1969 *Records of a Nation*. Archivists, when functioning as appraisers, "act as prognosticators of the future by determining what documentary evidence . . . will be preserved." The archivist is also a "limit-setter" and a "censor." "By one flick of the pen [approving a records disposition schedule] he can decide that the present and future will be denied knowledge of a particular matter except through the undependable memory of any surviving participants." Finally, the archivist:

> cannot be a specialist in all subjects, and he is unlikely to be a specialist in even a few subjects. . . . His decisions as to what to keep and what to destroy, therefore, may be questioned by individual researchers on specific subjects. There is no way out of this dilemma, for it would be impracticable to envision the consultation of thousands of specialists to advise in the appraisal of records.[3]

Even in supposedly simpler times, immense challenges and responsibilities confronted the individual responsible for the ultimate decisions about what should be saved or not.

Archival appraisal has always been a task that is partly a trip through a foreign country, no matter how rational archivists may have tried to make this function look. Have they believed in totally objective notions guiding appraisal, or were they really more concerned with acquiring anything that might be of value for someone, someday, in some way?[4] Have archivists and manuscripts curators approached appraisal as if they were pursuing an avocation or hobby, acquiring records in the same fashion they might acquire toy trains, baseball cards, or used lace by scouring their way through flea markets and antique stalls? There might be criteria, expertise, and planning, but all these are in reality subsumed by a somewhat serendipitous collecting approach.[5]

THE CONFUSING TERRAIN OF APPRAISAL

Archival appraisal seems to have drifted into a world of confused, conflicting, or complacent methods, theories, and practices—at least when seen by the typical archival practitioner. Some archivists in the field embrace specific guiding concepts, but others seem to operate with little knowledge of changing perspectives concerning this archival function. Still others desire only simplistic templates for making appraisal decisions, which explains the continuing popularity of basic manuals and textbooks, at least for those who argue that they must make daily decisions expeditiously. Some archivists believe that whatever they acquire is as good as anything else they could obtain, and others cautiously acquire records for use by a particular societal group—perhaps hoping to avoid the acrimonious debates plaguing the interpretation of the past and revisionist views of events still fresh in the memories of key players and observers. In our global society, archives and the past have become easy objectives or targets. In terrorism, ethnic cleansing, and civil strife, archives become assignments for destruction. In times of social tensions, archives become contested and confusing symbols because they are a symbol of authority and power. Historian Lawrence Levine, rejecting Allan Bloom's ideas, argues that Bloom's criticisms were not documented but based on his personal experience—formed "largely in the archives of his own mind."[6] Archives' role as authority and power should force archivists to reflect on why, how, and for whom appraisal is done, although many practitioners say they lack the time to do this.

Cacophony might be the most appropriate word to describe this state of affairs. There are many researchers (users of archives) who will rush ahead to form their own archives holdings and manuscript collections, either out of suspicion of what archivists are doing or because they want to join the cacophony produced by myriad individuals and groups all collecting archival records. One prominent retired historian writes, "To collect materials currently from those who create them can heighten one's realization that evidence is a product of limited human circumstance and purpose and can help one avoid the assumption that evidence has a universal quality." This historian argues that the "trick, of course, is to acquire evidence to describe the variations, and that effort places a premium on collecting manuscripts when they are created rather than depending on their later and chance assembly." This person sees the need to become "an entrepreneur in gathering historical information," forming partnerships to work with archives.

Archives could more actively facilitate the process of assembly, rather than leave it to chance. Arrangements between such "documentary entrepreneurs" and archives could be established as the entrepreneurs collect materials, in order to elicit the energies of entrepreneurs in enhancing the acquisition and preservation process.[7]

In other words, this user of historical records argues, don't let archivists make the decisions; make the decisions for them. The users of records know best, in this view.

Many archivists seem to agree. Someday researchers might be studying not the materials collected for their evidence and information but the historian who did the collecting and the archivist and archival repository agreeing to take in the collection. Now, for example, we study the habits and trends of pioneer archival collectors as much as, if not more than, what they acquired. In the nineteenth century, we understand autograph collectors were looking for signs of character, even when they shifted from their quest for the famous to the autographs of friends and acquaintances.[8] Others have suggested that the rise in autograph collecting was due to "technological changes," the "spread of literacy," "increased production and decreasing cost of writing paper," "improved postal systems," and an "interest in celebrities."[9] In the late twenty-first century, how will we understand the records selected a century before and then held by archives and historical manuscript repositories?

People *can* collect everything and anything, from the most arcane and seemingly useless materials to items connected to important events, personages, and institutions. The only consistency in such acquiring is the steady accumulating of materials, the archival equivalent of archaeological sites in which the debris of human settlement accumulates generation after generation. Although the donations of eccentric and eclectic collectors have formed the nuclei of important institutional collections, one must wonder how well this method can work for ensuring reasonable records for research as we move deeper into the era of digital records. Even though historians and collecting were practically synonymous at one time, the lack of study about collecting and its history in effect revealed its

sort of guilty pleasure.[10] (The lack of analysis suggests that no one
wanted to evaluate seriously an activity that just seemed to be so
instinctive and fun.) There is a sense that without the efforts of individual collectors, eccentricities and all, much would have been lost.
A manuscript dealer in 1890 wrote, "In America, with a few exceptions, credit for preserving the records of the nation's past must go
to the private collectors. About the deadest thing in the country is
the average Historical Society."[11] The situation was worse two centuries before. We know that individuals in England were collecting
public records as well as other stuff because of the "loose archival
practices of the period."[12] The reliance on private collectors has also
become part of the lore of the development of archives and historical
manuscript repositories, which identifies some collectors as saviors
of what might have been lost.[13]

APPRAISAL AND THE "EVERYTHING" PROBLEM

Collecting *anything* has its problems, because, as exemplified in the
museum literature, we cannot collect *everything*. A typical museum
curator (in an ethnographic collection) can argue that "it would be
far better to keep a few carefully selected examples of each category
of material in which we are interested and be content with accurate
plans, specifications, illustrations and histories of the remainder."
For this professional, "selectivity and the almost ruthless discarding
of irrelevant material" are crucial operatives, as are notions such as
"meaningful" collections, "in-depth research work," and "intimate
knowledge." Most notably, the "days of the haphazard, random
and unplanned collection of artifacts have long gone," as has the
value of an "enthusiastically collected miscellany of artifacts."[14]
Another museum professional goes even further: "Museum professionals are acquirers; we are inherently greedy collectors. Most of us
go into the profession because the desire to accumulate and bring
together objects of quality is in our blood. We are personally and
professionally devoted to adding to and improving our holdings—
that is what makes us tick."[15] How many holdings of archives and
historical manuscript repositories could claim to reflect such a tradition? Some exemplary, well-documented archival repositories can
and do, but many (perhaps the majority) might not. The identity of

an archivist is tied into his or her ability to appraise by *some* tradition, mindset, presupposition, or standard (different archivists will attribute their appraisal work to different influences). Margaret Cross Norton, many decades ago, declared that the "difference between a file clerk and an archivist is that the archivist has a sense of perspective. He knows that these documents have two phases of use; their present day legalistic use, and their potential historical value."[16]

We can see this duality when we turn to administrators' views of records. David Ehrenfeld, in his *Beginning Again*, critiques management by considering the desire of "documenting everything." "The true function of this modern tendency to document everything is plain. It serves to provide a source of undemanding work for managers who might otherwise not be terribly busy."[17] Perhaps the tendency by some archivists to sweep up everything is likewise the result of their desire for "undemanding" work. It is easier to simply sign off and receive records whenever they arrive than to argue about whether they fit into an institution's mission or hold up against some appraisal criteria; accepting anything is always easier than negotiating for other records with greater value for evidence, documentation, and research. This tendency to want to grab everything could be the result of the exploding quantity of records our modern age produces. Pierre Nora notes that "Modern memory is, above all, archival." He argues that the size of public archives has multiplied a thousandfold in the past few decades. "No society has ever produced archives as deliberately as our own, not only volume, not only by new technical means of reproduction and preservation, but also its superstitious esteem, by its veneration of the trace."[18] Although one might assume that this penchant should drive individuals to be much more highly selective and to follow rigorous criteria, we often see a sort of feeding frenzy in collecting—perhaps a reaction to trying to gather up sources other than the predominant government and organizational archives Nora has in mind. Individual collecting might occur out of suspicions about what government agencies and cultural organizations are doing in gathering archives, ranging from fears about not telling the complete story to those reflecting surveillance and intrusions of privacy. Some of the new intensity for collecting might be the result of growing concerns that each new electronic networking technology (from the telegraph to the World Wide Web) reduces the tendency to create essential records, let alone to create them in a form anybody would want to acquire.[19]

The "traces" Nora describes are everywhere, even seeming to be in demand. The lead editorial of the March 16, 1998, *New York Times,* "The Value of History," describes a group of JFK memorabilia and documents coming up for auction that concerned the editors. "But this time, it is not just a poignant trove of personal effects. The catalogue of 600 items for sale in New York this week includes not only a slim gold wedding ring, Caroline's bracelet and the registration for Jacqueline Kennedy's Ford station wagon, but old typed pages that resonate with history." The editorial describes documents on the admission of Red China to the UN, the 1962 Cuban Missile Crisis, and other noteworthy events.

> These are not things personal to the Kennedys. These are personal to the nation. Today, by law, such doodlings by Bill Clinton would be defined as Presidential records, government property. But the Kennedy papers . . . face the auction block, and an afterlife in someone's den. The National Archives is now hot to get them. The Archives has no money to buy such things. Perhaps it should. But instead, on Friday, it threatened to sue, on the basis of the ambiguous Kennedy deed of gift.

The records seem, indeed, to be significant, but more significant is the media coverage of the auction in helping us to comprehend a societal collecting mania *versus* the potentially more careful efforts of archival appraisal. The Kennedy auction brought out all of the strangest attitudes about collecting and collectors' interests in artifacts and historical records. Lori Spector, supervising the auction, states, "The sale is about the celebration of the life and career of one of this country's favorite Presidents."[20] A ludicrous view of acquiring is evident in a statement by Arlan Ettinger, the president of the New York auction house (Guernsey's) handling the Kennedy material. "Moments ago," Ettinger enthused, "some gentlemen walked in with an original wooden cigar box with the president's name and it's filled with beautifully conditioned cigars with his name on each one. You tell me a document in the world that's more exciting than that!"[21] The silliness continued as the auction proceeded:

> Ms. Shriver's secret bids highlighted the tension over the auction. Critics called it a tawdry sale of family items by people who had obtained

them through questionable means. But the auction's defenders, who pointed out that John and Caroline Kennedy benefited heftily from a $34.4 million auction of their mother's possessions in 1996, called it a just reward for collectors who spent decades frugally acquiring Kennedy ephemera.[22]

The Kennedy auction ended quietly. A few weeks after, some of the items auctioned were turned over to the John F. Kennedy Library and Museum, including his mahogany drop-leaf writing table, a 1961 memo about an upcoming meeting with Khrushchev, and two personal journals kept while on travel in Europe in 1951.[23] Yet the questions linger as to how archivists can conduct appraisal by assigning value to records in a society so willing to assign bizarre and cryptic values to ordinary records and objects associated with the events and times of the Cold War; archivists can seek to be deliberate, but can they prevail against the usually less-than-rational collecting psyche? To cacophony we can add compulsion. Cigars become important documents! What can we do to operate rationally in such a world?

THE PASSIONS OF COLLECTING

Now we also see the specter of two different kinds of potential compulsion—the Web and collecting—coming together. Here a collector of radios at Web auctions describes his "addictive" behavior:

> Early on, the activity seemed authentically connected to primal hunter-gatherer impulses deep within. But after a short while, it became clear that there was a good dose of obsessive-compulsive behavior mixed in. For instance, I once brought to the dinner table an alarm clock set to ring just in time for a final round of bidding. I have also rearranged a business trip to be at home for a critical auction. And, more than once, I have bought a duplicate of a radio I already own hoping to get one in better condition. I am sure that the addicting element is the "chase." Searching out, tracking, bidding, and winning is at least as rewarding as possessing the actual prize. I didn't realize this fully until, as a frequent bidder, I began receiving lists of radios for sale from other collectors. My interest in buying from these lists or from a radios-for-sale site is very low. How this addiction will end remains to be seen. Obviously, I am hoping to do it without professional help. It would be terribly demoralizing to pay the counseling

bills while thinking about the transistors that could have been bought with those precious funds.[24]

How many archivists might machinate to acquire yet another intriguing document or collection out of some compulsion, perhaps disguised as institutional policies and procedures? Although certain archival gems, such as a rare manuscript map or forgotten television news program, might be discovered and saved by such collecting, the use of resources and energies in such efforts needs to be weighed against more rational appraisal and other archival objectives.

The tremendous popular interest in acquiring bits and pieces of the past can be seen in fiction. Collecting records has become an obsession even within the fictional world of novelists, mystery writers, and New Age potboilers. We read about murders committed to acquire a rare and unknown manuscript by a famous writer; scholars chasing after letters with new revelations of a prominent English writer; spies trying to find a notebook of a famous writer; a sleuth trying to figure out the theft of a fourteenth-century illuminated manuscript from a Boston-area university; a doctoral student tracking down for his dissertation a trunk of love letters written by Warren G. Harding held by an elderly woman reputed to have been his mistress; a novel about the discovery of an ancient manuscript in South America promising to hold the secret or key to self-knowledge; and a mystery revolving about the discovery, theft, and quest for the first portion of the Samuel Clemens (Mark Twain) manuscript of *The Adventures of Huckleberry Finn*.[25] How many archivists wish their researchers were as interesting as the characters in such novels and mysteries?

Collecting is, indeed, a passion for both real and fictional characters, the latter typified by the speech given by a Jack Finney character longing to discover an original Shakespeare manuscript:

> I couldn't stand still. Hands jamming into my back pockets, I began walking up and down, before her, fast. "Listen, if you're a collector, you always have your—what?—your Holy Grail. A manuscript collector probably pictures himself in the back of some run-down, out-of-the-way secondhand bookstore. Finding a bundle of old papers at the back of a bottom shelf in a dark corner behind some books, where it's been for years. He unties it and looks through old paper after useless old paper. And then—down in the middle of the bundle—*there it is*. His hands start shaking because there under his eyes at last is the tiny

handwriting he has so often studied in reproductions of the man's signature. Just his *signature*, the only specimen of that handwriting ever
before found. Kept under glass and permanent guard in the British
Museum. Worth a million dollars, they think, if it were ever sold. Yet
now . . . here is page after page of that tiny, rusty-inked handwriting.
With notes in the margins! And then, *then* . . . far into this long handwritten script, he finds a speech. The first words have been crossed out,
but he can read them. And they say . . . they say 'To exist or die is my
dilemma,' and there's a pen stroke through them. And just above them
in even smaller letters is written for the first time in the world, in the
author's own handwriting . . . 'To be or not to be: that is—' "[26]

How many archivists secretly desire to make a discovery of this
sort? And is this the appropriate motivation to guide them in the
appraisal process?

In such collecting, there is a kind of archival "pot hunting" at
work akin to the methods of those who desecrate archaeological
sites by removing sought-after (collectible) objects in a manner that
destroys their context and value as evidence. One archaeologist
argues:

> There seems to be some fundamental human desire to collect things
> and display them in the privacy of one's home. . . . People collect every-
> thing, from barbed wire to beer cans, and many think of archaeology
> as the acquisition of objects. But when people collect archaeological
> finds, they are collecting a part of a finite resource that is rapidly van-
> ishing, a unique archive that can never be replaced. Every object they
> buy or dig from a site is the product of ancient human behavior. This
> behavior can be partly reconstructed from objects found in the soil, but
> much of our insight depends on the *contexts* (positions) in time and
> space in which the objects occur in the ground. Removing an artifact
> from its context is an irreversible act that cheats us all of knowledge.[27]

The aggressive, sometimes piecemeal acquisition of records and
manuscripts by both private collectors and institutions such as
libraries and historical societies can also affect contexts and constitute "irreversible acts." But when *anything* is collectible, do contexts
matter? When *everything* seems valuable, does any action leading to
destruction of some records or the evidence of records really seem
irreversible? When even garbage provides important clues to the
past, does it matter whether archivists have done much more than
randomly acquire interesting documentary debris?[28]

There might be something positive in all this. If a well-known psychiatrist can find value in the runaway obsession with Beanie Babies, then there might be something hidden in the intense competition to acquire a true piece of the Kennedy cross. "Eavesdrop on a group of children discussing their [Beanie Baby] collections and the conversations will, except for the high pitch of their voices, be eerily reminiscent of a group of Wall Street traders," writes Joyce Brothers.

> For those wondering whether this new sophistication is good or bad, it is simply a more complex version of the Monopoly we played when we were growing up. These kids are learning the ways of the market all by themselves. They are learning about the uses of the Internet for business; how to trade; how to price; how to traffic in market rumor and gossip using a newsletter; how to keep from being cheated; the difference between a check and a money order.[29]

Are archivists playing their own grown-up version of Monopoly when they enter the competitive marketplace (whether they seek donations, purchases, or a combination) for building their collections or holdings? Archivists need to reflect on how their actions really contribute to the purpose of archives, and most archivists generally assume that their mission is more than assembling random collections of interesting stuff for some ill-defined societal or scholarly purposes.

ARCHIVES AS MEMORY HOUSES

Some archivists and manuscript curators might argue that their repositories are akin to some sort of secular temple, "houses of memory" in a society often inclined to disregarding its past. Popular writer Paul Horgan subscribes to the power of records and personal papers, but in a way worth more reflection by archivists. "We all know the piercing sense of life which we are given by primary source materials—letters, diaries, eyewitness accounts, and the rest," Horgan writes:

> Even at their most artless they have power to move us according to our own degree of sensibility to life itself. But the writing of history is not devoted merely to collecting and publishing original raw materials. We put the weight of our whole structures upon them—but it is the design

we bring to our structures that in the end represents our whole achievement.[30]

Horgan provides an idea of the importance of the context of records, but he also points to the idea that there is something to the importance of records meriting more careful introspection and planning by archivists and manuscripts curators contemplating appraising and acquiring.

Drawing on Horgan, there are three structures (considered in a metaphoric sense) that affect how society values records and that lead to some notion about how records should be appraised by archivists. These "structures" emanate from the organizations and individuals creating the records, the archivists and colleagues evaluating records, and the researchers who could ultimately use the records for some purpose. The importance of the record-generating entity can be seen in the traditional archival science of diplomatics (recognizing records' forms and functions as being intimately connected to the record-generating process), newer ideas such as warrant (recognizing the authority for creating records), and function-based appraisal criteria.[31] Records professionals have long sought to provide a structure for evaluating records by either following informational and evidential values or scheduling records primarily for legal, fiscal, and administrative values. Finally, researchers traditionally have considered yet another structure. Historian Gertrude Himmelfarb argues that "rules governing footnotes . . . were a warrant . . . of accountability." She writes:

> Critical history puts a premium on archival research and primary sources, the authenticity of documents and reliability of witnesses, the need to obtain substantiating and countervailing evidence; and, at a more mundane level, the accuracy of quotations and citations, prescribed forms of documentation in footnotes and bibliography, and all the rest of the "methodology" that goes into the "canon of evidence."[32]

This latter structure suggests, of course, how all three overlap to some degree and provide some authority for appraising records, that is, determining what records will be allowed to survive for a longer period than others. The problem is that many archivists sometimes have allowed collecting to take the place of careful consideration of how these various structures work or do not work, or how they are rational or ambiguous.

The problem faced by archivists and manuscript curators can be seen in their struggle to apply theory to such a task as appraisal. Frank Boles, in his 1991 book on appraisal, writes that "The archival community's hope is that rational planning and decision making can eliminate, or at least minimize, the undesirable consequences of destroying information."[33] Efforts to be more rational can lead to problems, however. Boles's review of my book on documenting localities argues that the theory is not useful because there are no practical examples, that my approach "essentially repudiates much of the American experience of archives," and that it also "runs out of the profession those individuals" seeing value in collecting. Boles argues, "I believe the term 'archivist' should be used inclusively to incorporate all those who deal with documentary heritage recorded through some representative process rather than exclusively to create an ideological admissions test for 'archivists.'"[34] Even with his misreading of the book, the scenario offered by Boles is interesting: It must be, for the archivist, business as usual. Collect, acquire, take in. American archivists have become fixated with democratic notions like representation and a pragmatism that seems to resist the more European-like comfort with ideology.

Archivists like Boles can take solace from observing that rampant collecting *is* the order of business for archivists. But it leads us in dangerous directions. David Bearman argues that we can do without the "comprehensive record." "We can construct most satisfactory versions of the past from the fragments we possess." Bearman might have been reacting to the chaotic state of the conceptualization of archival appraisal/collecting.

> The sooner we admit to the futility of efforts to accumulate a comprehensive and unbiased record for some future generation, the easier it will be to argue our benefit to the present and to compete for resources with other essential services.[35]

No more ideology, working with others, comfort with documentary fragments, and more realistic notions all seem to provide some hope for archivists—*except* that they cannot *all* be operative.

Bearman's ideas reacting against archivists' grasping for comprehensiveness, an archival theorist like Luciana Duranti constructing positivist views of knowledge and evidence, or the sea change rep-

resented by thoughtful archival postmodernists like Brian Brothman, Richard Brown, Terry Cook, and others, are worth more than a
few moments' thought. In these writings, we can see that acquisition
without purpose or appraisal with *no* objective is neither mandatory
nor meritorious. What would we be left with?

Fortunately, some have been bold enough to tell us. William
Maher, in his 1992 book on academic archives, argues against "general rules" for appraisal, instead preferring an application of archivists' "own appraisal criteria to each group of records they
consider." He contends that the "elements of appraisal can be item-
ized, but the exact method for deciding the value of a given records
series remains unclear." Instead, "Appraisal is primarily a decision
based on the archivist's knowledge, experience, and instinct."[36]
Think through this argument logically. It means that when archivists encounter records, they apply their individual knowledge to
an appraisal. But what determines *when* an archivist encounters
records? Is this a completely serendipitous process? And will the
knowledge, experience, and research of one archivist be as good as
another's for a particular kind of record? Maher's comments imply,
as well, a kind of cumulative experience coming from archivists, but
how could this experience be appropriately accumulated? Isn't it
codified in the kinds of "general rules" or theory he rejects?

I am not arguing for a broad theoretical premise or some kind of
universal law for appraisal, although I believe archivists must have
clear and precise objectives in appraisal just in order to know how
best to utilize their always-limited resources. Nor am I arguing that
seemingly random collecting—which is more reactive and ad hoc
than random[37]—will not result in some records of immense value
and importance being saved. Obviously, it has had this result in the
past and it will again. What I am suggesting, instead, is that archivists need to understand the limitations and more clearly document
the purposes and results of their appraisal processes and decisions.
Examples abound that demonstrate why this is important. I believe
archivists who hold to a particular *weltanschauung* and are armed
with a careful documenting of the appraisal process will be in better
shape (better in fulfilling their mission, managing their resources,
and accounting for their appraisal choices) than archivists who
acquire in an ad hoc or unstructured manner. And archives will benefit accordingly.

REEVALUATING ARCHIVAL APPRAISAL

We need to think carefully and clearly about any activity, including archival appraisal. What effect has the rampant collecting of past generations had on the way archivists presently approach appraisal? For example, a commentator on urban historic preservation notes that its "apparent objective . . . is to preserve history, but the more preservation succeeds in a given urban district, the less historical the result becomes. As the restoration moves forward, the district increasingly resembles a stage set."[38] What do all the records in all the archives and historical manuscript repositories represent? Is it a sort of documentary Hollywood landscape? It was *precisely* such questions that prompted in the early 1980s the beginning of a complete rethinking of the methodology of appraisal. That this rethinking has not permeated all practice does not indicate that such reflection is unimportant. Instead it means that appraisal still has not gained the priority in the spectrum of archival functions that it should have (except that the recent writing about appraisal has moved the *sense* of its importance to the forefront of archival work). There is, however, still a gap between the conceptualization of appraisal and its practice in archival repositories.

It is not just the implications of past private collectors that need to be constantly reconsidered, but the actions of past archivists and manuscripts curators, also. A persistent theme in writings and presentations by archivists about appraisal is a sort of sanctity of the decisions of past archivists and records professionals. To tamper with their decisions is to somehow allow subjectivity to impinge on the normal accretions of records and records systems. This sort of view ignores the very subjective processes and biases that must affect any individual's decision, regardless of accumulated experience, education, and expertise. Museum professionals have been more sensitive to such issues. Susan Pearce suggests that "every time we take a museum decision, we are carrying out a philosophical act which arises from a cultural context and has cultural implications, and the more we understand about this, the better for all concerned." Pearce ponders about how, in some cases, it is the process of collecting that is worth studying rather than the object acquired. She writes:

> The point at which an object passes from "rubbish" or "transient" to "durable" lies in the act of collecting; it is this which produces the

transformation of material into the heritage mode. . . . Collecting seems to operate in that obscure zone between cultural ideas of value and the deepest levels of individual personality.[39]

Indeed, the archivist's act of appraising a record as archival does something to that record that no other act can do, and this certainly relates both to the power within records and the transferal of some of that power to the records professionals and their repositories. In the introduction to their book on memory and history in twentieth-century Australia, Kate Darian-Smith and Paula Hamilton suggest this process. They note, "Through their selection of items from the written, visual and material objects that circulate in our society, public collecting institutions award a social value to specific objects and thus prescribe our historical consciousness."[40] This argument can be applied to archives, but whether all archivists understand it or embrace it is doubtful. Most archives and many archivists gather records without considering such implications and with no real conceptual model in mind. They often rush to save endangered records and, more often than not, accept records as they are offered.

Collecting, as appraisal, is not neutral. One cultural historian considers "systematic cultural intervention" the process by which:

someone (or some institution) consciously and programmatically takes action within a culture with the intent of affecting it in some specific way that the person or institution intervening thinks desirable. The action taken can range from relatively passive (say, starting an archive or museum) to relatively active (like instituting a cultural revitalization effort). Its intent can be either positive (as in a sensitive revitalization effort) or negative (as in the prohibition of ethnic customs, dress, or language). Moreover, a negative effect may follow from a positive intent, and vice versa.[41]

All the hand-wringing by archivists about appraisal cannot enable them to ignore such a reality. This reality is a type of gravitational pull that brings all archival appraising back to earth's subjectivity and weaknesses. The questions one ponders, of course, concern how aware an archivist is about such matters and whether such awareness is all that important. Understanding archives requires some understanding of such matters, but the theoretical approaches to appraisal, whatever they are, might be more critical for how they enable an archivist to handle the vast documentary universe. Documenting the appraisal approach becomes important only for suggesting to the ultimate user of archives how the selection was made.

This effort to document fully appraisal should turn the archivist
back to reconsidering what collecting and collections represent. A
new interest in records and record-keeping systems has emerged in
the past decade, primarily because of the push and tensions of more
dynamic electronic systems. But the historic interest in the nature of
records creation extends back to the beginnings of archival science
(with the Dutch and their notion of the organic nature of records),
and this interest should have long ago been applied to the formation
of collections. Even random collecting has a system. Robert Alan
Shaddy, in his reading of memoirs by collectors of a century ago,
states:

> The collection, in effect, allowed the collector to truly know and under
> stand the past and its inhabitants. It was perceived by collectors that
> the collection allowed the transcending of time and space, and that the
> collector, as a result of his sentimental communion, could freely roam
> through the past. It seems, from examining their published recollec
> tions and reminiscences, that collectors used inanimate objects . . . as a
> way of coping therapeutically with the modern world.

Collecting is "more than a mere 'hobby' or an indulgence; the true
collector manifested a mania."[42] The formation of a records system—generated by legislative or administrative mandate or formed
because of professional best practices and cultural influences—may
be akin to the formation of "collections." In fact, the tendency of
many American archivists to use the word "collections" to describe
their individual holdings of records, chastised by some theorists as
both imprecise and careless of the differences between more systematic records and personal and idiosyncratic documentation, could in
fact have merit. Records systems create and acquire records documenting transactions clustered about functions; while the collecting
psyche is not as obvious, it still builds documentary schemes with
some similarity to collections.

The core of this problem resides, perhaps, in how archivists
approach appraisal. Frank Boles wrote at the beginning of the 1990s
that, "As it is used by most archivists, appraisal has come to mean
evaluating the informational content of a record with an eye toward
determining whether or not it is sufficiently important to merit long-

term retention."[43] Given the general obsession with acquiring, the multitude of records to be examined, and the seemingly infinite possibilities for informational value, this seems like an optimistic yet impossible task. Is collecting the same as archival appraisal? The answer might be no. Edward Kemp, twenty years ago in a book on "manuscript solicitation," demonstrated this by listing numerous benefits to cultural institutions in acquiring historical manuscripts but nothing that was systematic or carefully reasoned. The concept was somehow that if things were not collected, many valuable items would be lost. But this paled in comparison to the idea of prestige and other such tangible benefits of acquisition for the institution.[44] Now, there is a large body of writing challenging the kind of thinking espoused by Boles and building on the tradition going back to Schellenberg and others and forward to the more recent thinkers focusing on notions like functional analysis, macroappraisal, and related ideas. However, the real point is that most archivists may not systematically conduct appraisal at all and often resort to notions like evidential and informational, or primary and secondary, values because they are commonly used and accepted within the field.

THE INFLUENCE OF THE
IDEA OF COLLECTING

Why has archival appraisal developed in the way it has? The answer to this question might be little more complicated than the overwhelming influence of historical manuscript collecting on the professional development of archives. One European commentator on North American archives notes first that above all archives are essential for administration, but that the tradition was not as strong in the United States:

> The first driving force behind collecting archives in this country was historical interest. Historical societies started to collect archives because of their historical value even before public archives existed. The result in the United States is an archival system split in two. . . . The societies also influenced the view and use of archives. They were collected and preserved for use by scholars, not by ordinary citizens. They were seen as useful for historical research, but as having no importance as legal evidence. The fact that the historical societies were

able to collect public archives again points to the weak position of public administration.[45]

Sweeping out attics, as occurred in American historical pageants a century ago,[46] has been carried over to the continuing efforts of historical records programs and even institutional archives. This sweeping is seen in the preface by Edgerton G. North, president, in the centennial history of the Long Island Historical Society:

> Generations are usually measured as a score of years or so; thus a century will encompass about five generations. Picture then, if you will, the historical accumulations of five generations of thrifty collectors which have been willed, donated, or otherwise bequeathed to the Long Island Historical Society over the years and you will gain some conception of the magnitude of the holdings of the Society at the end of its centennial year. Granted that some of this gratuitous store is ephemera of the purest dross; on the other hand, and to a large extent, it also represents selective collecting by those who were bound by qualitative rather than quantitative criteria.[47]

This is the idea of historical societies and museums as memory houses. Howard Mansfield notes:

> If you look at the history of most respected antiquarian organizations, usually you will find a founder who would not even be hired by his own organization today. The founders are magpies, bower birds who gather everything in sight as a rapturous prayer to the world: Look at this and this and this: so wonderful. They must love it, weave it into their collection before it vanishes from the earth. The world, in their sight, remains always new. Then come the art historians and the skilled art technicians to preserve the hoard and draw up "rationales" for how to present this collection to the public, storylines, actually, a narrative for the jumble. But all that comes later in the first blush of collecting, it is like love. . . .[48]

If unbridled appraising is an act of love by the archivist for records, then we might need a divorce.

Do archivists collect with such passionate intensity? Archivists have not been as ambivalent about this as one might expect. English archivist J. H. Hodson, in his basic textbook, wrote that acquiring records is "probably the most exciting, certainly the most satisfying, part of the local archivist's work." Why? "Nearly all archivists are instinctive collectors. They like to acquire collections of records; the bigger . . . , the older, and the more important, the better."[49] This is the start of his chapter on acquisition and appraisal. Twenty years ago, Ken Duckett could state that "Few curators of manuscripts, either at the historical society or the university, are asked to justify collecting manuscripts."[50] For a while archivists even looked at collecting as a *temporary* activity. Forty years ago, an archivist wrote, "In America, I think we *know* where the manuscripts are. They are flowing into the repositories, sometimes with more or less temporary interruptions in the hands of private collectors."[51] Such knowledge, flow, and connection between private and public acquisition have proved to be inaccurate. Now, archivists need to seek more aggressively not just an understanding of appraisal methods but of the collecting phenomenon.

There have been efforts to grapple with this phenomenon, seeing a "magical" attribute in the original manuscript. Dana Gioia describes this "magic value":

> The scholarly alibi of libraries that they acquire literary manuscripts for intellectual reasons . . . is inadequate at best. Those needs could be better served by microfilm or photocopies at a negligible fraction of the expense. . . . An institution of learning seeks significant manuscripts because they possess qualities that scholarship cannot entirely reproduce—an authentic, holistic connection with the great writers of the past. It is not the intellectual content of the manuscript that is important but its material presence—ink spots, tobacco stains, pinworm holes, and foxing included. . . . That the magic value of manuscripts surpasses their meaningful value can be further attested by the passion both private collectors and public institutions exercise in obtaining the personal effects of famous writers. . . . The new owners hope mysteriously to gain some part of the original celebrity's power or allure.[52]

Of course, what such value says about the increasing responsibility of archivists for electronic records and record-keeping systems is uncertain. The beauty of records will have to shift from an old antiquarian sensibility to the more technocratic beauty of design and order.[53]

EXPLAINING APPRAISAL

Although there is nothing inherently wrong in developing elaborate theories of appraisal, archivists also need to develop methodologies that project their knowledge about the process to the researchers who ultimately use their records. Perhaps we are considering an "informed subjectivity" discussed by media experts. "We seek a new informed subjectivity, one in which point of view is prized, not hidden." "Informed subjectivity preaches opinion that is fair, openly acknowledged, and clearly argued—that is drawn from facts and research."[54] I would argue that such an "informed subjectivity" constitutes providing more observation about *how* archivists have conducted past appraisal decisions. There are many reasons for doing this, but, at its most elemental, archivists need to leave behind a detailed account of how they have determined what records are brought into the archives, including a documentary trail of records that have been destroyed. Given that the act of appraisal is the most important archival function in that it affects all other archival functions and shapes the documentary heritage, documenting the process is a fundamental part of archivists' accountability to each other (in that they can share appraisal information), to researchers, and to society.

Edward Linenthal, in his study of the origins of the Holocaust Museum, notes that "The act of collection itself—quite apart from the results—was a vibrant form of memory work. The design team acted as archaeologists of the Holocaust, digging into the attics of homes, weighing the impact of the physical remnants of a camp, in order to make the Holocaust 'real' through physical contact. The signing of agreements and the physical exchange of artifacts themselves became acts of Holocaust commemoration."[55] Common records can become important, partly because of their connection to significant events but also because they are imbued with value as survivals.

> Railroad maps, like political maps, are not usually considered the most visually exciting form of cartography, but to those who need to consult them, they provide data of infinite value. Like many other map forms, they were often regarded as ephemera, and thus all but a few copies have perished. Fortunately there are some collectors of such materials, so we have a record of the significance of railroad maps in the nineteenth century and beyond.[56]

Archivists need to realize that appraisal is part of a larger process of building public memory and a process connecting to other societal events related to the past. Paul Connerton, in *How Societies Remember*, informs us that societies remember via a complex array of rituals, commemorations, artifacts, personal representation and activities, and, of course, writing and texts. It is what makes collecting so attractive. We want to acquire all and anything that triggers a recollection or that symbolically evokes collective remembrance.[57] But this broader symbolic role of archives in public memory cannot be limited to systematic or scientific or rational exercises. Michel-Rolph Trouillot, in *Silencing the Past*, also understands that "average citizens" "access history through celebrations, site and museum visits, movies, national holidays, and primary school books." This leads him to speculate that the "making of archives involves a number of selective operations: selection of producers, selection of evidence, selection of themes, selection of procedures—which means, at best the differential ranking and, at worst, the exclusion of some producers, some evidence, some themes, some procedures." For archivists this is especially relevant: "History does not belong only to its narrators, professional or amateur. While some of us debate what history is or was, others take it in their own hands."[58]

Collecting as a transforming process has been well documented in the raiding of native people's artifacts and documents. In one study of the gathering of objects from Native Americans in the Northwest, it was considered that

> Objects become "artifacts" or "treasures" by a particular process. In themselves, they are merely artificially contrived bits of wood, stone, fur, or bone. Within their original setting, they possess whatever meaning that society may give them; they may even be valued as process rather than as products or possessions. They may be commodities or they may be sacred. Even these values will change as Native society changes. When Western ethnologists and collectors enter, the objects move into another orbit of value, one determined by Europeans. In this orbit they have a different value, higher in monetary terms than the one they are given in their indigenous sphere.[59]

Could it be that the records and manuscripts gathered into archives are valued as much for their *process* of saving as for their evidential and informational values traditionally enumerated by archivists, manuscripts curators, and records managers? In the debates about the contemporary meaning of the past, the textbooks targeted for criticism were, in the opinion of some observers, not the source of the real debate but part of "symbols, overloaded with emotional meaning, totems of moral conviction. For many people—administrators, teachers, and parents—textbooks are symbols to start with: signs that some larger community exists."[60] Perhaps, archives are mainly cultural symbols, to be administered and studied as such.

Archivists need to have some clear and achievable objectives in mind as they appraise. My own predilection is to emphasize evidence over information as a mechanism for formulating appraisal theory, methodology, and practice. Evidence provides some precise legal, fiscal, and administrative parameters while at the same time capturing a considerable amount of records that can be used by a broad number of researchers and scholars. But the point here is that no matter how archivists approach appraisal, they need to be aware of the unanticipated values and societal attributes that the appraisal process and result (the actual records) will undoubtedly entail. What might be saved for evidence might ultimately come to possess a cultural or symbolic value, and even vice versa. A researcher might be just as much or more interested in *how* the records got to the archives than in the records themselves. And, as an extension of the idea of provenance, this is really an intrinsic part of the evidence.

NOTES

1. The idea of archival appraisal representing a "foreign country" is a play on David Lowenthal's ideas in *The Past Is a Foreign Country* (Cambridge, Mass.: Cambridge University Press, 1985). Lowenthal's work challenges the more complacent view that the past is a stable, placid, completely rational place to visit or understand.

2. Some of this equivocating has been captured in my essay examining the primary archival appraisal literature of the twentieth century; see "The Documentation Strategy and Archival Appraisal Principles: A Different Perspective," *Archivaria* 38 (Fall 1994): 11–36.

3. H. G. Jones, *The Records of a Nation: Their Management, Preservation, and Use* (New York: Atheneum, 1969), 80, 82, 85.

4. That this kind of debate continues can be seen in the more recent exchange between Frank Boles/Mark Greene and Luciana Duranti. See Luciana Duranti, "The Concept of Appraisal and Archival Theory," *American Archivist* 57 (Spring 1994): 328–344, and Frank Boles and Mark A.

Greene, "Et Tu Schellenberg? Thoughts on the Dagger of American Appraisal Theory," *American Archivist* 59 (Summer 1996): 298–310.

5. I argued for the validity of the serendipitous approach in "The Archivist and Collecting: A Review Essay," *American Archivist* 59 (Fall 1996): 496–512, now incorporated as part of the next chapter of this book.

6. Lawrence W. Levine, *The Opening of the American Mind: Canons, Culture, and History* (Boston: Beacon Press, 1996), 23.

7. Samuel P. Hays, "Manuscripts for Recent History: A Proposal for a New Approach," *Journal of American History* 77 (June 1990): 212, 213, 215–216.

8. Tamara Plakins Thornton, *Handwriting in America: A Cultural History* (New Haven, Conn.: Yale University Press, 1996), 86–88, 110–118.

9. Donald H. Rieman, *The Study of Modern Manuscripts: Public, Confidential, and Private* (Baltimore, Md.: Johns Hopkins University Press, 1993), 24–26. For an earlier but similar assessment, see the introduction in Clifford Lord, ed., *Keepers of the Past* (Chapel Hill: University of North Carolina Press, 1965), 6.

10. R. Richard Wohl, "A Collection of Collectors: Some Varieties of Peculiar Passion," parts 1 and 2, *Manuscripts* 8 (Summer 1956): 244–250; (Fall 1956): 303–311. "Surely it is one of the anomalies of American intellectual history that the role of collecting has not been given more notice and study in describing how humanistic and historical scholarship took root, and developed, in this country," writes Wohl. "For many special subjects and for a considerable period in our history—in some cases, right into the twentieth century—the terms 'historian' and 'collector' were well nigh synonymous" (245).

11. Quoted in Kenneth Duckett, *Modern Manuscripts: A Practical Manual for Their Management, Care, and Use* (Nashville, Tenn.: American Association for State and Local History, 1975), 9.

12. Lester J. Cappon, "Collectors and Keepers in the England of Elizabeth and James," in *Sibley's Heir: A Volume in Memory of Clifford Kenyon Shipton* (Boston: The Colonial Society of Massachusetts, 1982), 152.

13. Steve Kemper, "Signs of the Times," *Smithsonian* 28 (November 1997): 134–140.

14. J. Geraint Jenkins, "The Collection of Material Objects and Their Interpretation," in *Museum Studies in Material Culture*, ed. Susan M. Pearce (Washington, D.C.: Smithsonian Institution Press, 1989), 120.

15. Alan Shestack, "The Museum and Cultural Property: The Transformation of Institutional Ethics," in *The Ethics of Collecting Cultural Property: Whose Culture? Whose Property?*, ed. Phyllis Mauch Messenger (Albuquerque: University of New Mexico Press, 1989), 97–98.

16. Thornton W. Mitchell, ed., *Norton on Archives: The Writings of Margaret Cross Norton on Archival & Records Management* (Carbondale and Edwardsville: Southern Illinois University Press, 1975), 9.

17. David Ehrenfeld, *Beginning Again: People and Nature in the New Millennium* (New York: Oxford University Press, 1993), 53.

18. Pierre Nora, "Between Memory and History: Les Lieux de Memoire," in *History and Memory in African-American Culture*, eds. Genevieve Fabre and Robert O'Meally (New York: Oxford University Press, 1994), 290.

19. See, for example, Rieman's comments on the telephone and the typewriter in his *Study of Modern Manuscripts*, 33, 35, 36.

20. Quoted in Dan Barry, "Bidding on the Bric-a-Brac of Mystique," *New York Times*, 19 March 1998, A19.

21. Quoted in David Rhode, "Kennedy Items Turned Over to Archives," *New York Times*, 18 March 1998, A21. Other articles: David Rhode, "Collectors Covet Bits of Camelot," *New York Times*, 20 March 1998, A19; N. R. Kleinfeld, "Whose JFK Memorabilia?" *New York Times*, 13 March 1998 (mentions that the government identified 14 lots belonging to it); Frank Bruni, "Angry Kennedys Speak Out on Auction," *New York Times*, 17 March 1998.

22. David Rhode, "Maria Shriver Buys Diaries in Secret Bids," *New York Times*, 21 March 1998, A13.

23. Thomas Farragher, "Kennedy Artifacts Arrive at New Home," *Boston Globe*, 16 May 1998.

24. Jeff Kennedy, "Radio Daze," *Technology Review* 101 (November/December 1998): 71.

25. Robert Banard, *The Case of the Missing Bronte* (New York: Dell, 1983); A. S. Byatt, *Possession: A Romance* (New York: Vintage Books, 1990); Bill Granger, *Hemingway's Notebook* (New York: Warner Books, 1986); Robert B. Parker, *The Godwulf Manuscript* (New York: Dell Publishing Co., 1973); Robert Plunket, *My Search for Warren Harding* (New York: Laurel, 1983); James Redfield, *The Celestine Prophecy: An Adventure* (New York: Warner, 1993); Julie Smith, *Huckleberry Fiend* (New York: Mysterious Press, 1987).

26. Jack Finney, *Marion's Wall* (New York: Simon and Schuster, 1973), 106–107.

27. Brian Fagan, *Archaeology: A Brief Introduction* (Boston: Little, Brown and Co., 1978), 7.

28. One of the challenges in doing what passes for appraisal derives from the fact that remnants, whether purposefully or accidentally saved, can take on values of immense importance over time. We know, for example, that historians and other students of the past have long worked with fragments. Daniel Boorstin describes the "casual and accidental causes of preservation, survival, and accessibility" of documents and the fact that historians have always dealt with a "random record" of the past (Daniel J. Boorstin, *Hidden History* [New York: Harper and Row, 1987], 6, 8). Archaeologists often find the most valuable information in garbage. "Garbage is among humanity's most prodigious physical legacies to those who have yet to be born; if we come to understand our discards . . . then we will better understand the

world in which we live." Although "historians are understandably drawn to written evidence . . . , garbage has often served as a kind of tattle-tale, setting the record straight" (William Rathje and Cullen Murphy, *Rubbish! The Archaeology of Garbage* (New York: HarperPerennial, 1992), 4, 12.

29. Joyce D. Brothers, "Beanie Bonanza: Soft Toys Offer Kids Hard Lessons About the Market," *Wall Street Journal*, 5 June 1998, W13.

30. Paul Horgan, *A Certain Climate: Essays in History, Arts, and Letters* (Middletown, Conn.: Wesleyan University Press, 1988), 21.

31. The literature is extensive on these approaches, but a sense of what they have to offer can be seen in the following: Richard Brown, "Macro-Appraisal Theory and the Context of the Public Records Creator," *Archivaria* 40 (Fall 1995): 121–172 and "Records Acquisition Strategy and Its Theoretical Foundation: The Case for a Concept of Archival Hermeneutics," *Archivaria* 33 (Winter 1991–92): 34–56; Wendy Duff, "Harnessing the Power of Warrant," *American Archivist* 61 (Spring 1998): 88–122; and Luciana Duranti, *Diplomatics* (Metuchen, N.J.: Scarecrow Press, 1998).

32. Gertrude Himmelfarb, *On Looking Into the Abyss: Untimely Thoughts on Culture and Society* (New York: Alfred A. Knopf, 1994), 127, 136.

33. Frank Boles, *Archival Appraisal* (New York: Neal-Schuman Publishers, Inc., 1991), 4.

34. See his review in the *American Archivist* 60 (Fall 1997): 460–463.

35. David Bearman, *Archival Methods* (Pittsburgh: Archives and Museum Informatics, 1989), 63, 65.

36. William J. Maher, *The Management of College and University Archives* (Metuchen, New Jersey: Society of American Archivists and the Scarecrow Press, Inc., 1992), 27, 37.

37. I am sure that archivists who seem to acquire in a random fashion could justify their labors as resting on the notion that this is as good as any other means for an archives to acquire records. And I am sure the astute observer of such archives and archivists could discern other than randomness in the predilections, attitudes, and approaches of the archivists.

38. O. B. Hardison, Jr., *Disappearing through the Skylight: Culture and Technology in the Twentieth Century* (New York: Viking, 1989), 116–117.

39. Susan M. Pearce, *Museums, Objects and Collections: A Cultural Study* (Washington, D.C.: Smithsonian Institution Press, 1992), 11, 35.

40. Kate Darian-Smith and Paula Hamilton, eds., *Memory and History in Twentieth-Century Australia* (New York: Oxford University Press, 1994), 4.

41. David E. Whisnant, *All That Is Native and Fine: The Politics of Culture in an American Region* (Chapel Hill: University of North Carolina Press, 1983), 13–14.

42. Robert Alan Shaddy, "A World of Sentimental Attachments: The Cult of Collecting, 1890–1938," *The Book Collector* 43 (Summer 1994): 186, 187. See also, for the nature of collecting, Russell W. Belk, Melanie Wallendorf, John

F. Sherry, Jr., and Morris B. Holbrook, "Collecting in a Consumer Culture," in *Highways and Buyways: Naturalistic Research from the Consumer Behavior Odyssey*, ed. Russell W. Belk (Provo, Utah: Association for Consumer Research, 1991), 178–215.

43. Frank Boles, *Archival Appraisal*, 19.

44. Edward C. Kemp, *Manuscript Solicitation for Libraries, Special Collections, Museums, and Archives* (Littleton, Colo.: Libraries Unlimited, 1978).

45. J. Peter Sigmond, "Divergences and Convergences of Archives: A European Looks at North America," in *Second European Conference on Archives*, International Council on Archives (Ann Arbor, Mich.: ICA, 1989), 8.

46. See David Glassberg, *American Historical Pageantry: The Uses of Tradition in the Early Twentieth Century* (Chapel Hill: University of North Carolina Press, 1990).

47. Walton H. Rawls, ed., *The Century Book of the Long Island Historical Society* (New York: Long Island Historical Society, 1964), v.

48. Howard Mansfield, *In the Memory House* (Golden, Colo.: Fulcrum Publishing, 1993), 16–17.

49. J. H. Hodson, *The Administration of Archives* (Oxford, England: Pergamon Press, 1972), 79.

50. Duckett, *Modern Manuscripts*, 19.

51. Francis L. Berkeley, Jr., "History and Problems of the Control of Manuscripts in the United States," *Proceedings of the American Philosophical Society* 98 (June 1954): 176.

52. Dana Gioia, "The Hand of the Poet: The Magical Value of Manuscripts," *Hudson Review* 49 (Spring 1996): 22, 25.

53. David Gelernter, *Machine Beauty: Elegance and the Heart of Technology* (New York: Basic Books, 1998).

54. Jon Katz, *Media Rants: PostPolitics in the Digital Nation* (San Francisco: HardWired, 1997), 6.

55. Edward T. Linenthal, *Preserving Memory: The Struggle to Create America's Holocaust Museum* (New York: Viking, 1995), 164.

56. Norman J. Thrower, *Maps & Civilization: Cartography in Culture and Society* (Chicago: University of Chicago Press, 1996), 141.

57. Paul Connerton, *How Societies Remember* (Cambridge: Cambridge University Press, 1989).

58. Michel-Rolph Trouillot, *Silencing the Past: Power and the Production of History* (Boston: Beacon Press, 1995), 20, 53, 153.

59. Douglas Cole, *Captured Heritage: The Scramble for Northwest Coast Artifacts* (Norman: University of Oklahoma Press, 1985), xiii.

60. Todd Gitlin, *The Twilight of Common Dreams: Why America Is Wracked by Culture Wars* (New York: Henry Holt and Co., 1995), 23.

3

The Archivist and Collecting: How Others Might See Archivists as Collectors

Whereas it is virtually impossible to define collecting, and, narratively speaking, to mark where that activity begins, a collecting attitude is unmistakable and distinct.

Mieke Bal, 1994[1]

During the past quarter-century, the number of repositories for research purposes has increased notably, and all these repositories are engaged in collecting records. It is a pursuit that has always been highly individualistic and competitive, but whether these characteristics are for better or for worse is open to argument.

Lester J. Cappon, 1976[2]

Archival collecting, the acquisition of historical manuscripts and archives, has been a primary activity of the North American archivist from the faintest origins of the modern profession, whether we dress it up with terms such as *acquisition* or *appraisal* or with some other professional jargon. As a profession, in North America at least, archivists continue to be absorbed with the physical possession of records, documentary remnants, and a wide spectrum of other objects they could term *artifacts* or that they often treat as artifacts. Archivists describe their motivations for such acquisition as ranging from the preservation of documentary materials to the service of scholarship, but, despite the long history of collecting archives and historical manuscripts, it is not an activity that has been the topic of sustained scrutiny by the archival profession.

Collecting became more difficult in the late twentieth century for a variety of reasons: shrinking archives resources, increasing records quantities, more complex record-keeping technologies, and a society seemingly torn asunder by multiculturalism and related ideologies. (What can archivists possibly acquire to meet constantly changing and often conflicting needs?) We could add to these challenges the debates about the archival mission and appraisal theory and practice. The archival community certainly needs to reopen discussion about collecting, whether it is the profession's relationship to autograph dealers or individual collectors or the issue of the physical custody of digital record-keeping systems.

To a certain extent, the archival profession has allowed a sort of free-market approach in the acquisition of archival records. Archivists collect institutional records rather than nurture the development of viable institutional archives; even institutional archivists seem prone to refer to their holdings as "collections," a reference perhaps no more significant than a convenient shorthand but one that seems dangerously more than semantic. Archivists more often than not compete rather than cooperate in our collecting (an issue that Lester Cappon alluded to more than two decades ago in the article quoted at the outset of this chapter). Archivists even sometimes overlook the problems with managing certain kinds of record-keeping technologies so that they still try to acquire them in ways that may not really protect the records themselves. And archivists even participate in the autograph trade, ignoring some of the logical issues this causes for security or how the acquisition of such records has often compromised their provenance (and as a consequence their "recordness").

The marketplace approach has many problems. Following Christopher Lasch, this "market appears to be the ideal embodiment of the principle . . . that [individual repositories] are the best judges of their own interests and that they must be therefore be allowed to speak for themselves in matters that concern their happiness and well-being. But [individual repositories] cannot learn to speak for themselves at all, much less come to an intelligent understanding of their happiness and well-being, in a world in which there are no values except those of the market."[3] Left to the marketplace, archives become like history textbook writers trying to fit in everything and doing it on an equal playing field; the "textbooks fall apart" or do not get written at all,[4] and the archives become repositories of lots of interesting stuff without real coherence or focus. Or, like the marketplace, archives can become like the old *Wunderkammern*, wonder-cabinets, museums "where natural wonders were displayed alongside works of art and various man-made feats of ingenuity."[5] In this type of analysis, we can understand that this marketplace is an extension of a complicated set of activities, attitudes, and aspects that constitute collecting and that can endanger the nature and purpose of archives.

As I was writing this chapter, I was also reading the daily reports on the sale of John F. and Jacqueline Kennedy "stuff" (is there a better term to describe the incredible diversity of objects ranging from old golf clubs to fake pearl necklaces?) and the extraordinary prices it fetched. The media, not surprisingly transfixed by the sale, made many references to the price of "history" and provided a window into the mind and world of the collector. As far as the media are concerned, there really seems to be little difference between what goes on at a bizarre Sotheby's auction and a museum or archive. Popular columnists, writing about archives and their acquisition, have often revealed this sentiment. Cullen Murphy, in a recent *Atlantic Monthly*, made reference to the National Archives' efforts and the recent PROFS case's (the PROFS case, named after a particular e-mail system, concerns the effort by the Reagan-Bush administrations to delete e-mail concerning their activities in the controversial Iran-Contra affair) impact on the preservation of electronic mail with wonderment about the need to save all these records. "I cannot help wondering," Murphy wrote, "whether as a nation we are compiling archives at a rate that will exceed anyone's ability ever to make sense of them." He turned to an archaeological metaphor. "Is it preposterous to begin thinking of some of our archives as the new tells? . . . But there are too many of them for more than a few ever to be excavated systematically and understanding what's in even those few takes decades if not centuries."[6] Thinking of archives as archaeological sites and collections enables one to miss the larger issues of the value of archives for evidence, accountability, and even corporate memory. Wrestling with the psychology and nature of collecting is important for the archivist and the archival program; if nothing else, doing this forces archivists to come to terms with their institutional and societal missions. It makes archivists wonder if there is any more point to their work than trying to fill their repositories with high profile archival fonds and manuscript collections.

I have certain viewpoints about the issue of collecting: collecting is not appraisal, it can destroy the value of archival records, and it is sometimes irresponsibly carried out. While a decade ago Richard Berner could write that "collecting has taken on a coherence that was previously lacking," I disagree with this assessment, then and now.[7] While the discussion about archival appraisal over the last decade of the twentieth century brought about more precise terminology and some intriguing arguments for macroappraisal as a coherent, principled, scholarly activity, the practice of appraisal has not kept pace; it still appears to be malformed collecting to satisfy ill-defined users' or other needs.

The purpose of this chapter is, however, not to describe these perspectives. My intention is, instead, to analyze recent studies concerning collecting that I believe will be valuable to archivists in their deliberations about this important issue. Looking at collecting from a variety of other disciplines and perspectives can do wonders for our own understanding of the role of collecting in the crucial function of archival appraisal. It can awaken us to the crucial differences between appraisal and collecting.

THE BIG QUESTION: WHY COLLECT?

Archival professionals who advocate relentless collecting suggest many reasons acquisition is so important. Many of these reasons are good: protection, physical and intellectual; accessibility; impending destruction; and appropriate professional care. But are there other reasons? For example, why is it that we see the rationale for collecting expounded within a professional rationale, while many archival repositories fail to develop adequate acquisitions policies or will readily ignore these policies when the possibility of a good acquisition is identified?

Werner Muensterberger's *Collecting* is worth considering for some answers to this kind of question.[8] Muensterberger, identified as a practicing psychoanalyst, has attempted to probe into the psyche of the collector. His assessment of the "unruly passion" is itself unruly (the book is often repetitive and not particularly well organized), but *Collecting* is often illuminating about the activity of the collector (and it is also fun to read). The book is based on historical case studies, interviews with living collectors, and an analysis of existing studies. While Muensterberger is considering the individual collector, I wonder whether many of the characteristics he identifies aren't also applicable to archives, historical manuscripts repositories, and special collections in which either their leaders have expressed unbridled enthusiasm for collecting or the program originated with the core gift of manuscripts from an individual collector?

Muensterberger's evaluation revolves about his sense that collecting is an exercise intended to overcome certain personality disorders. There is the matter of trying to overcome personal uncertainties: "Repeated acquisitions serve as a vehicle to cope with inner uncertainty, a way of dealing with the dread of renewed anxiety, with confusing problems of need and longing."[9] Loneliness seems to be an issue: "Irrespective of individual idiosyncrasies of collectors, and no matter what or how they collect, one issue is paramount: the objects in their possession are all ultimate, often unconscious assurances against despair and loneliness."[10] Muensterberger concludes his study, in fact, with a suggestion that collectors are in constant search for meaning: "The objects they cherish are inanimate substitutes for reassurance and care. Perhaps even more telling, these objects prove, both to the collector and to the world, that he or she is special and worthy of them."[11] Is this why many archivists seem content in university *special* collections? Is this why so many university archivists and other institutional archivists try to collect without developing or working with records management programs?

Collecting may be both a crucial aspect of one's identity and a kind of religious exercise. The objects being acquired, suggests Muensterberger, "contribute to [a collector's] sense of identity and function as a source of self-definition."[12] There seems to be a common element among collectors in that "they need to convince themselves that what they own is special, if not the 'best,' or 'the ultimate.'"[13] This may relate to the religious nature of collecting: the "collector, not unlike the religious believer, assigns power and value to these objects because their presence and possession seem to have a modifying—usually pleasure-giving—function in the owner's mental state."[14] Muensterberger compares collecting to the "accumulation of relics" as a search for evidence: "The objects are regarded as testimony that death is not final and the end of all existence; that one does not have to face abandonment, the dread of being left alone and, ultimately, demise and nothingness."[15] The repeated references to the *symbolic* importance of archives, seeming to reemerge as more and more archivists turn to working with electronic record-keeping systems, often carry with them a kind of religious reference.

Collecting also examines a typical aspect normally associated with collecting, its pleasure. Muensterberger argues that "for the dedicated . . . collector . . . the experience is not simply recreational but an enriching respite from the sometimes frustrating demands of everyday life."[16] Put in a more blunt fashion, "Objects in the collector's experience, real or imagined, allow for a magical escape into a remote and private world."[17] Is this the source of the popular perception of archives as a refuge from the problems of the real world? Is the fact that so many archives are unable to build broader public profiles or to work with more sophisticated record-keeping technologies while they struggle with processing backlogs a reflection of this kind of attitude? Is the stack area that "remote and private world"?

Russell Belk's *Collecting in a Consumer Society* examines the rationale for collecting by considering this activity as a "special type of consuming," a topic that has not been generally considered by other scholars.[18] Belk considers the nature of the consumer society, the history of collecting, and then provides parallel analysis of individual and institutional collectors. Although he draws on the psychological studies of experts like Muensterberger, Belk is relying more on his own field of business administration to understand why we collect and how we rationalize the process of collecting. He runs through how collectors explain their activity, including many explanations that will sound familiar to archivists (such as acting as the "savior of lost, neglected, or endangered objects"[19] or acquiring objects that will preserve memories and a sense of the past).

Belk's chapter on institutional collecting is worth a close reading by archivists because it is the closest to their own situation. Unfortunately, Belk chooses to stress the museum in his discussion rather than drawing in other institutions such as libraries and archives that also collect. Belk makes some strong distinctions between institutional and individual collectors, saying, for example:

> While a curator may be possessive toward a collection and regard it as "mine," the fact remains that unlike an individual collector, a museum curator does not own the objects in a collection and lacks the individual collector's total control over their fate.[20]

But he considers other important issues when viewing institutions such as museums in the context of a consumer society. Belk notes that museums view themselves as competing with the department store, shopping mall, and theme park, and he also suggests that in drawing on the efforts of individual collectors in forming the nucleus of institutional collections, museums must keep in mind that these collections and their acquisition do not result in representative holdings (they have already been formed for other reasons and purposes). In other words, Belk's work is a way of reminding archivists to reconsider the context for their own appraisal. What would archivists see as their main competitor in their social context (the information resources manager, the World Wide Web, or what?)? How does the archivist take into account the efforts of institutional records creators and individual collectors when appraising these records?

A more promising volume on the nature of collecting is Susan Pearce's *On Collecting*.[21] Pearce, an English museum educator, argues that she wrote this book in order "to treat collecting as a social phenomenon, which should be examined from the perspective of its own proper critique rather than as a loosely historical bundle of anecdote."[22] This is, Pearce hopes:

> an investigation into collecting as a set of things which people do, as an aspect of individual and social practice which is important in public and private life as a means of constructing the way in which we relate to the material world and build up our own lives.[23]

In addition to a sweeping introduction and summary, Pearce includes three long sections on "collecting in practice," the "poetics of collecting," and the "politics of collecting." Revealing that this is a topic that has been of interest to her for some years, Pearce summarizes and critiques the diverse literature, draws in other disciplines and their own institutional and case studies, and liberally discusses particular cases as illustrations.[24] Although dwelling on the European scene, Pearce's encyclopedic scope, carefully woven themes, and well-written and interesting prose supports a book that might be the best single-volume study on the topic, and it contains innumerable insights of interest to American archivists.

Although there are far too many detailed discussions to relate them all, I believe it is appropriate to mention some as a window into how we archivists might have built our own worlds through collecting, acquiring, or whatever we deem to term it. Pearce writes that the "selection process clearly lies at the heart of collecting,"[25] chronicling that objects collected "have passed from the profane— the secular world of mundane, ordinary commodity—to the sacred, taken to be extraordinary, special and capable of generating reverence."[26] Have we not also heard archivists speak of their "collections" in this way? There are also lessons from the historical review of collecting.

> Just as the Roman public temple collections have given us some of our institutional vocabulary, particularly the word "curator," so the Roman private art collections have provided characteristic collecting rationales which lay stress on the moral and ennobling qualities of accumulated art.[27]

In the United States, at least, many archivists still prefer to call and to think of themselves as curators, handling special collections entrusted to them as signposts to the past. Pearce believes that "collections are therefore both the product of a personal life . . . and a means of structuring that life span, of giving tangible form and content to the experience of time passing,"[28] and she includes a lengthy analysis of the reasons collectors collect that certainly suggests some useful things about the origins of preformed collections offered to archives and manuscript repositories and about the collecting impulses of archivists themselves. If nothing else, Pearce provides some powerful insights into the collecting impulse that archivists and manuscripts curators must document as they appraise and describe both collections and fonds that might have been treated more like collections. Collections are a way to beat time, to gain immortality, and:

museums . . . are the natural heirs . . . of deep-rooted preoccupations
in the European psyche which revolve around the capacity of material
to create relationships between gods and men, the sacred significance
of relics, and the need for a building in which sacred wealth can be set
aside on behalf of the community.[29]

Are archives any different from museums in this sense?

Pearce also provides some insights into collecting that could sig-
nal to archivists new ways of reflecting on their holdings. At one
point she notes that "collections which have come to us from the
earlier periods are attracting considerable attention as historical
documents in their own right . . . ,"[30] yet as archivists we have
tended not to study our own holdings, their origins, the changing
ideas about the mission of accumulating such records, and other
concerns. If you, as an archivist, accept a collection of historic manuscripts concerning Thomas Jefferson's perspective on slavery, are
you gaining a Jefferson fonds or a particular collector's fonds, and
how does the difference in origin affect the records' evidence?
Pearce writes:

Collections are psychic ordering, of individuality, of public and private relationships, and of time and space. They live in the minds and
hearts of their collectors, for whom they act as material autobiogra-
phies, chronicling the cycle of a life, from the first moment an object
strikes a particular personal chord, to specialized accumulation, to
constructing the dimensions of life, to a final measure of immortality.[31]

If we can accept Pearce's assessment, then how do we strive to
describe such a collection? At another point, Pearce suggests that
"material objects, like all other kinds of objects, are constantly created and recreated by human beings through their symbolic desig-
nation of them and their actions toward them,"[32] yet archivists have
seemed to be more compelled to try to determine past actions of
archivists in order to preserve their decisions and their holdings,
failing to understand that any record kept for one time as evidence
may be determined at a later time to not be the necessary evidence.

There are also reassuring aspects of Pearce's study about some of
our own most cherished archival principles. Pearce mentions:

Information cannot come from single specimens, only from groups:
the knowledge involved is essentially collective, and the collected exis-

tence of the many millions of pieces just referred to are essential to the existence of the system. Perceived relationships are of the essence; reality lies not in an individual item but in the relationship it bears to others which are like and unlike it.[33]

Here we have affirmation of a principle very similar to the archivist's notion of provenance and context.

ANOTHER BIG QUESTION:
HOW IS COLLECTING DONE?

Although it is quite clear that the psychology of collecting remains the more intriguing topic, the dynamics and practicalities of acquisition have also been the focus of an increasing number of studies, popular and scholarly. One reason might be that the increasing splintering of society into many cultural and ethnic groups has brought with it more complicated issues ranging from repatriation of objects to the religious or symbolic importance of artifacts and collections to particular groups, and this new interest brings new perspectives on the marketplace for antiques, museum-quality objects, books, and manuscripts. Practices once well accepted seem not so clear or clean.

Much has been written, for example, about the ethics of collecting. The Messenger-edited collection of essays, *The Ethics of Collecting Cultural Property*, is as good a place as any to start.[34] Consisting of sixteen essays written by archaeologists, art dealers, museum curators and administrators, lawyers, public policy people, government officials, and scholars, the volume focuses on cultural property as archaeological or ethnological objects. *The Ethics of Collecting* is really a collection of case studies, including descriptions of Native American perspectives, the antiquities trade in Arkansas, international looting of Mayan objects and of objects of other native peoples in different countries, the role of museums and collectors in the preservation of these objects, and legal cases concerning the repatriation of these objects. Karen J. Warren's introduction to the volume alludes to the "cacophony of voices over cultural properties," and this volume seems to be a testament to this cacophony. There is a lot of disagreement and debate, something you would expect given the diversity of perspectives represented in this publication. Yet there is much to be gained from reading the range of perspectives provided here. If I had to determine one statement suggesting the primary viewpoint that emanates from the book, I would choose one from the essay by David Sassoon on the antiquities of Nepal:

> Over the years, we have listened to the perspective of the nation's art dealers, and we have listened to the perspective of the nation's scholars. But there has been nobody who has given voice to the perspective of the villagers who wake up one morning to find their God missing from the temple.[35]

This volume gives a voice to the people.

Why should archivists want to read a volume of essays like this? After all, it is not about archives and manuscripts. I believe there are two reasons. First, there has been a stronger effort by the international museum community to regulate the acquisition and trade of antiquities, and while these efforts have been uneven, they still represent a significant improvement over what, if anything, has occurred in the companion trade in autographs and manuscripts. Second, the collection of essays is useful for providing a host of insights into the general nature of collecting and the implications of collecting. Some examples will suffice to suggest what I mean by this. Alan Shestack, in his essay on art museums, argues:

> Museum professionals are acquirers; we are inherently greedy collectors. Most of us go into the profession because the desire to accumulate and bring together objects of quality is in our blood. We are personally and professionally devoted to adding to and improving our holdings—that is what makes us tick.[36]

This should sound familiar to archivists. Shestack goes on to add that this quality includes acquiring even objects suspected of being acquired through less-than-appropriate means. Orrin C. Shane, III, in a commentary on one section of essays, relates public and private collecting to each other, noting that "it is the demand for illicit cultural property created by private collecting that fosters the looting that supplies illicit material."[37] Both of these insights can be, but have not been, discussed by archivists.

To the collections of scholarly essays, we can add—in a quite useful manner—more popular studies of specific cases in the annals of collecting. For whatever reason, an interest has developed in the antiquities and art trade, probably spurred on by unrelated events such as the fabulous prices some of these objects have fetched in the auction house (and the interest of the media in these tales), the chaotic collapse of the Eastern Europe Communist Bloc and the escalating smuggling of art and historic objects, and the half-century anniversary of the end of World War II, which brought with it some bizarre chronicles of how warfare encourages systematic looting of other nations' museums, libraries, and archives.

There are too many works to describe all in detail, but a few merit interest and comment. Dan Hofstadter's *Goldberg's Angel: An Adventure in the Antiquities Trade* is a journalistic telling of the pillaging, buying, and recovering of four early Christian devotional mosaics leading to the 1989 case of *Cyprus v. Goldberg*, described by the author as important landmark litigation because it recovered artworks of "unknown provenance" bought on good faith by an American dealer.[38] Hofstadter describes a story that is as complicated and as intriguing as Dashiell Hammett's *Maltese Falcon*, but the points relevant to this chapter are in the discussion about the cast of characters involved. None seem truthful. Lies abound. As Hofstadter comments, "Even the most respectable dealers, collectors, and curators depended on a class of audacious brokers . . . from which they hypocritically averted their eyes."[39] Can the autograph trade be any more respectable than this? How will we ever know because nearly every work on this subject, one intertwined with the history of the American archival profession, has been written by insiders in the trade?

Thatcher Freund's *Objects of Desire: The Lives of Antiques and Those Who Pursue Them* is a popular treatise similar to the Hofstadter volume.[40] Freund traces the manufacture, use, subsequent ownership, and transition from utilitarian objects to prized antiques of two disparate pieces of furniture—an eighteenth-century Pennsylvania blanket chest and a Chippendale card table of the same century. Freund's work is a sympathetic one, for he is obviously a lover of both antiques and the quest for antiques. Again, we gain insights into the marketplace for such objects, and we begin to understand the reasons monetary values fluctuate and certain objects gain the prestige they do. About the card table, Freund writes:

> Money makes some things beautiful, and the card table, they knew, was worth a lot of money. It was valuable because some people wanted it in their homes and because museums wanted examples in

their American wings. It was valuable because someplace a market existed for it and because out in the world of American furniture—where the dealers fought and lied and stole things from their friends—some people could tell a great card table from a good one.[41]

This description might appear to be as far from the issue of archival collecting as one could get, except that there has not yet to date been an objective analysis of the impact of the autograph market, the market in nostalgia (typified by the Kennedy auction), and the involvement of archival and historical manuscript repositories in the marketplace on the prices of documents, the urge to acquire such documents, and the competition for important archival fonds and collections. Books such as Freund's can remind archivists that the issues of acquiring document collections by purchase can be a complicated matter; these perspectives might even suggest that archivists might think twice before becoming involved in the marketplace.

There has been a growing interest in the plunder of art and other national treasures during World War II, and this looting is certainly another form of collecting (although certainly it is the most perverse form). Lynn Nicholas's *Rape of Europa* is by far the most comprehensive, informative, and disturbing of these new studies. It examines the Third Reich's carting off art from over Europe as well as the Nazi notion of "degenerate art" and its destruction or removal from public view.[42] There are many tidbits about intriguing activities in her book. She writes about the many auctions just before the onslaught of World War II and how many art museums around the world formed or added to their core collections. The many traveling art exhibits in North America were intended to protect the collections of European art museums. Nicholas describes how the art museums, art scholarship, and antiquities and art trade within the Third Reich were all bent to supporting both the nationalistic aims of that despotic regime and the personal aggrandizement of individual collectors:

All this preservation, confiscation, and dealing would be carried out by a complex group of bureaucracies, often in ferocious competition, whose utterly cynical exploitation of those in their power was justified within true Nazi bosoms by an equally complex series of legalisms and rationalizations.[43]

As the author also points out, all of this wheeling and dealing was meticulously documented by a political power expecting to be in power for a very long time. Although Nicholas does not psychoanalyze the activities and reasons of the Third Reich and its leaders, preferring to tell the story of the illicit trade and of the tidy group of Allied experts who tried to put all the pieces back together after the war, *The Rape of Europa* is, in fact, another study of the powerful allure of collecting. At the conclusion of her book, she notes that her story does not have an ending because many of the art works and other treasures were "lost" or remained "in hiding." Her characterization of the whole affair as "cynical and desperate games of ideology, greed, and survival"[44] is not that far from the seamier side of much of the collecting that still goes on today in the antiquities, art, and autograph trades.

More relevant for archivists is Kenneth Rendell's *History Comes to Life*, his most recent volume on collecting autographs and historical manuscripts.[45] Rendell is well known to archivists for both his publications and his well-known work on recent forgeries. This book consists of two parts. The first is a brief series of chapters on why people collect, what can be collected, the determination of values, and the detection of forgeries. The second part is a series of topical descriptions of "areas of collecting" with brief descriptions of the rarity or availability of certain autographs with numerous reproductions of signatures and photographs of certain types of records. *History Comes to Life* is, it seems, an update or replacement of the earlier reference works for collectors published by another dealer, Charles Hamilton.[46] Rendell's volume is an unabashed invitation to start collecting, typical of this genre.

Two aspects of this book are noteworthy, one interesting and the other quite disturbing. First, Rendell's volume is obviously intended to establish his credentials as an authority, and some of the references to himself and his work fit well into the type of analysis of collecting done by Muensterberger, Belk, and Pearce. Consider this assessment of changing trends of manuscript collecting:

> By the late 1980s, the entire business of historical letters and documents had very significantly shifted its focus from institutional to private collectors. This was a result both of decreased institutional budgets, particularly as the availability of major collections declined,

and my own personal preference for wanting to share more directly in the enthusiasm and fun of building private collections.[47]

Admittedly this is hard to read. Is he describing his *own* business? Or is he stating that *he* was a major influence on the changing trends of the trade in this decade? Or is Rendell merely describing his following of the shifts in interest and activity of the market?

The more important issue, however, is the second major focus on the reasons and justifications for the market. Although Rendell's explanation of the reasons people collect is simplistic ("while many may think of collecting as an intellectual pursuit, it is an emotional one as well"[48]), he has written the book not to explain what collecting is about but to encourage it ("many of our clients are as fascinating and well known as the people whose letters they are collecting"[49]). And this is where the archivist should be concerned. Although Rendell is certainly not advocating illegal activity, he is making some statements that are dangerous: "A collector should not be bound by any rules of collecting except those created by his or her own interests and ideas."[50] What Rendell is stating here, of course, is the desirability of forming one's own collecting focus, but how will this statement be read by the individual who works for an archives or historical manuscripts repository or by an individual who is upset that so many valuable and important records are held by institutions? In fact, throughout the book, one senses Rendell's wistful longing for the good old days when institutions were not the owners of many of the important collections. There are other questionable statements as well: "As budget problems have plagued libraries, it has made sense to convert unwanted collections into funds needed for other activities."[51] Here is a statement that should have been accompanied with some indication of the legal and ethical matters and complexities of an institution doing this.[52] Instead, one can imagine the energetic collector beginning to call repositories to try to make deals for their holdings.

Rendell's writings are valuable to archivists for two reasons. Like earlier writings by Charles Hamilton and other autograph dealers, they are rich sources of reproductions of autographs and prominent forgeries. They are more important, however, for orienting archivists to the autograph trade, a trade we need to be more critical toward and that deserves significantly more study and reflection. We could rename Rendell's book *Autograph Dealing Comes to Life*.

CASE STUDIES IN COLLECTING

Two of the books considered in this part of the chapter are case studies. One is a serious, legitimate case study in nonprofit management that actually focuses on one institution's problems with unregulated acquisition. The other publication is intended to be a broad analysis of book collecting, but it turns out to be a series of biographical sketches and vignettes about both book and manuscript collecting.

Although Kevin Guthrie's study of the New-York Historical Society is an analysis of nonprofit management, it is also a case study of the dangers of unmanaged collecting.[53] For most archivists, the story of the New-York Historical Society is a familiar one. The Society is one of the venerated historical societies, founded in 1804, and as a result it is part of the ancient history of the American archival profession. Long before the establishment of government archives or institutional archives, organizations like the New-York Historical Society were the primary means of protecting this nation's documentary heritage. This institution assembled an outstanding collection of historical manuscripts, historical artifacts, prints, and photographs exceeded by few other repositories. For many archivists and manuscripts curators, societies like this represent the preeminence of collecting venues. But as recent articles in the *New York Times*, *Museum News*, and other newspapers and journals have indicated, the New-York Historical Society has fallen on hard times. For much of the past decade, leadership at the institution has changed often, staff relations have deteriorated, desperate calls for financial support have been sounded, hours and services have been curtailed, and partnerships have been sought as saviors. What went wrong?

The primary question Guthrie seeks to answer in his book relates to the New-York Historical Society as collector. "With such highly esteemed collections and seemingly broad support," the author muses, "how could the Society be in such trouble?"[54] Although Guthrie provides the answer later in the book that these collections are "cultural assets" and valuable not because of any cash value but "by the relevance of that asset to the broader cultural purposes and capacities of the institution to which it belongs,"[55] it is also true that the threat to the Society's collections stimulated public consternation about the fate of the New York institution. Still, the sobering conclusion by Guthrie is that "although few people question the cultural value of the millions of manuscripts, books, prints, and other historical documents and artifacts held by the Society, they are not the kinds of assets that inspire and excite contributors."[56] But for the purposes of this chapter, it is Guthrie's insights into the Society's collecting activities and emphases that are interesting. This study of the New-York Historical Society suggests that the source of much of the institution's later financial and managerial problems was its collecting. Early in the book, Guthrie's comment that "an emphasis on acquisitions, particularly to the extent that quantity was regarded as important, could be dangerous"[57] serves as a sort of understatement. He argues that the "Society had a long history of accepting anything and everything that was given to it with little regard for the quality of the gift, the institution's capacity to absorb it, or the relevance of the gift to the Society."[58] Later, Guthrie concludes, the:

> Society's history provides a dramatic illustration of what can happen when the relationship between an institution's mission and its collections is not carefully managed. The uncritical accumulation of materials for many, many years played a major role in creating financial obligations that far exceed the Society's present capacity to meet them.[59]

What are the specific points made by Guthrie about the mismanagement of the Society? There was a constant battle throughout the Society's history to gain control of the collections.[60] Deaccessioning, needed to help the Society rid itself of items recognized as outside the scope of any rational mission, was handicapped because of the poor records maintained about the collections.[61] The Society found itself unable to choose priorities in its research library or more public museum function,[62] and even staff competed for priority recognition as the Society declined to the point of oblivion.[63] Board members were not selected because of their managerial or other expertise but because they were collectors or interested in the collecting activities of the Society.[64] The lack of control of the Society's holdings even scared off partners who had similar interests.[65] And, finally, the Society for decades prided itself on its independence from both professionalism and public and government benefactors. Evident in Guthrie's study are the results of unbridled collecting and the mistaken assumption that building great collections should be the primary mission of cultural repositories like the New-York Historical Society.

Nicholas Basbanes's *Gentle Madness* might be the most disappointing of the volumes considered in this chapter.[66] Basbanes, a former literary editor and now columnist, claims that his book is the result of eight years of "investigative journalism" with a thesis that "however bizarre and zealous collectors have been through the ages, so much of what we know about history, literature, and culture would be lost forever if not for the passion and dedication of these driven souls."[67] For those looking for a well-written and interesting book about individual book collectors (and we should note that there is a substantial discussion about manuscript collectors as well)—that is, stories about the hunt for books, the building of particular collections, the market for books, and the donation of some of these personal collections to institutional repositories—*A Gentle Madness* will be an entertaining addition to the bookshelf and good beach reading. Those looking for what Basbanes calls his thesis, the relationship of book collecting to knowledge and scholarship, will be disappointed.

A Gentle Madness is an antiquarian's delight, meaning that those who enjoy collecting books will like it (and in many ways I really like this book as well). The book does not provide any real understanding of collecting, failing to delve into motivations or to develop themes that tie various collectors and their activities together, and it takes for granted that accumulating collections of books will generate or sustain meaningful and useful scholarship; in the entire volume there is not a single discussion about *how* the book collections are or could be used. In fact, there are many references to the origins of personal collections, making one wonder whether such assumptions are merited at all. In one account of the reason one collector started acquiring documents, Basbanes provides an example of what I am discussing:

> Karpeles explained that his fervor was inspired by nothing less than a midlife epiphany, a revelation that came in 1978 when he was forty-two years old and visiting the Huntington Library in San Marino with his wife, Marsha. "We looked in an exhibit case and we saw something that we could not believe was there, something we felt belonged in the Smithsonian Institution," he said. "It was a pass that President Lincoln had given to one of his bodyguards the night he was killed." We asked some questions and we found out that this little pass is nothing, that there are documents changing hands all the time that would make you

faint. Right there, I decided I would go into this, and I would go into it with a vengeance. I would see how many of these great documents I could get before people realized what they were selling.[68]

Whether or not this collection comes back to an institution seems almost beside the point. Here is testimony of a collector competing with repositories and going after individual ("great") documents, perhaps even destroying the evidence of the records in question by ruining their context and making them into artifacts serving a completely different purpose. The irony of the Basbanes book is that the long chapter on the book thief Stephen Blumberg paints a character portrait that seems in perfect harmony with the many other collectors described. The value of this book is that perhaps it reveals something of the obsessive nature of such collecting that should cause archivists and manuscripts curators to question their own collecting activities and motivations.[69]

MAKING THE RECORDS SPEAK: ARCHIVAL APPRAISAL, MEMORY, PRESERVATION, AND COLLECTING

Acquisition policies, collection development concepts, archival values, reappraisal approaches, and a host of other methods, worldviews, and theories have become the persistent topic of archival professional sessions, journal articles, and listserv discussions focused broadly on the nature and purpose of archival appraisal. When I sat down to write this part of the chapter, the National Archives of Australia were embroiled in a public controversy about plans to reappraise and deaccession some of its holdings,[70] the United Kingdom's archives list was discussing the public perception of archivists (dredging up those stereotypes of dusty, mild-mannered individuals squirreling away old documents), the Smithsonian Institution was under attack about new alliances with businesses and private individuals concerning the content of its exhibitions,[71] and Americans were captivated by Nicholson Baker's scathing denunciation of library and archives preservation practices, the heart of which was based on misconceptions about the nature and mission of libraries and archives.[72] Archives and archivists were in the news, but not in the positive way that they might have hoped for.

Archivists have become more sophisticated in how they consider appraisal, but the public perception of what archives are about, especially in their selective identification and preservation from the vast documentary universe, is still weak. Although I know of books, research projects, and Web-based tools in the works to try to strengthen the public's understanding of the archival mission and appraisal's role in that mandate, it is clear that archivists have a long way to go in correcting misperceptions—but efforts are being made.[73] Nicholson Baker is outraged that original printed and other artifacts are reformatted and discarded, and he seems to suggest that *all* books, newspapers, and other textual documents must be saved. His reviewers have been forceful in saying just that. Australian historians, journalists, and citizens are confused that most, if not all, records are eventually scrapped or angry that records once thought important enough to be stored in their national archives could now be removed. Despite a century of a modern archives movement, archivists are still not understood, and much of this misunderstanding revolves around the crucial function of appraisal—or, if you will, how and why archives are formed.

Certainly, archivists need to explain, clearly and patiently, how they appraise and ultimately acquire records. In the meantime, archivists can learn much from how others seem to be writing about selection and preservation issues closely akin to the archival appraisal function. Susan Crane's study of collecting in early nineteenth-century Germany reveals much about how historical collections are formed.[74] Crane's edited volume on memory and museums provides a glimpse into the similarities and differences between archives and museums, as well as giving a prototype for similar investigations into archives.[75] And Howard Mansfield's popular discourse on preservation (he uses the term "restoration") should suggest to archivists just how difficult it is to persuade the public of the difficult decisions archivists and other record professionals face in forming archives.[76] A documentary heritage does not appear magically, but it is the result of many factors, incidents, and accidents—along with the dedicated work of archivists.

All three books are noteworthy in their own right, and each could be analyzed merely for what it suggests about museums and historic preservation. Crane's edited volume on museums and memory fits nicely into an expanding literature on these topics, and it is one of the few efforts to relate the two in a direct fashion. Crane's study on collecting and public memory also relates two subjects that are receiving considerable new attention, and her conclusions about the impact of the movement from individual collecting to organized (voluntary and government sponsored) acquiring will probably lead to new scrutiny of the development of historical organizations in other nations and eras. And, finally, Mansfield's popular ruminations on preservation give us insight into the way many Americans view the maintenance of historical objects, traditions, and sites. Crane's book on German collecting examines "two conceptions of historical consciousness." Crane, a professor of modern European history, writes:

> First, the "historical sublime," represented the initial, highly emotional historical sensation or revelation in the presence of certain objects. The second, secondary experience of historical consciousness was received upon encountering historical objects that had been collected, preserved, and presented for repeated viewing in a collection which attempted to instill coherent meanings through a narrative context—and succeeded insofar as viewers began to think historically.[77]

In this era, two centuries removed, we discover an almost religious quest with the use of objects and rapidly emergent historical preservation societies, academic disciplines, and public museums and other repositories—all very familiar to us today but very innovative and sometimes controversial in the early nineteenth century. Tying her study to the vast scholarship on public history, Crane writes, "This is a study of how we begin to remember history,"[78] and it looks very similar to what was happening in the United States at the same time.

Crane commences her analysis by considering the emergence of the historical sublime (much as transpired in religious experience or in the described experiences of Romantic poets) and the role of collectors in enumerating ruins and gathering artifacts and older documents. It is a fascinating chapter, as we marvel today at the popularity of eBay, antiquing manuals, and television antique shows. Ruins, for example, became important because of their "ability to refer to already existing historical knowledge,"[79] but it was a deeply personal process: "Ruins and decrepit buildings are one and

the same until someone 'sees' otherwise.''[80] Ruins, manuscripts, and
artifacts were all acquired in unprecedented ways, with a new role
for government authorities publishing lists and building and opening repositories. Such collecting has a universality that should resonate with us today. Crane notes:

> Once the inspiring object has been marked for preservation, it is usu-
> ally removed from its context (the physical context of its site or the
> emotional context of its sudden apparition) and placed in a collection
> which then creates a new historical context of visibility and explicabil-
> ity, as well as a site in which that object and that experience can be
> revisited.[81]

In other words, the collective process of establishing associations to
expedite the gathering and preserving of historical artifacts created
situations in which individual collectors no longer had control over
how they viewed or experienced such objects or history. No coherent collective memory developed, but rather contested memories
emerged, pitting individuals, organizations, and the state against
each other.

Crane's study also documents the transition from individual to
collective collecting, chronicling the origins of what often remains
today an uneasy relationship. She traces the formation of historical
associations, part of a broader movement of providing a "political
forum for liberal nationalism" and serving the "cultural interests
and ambitions of the rising bourgeoisie,"[82] another parallel with
events in the United States in the same era. An additional impetus
to the formation of historical organizations was the concern that
individual collections would disappear unless an opportunity was
provided to join them into more publicly accessible repositories, a
trend that in our own era has given rise to tensions between individual and institutional collecting. Collectors themselves wrote memoirs, articles, and voluminous correspondence explaining their
work, with at least one eye to preserving not just their collections
but the reasons for their efforts. Someday an observer might look on
the archival literature on appraisal in this same light, as part of a
self-conscious effort to explain ourselves or to justify our own selection efforts. In fact, these associations stressed collecting to such a
degree that they made little effort to interpret the collections, sometimes out of fear that museums and libraries indulging in such inter-

pretation might anger the political authorities (a topic that became much more of an issue in Germany in the era of Nazism and its aftermath).[83] In this present era of congressional scrutiny and media coverage of exhibition controversies such as occurred with the Smithsonian and the use of the *Enola Gay* fuselage, it is interesting to see how such concerns are not new at all.

Regardless of the intentions about interpretation, the nineteenth-century German museums and other repositories were new, and they provided a new context for the objects stored and exhibited there. Crane suggests that the objects were placed in a new historical context "in which the presence of the past could be alluded to while the present's interest in the past was displayed."[84] We might argue that if the new placement of objects changed their meaning, then this process would make the selection of what came into the museums all the more crucial. Crane senses this:

> The new definition of what constituted a historical object, and how it came to be collected, preserved, displayed, and interpreted—and by whom—was perhaps the single most important development in the museology of this time.[85]

The emphasis on what happens to museum and other objects is very illuminating for any group, certainly archivists, involved in decision making about preservation, although this is a process only beginning to receive scholarly treatment and certainly one that is not understood by the public (and one that is prone to attract somewhat hysterical commentaries in newspaper coverage). The relevance of Crane's study for archivists resides not just in her depiction of a period of the formation of institutions like museums and archives but in her description of the way artifacts and objects are seen and change. She describes how in the early nineteenth century, Germans did not collect or display objects because of their age. Crane surmises, "The historicity of an object lies not in its age but in its capacity to bear the meanings attached to the perception of the object in the present. The object must excite a sense of history in the viewer."[86] Left apart from such collections, the Germans believed, the objects face not only physical deterioration but a loss of meaning. As Crane writes, "Once the context of meaning was secured in the museum, the objects themselves became less important than the site in which they were brought together."[87] The meaning of objects derives from being part of a collection, specifically a museum. Some archivists, like Hans Booms, have argued a similar view in the formation of twentieth-century archives,[88] and it is interesting to understand that the implications of the process of collecting have been scrutinized and speculated about for a very long time. Still, it is an issue deserving more analysis.

An interesting parallel is the publication of new scholarly journals. Crane notes that many journals were founded between 1770 and 1850 and employed "museum" as part of their title, functioning as vehicles for bringing together source materials and creating a network of scholars. Crane argues, "We think of modern museums as social contexts, places of meetings, as well as repositories of historical or art objects. In this sense, nineteenth-century journals performed a similar function, only the meeting place was mental rather than physical."[89] These journals, publishing facsimiles of art and artifacts, served scholarship and also gave the "viewer a sense of the historical and a desire to participate in preservation."[90] These journals and various historical associations and museums also existed in the United States, prompting one historian of this phenomenon to refer to this same era as a period of "documania."[91] Such analysis should also make one wonder how future historians will consider our time and the archives field, especially as archivists wrestle with how to use the World Wide Web for making the public and scholarly communities aware of archives. While debate continues in the field about the content and purpose of archives journals (usually in the guise of how much practice versus theory should be represented in their pages), to an outsider the growth in the number of journals and specialized archival repositories and increased access to archival records through digitization will prompt some discussion about this meaning. Certainly the pioneering German collectors, historians, museum officials, and preservationists were having similar debates, expressing their sense of increased concern about the past and societal memory.

Crane ends her book on an interesting note, the personal experience of interacting with an historical object. She thinks that "what history means to a culture . . . is measured by its repetition. . . . The repetition occurs with each writing, each visit to a museum, each reading of a text." Crane sees that these remaining objects are "empty forms readily available for the frequently repeated filling-in of historical memory," and she sees that this "filling-in" is very personal.[92] Yet, her book argues how the individual connection to the past actually seemed to be lost as historical organizations were established and individual collectors banded together to preserve the remains of that past. There is an ironic note in her analysis, not unlike what some archivists representing repositories have probably experienced when they discussed mutual concerns with individual collectors. A historical consciousness seems to be both lost and gained.

Crane's edited volume, *Museums and Memory*, has a broader purpose and is less focused on either chronological or geographical eras, but it can certainly be read as a companion to her book on nineteenth-century German historical collecting. With essays about three themes—thinking through the museum, memories in the museum, and collections and institutions—the book explores how museums and memories "shape each other"[93] in the United States, China, Japan, and Germany from the disciplines of anthropology, art history, museology, and history. Crane, in her introduction to this volume, is interested in museums because of their storage of memories. "Like an archives," she writes, a museum "holds the material manifestations of cultural and scientific production as records, articulated memories removed from the mental world and literally placed in the physical world. Like an archive, it has its own sense of organization, but that sense is deeply complex."[94] The allusions to archives are fascinating, making an archivist, like myself, wonder why we do not yet have a book called *Archives and Memory* (although we are moving ever closer to such scholarship). Although we are beginning to find more interest in archives by historians of culture and memory, many of these studies stretch their definition of archives far beyond how archivists have approached their work (either stimulating them to rethink how they define the term and their work or burying a more literal sense and importance of archives so far into postmodernist jargon as to give little to compare with or relate to the archival work and mission).[95]

The eleven essays in this volume provide many stimulating ideas archivists should mull over in relation to their own work and profession. Michael Fehr's essay about a German museum contends that a museum "has no meaning at all if it is not related to a context shared by a community,"[96] making an archivist pause about how this corresponds to archives, most of which have connections to local communities. Susan Crane's essay on the Museum of Jurassic Technology in

Los Angeles includes her statement that "If early modern curiosity cabinets included objects such as fossil men, giants' thighbones, mermaid tails, and unicorn horns, we must consider the possibility that these were not expressions of irrationality, antiscientific or mystical in their conception, but rather were consistent with the scientific imaginary of the time, structured within a concept of Nature's inexhaustible plentitude."[97] Crane's assessment of early museum collecting suggests the difficulty of imposing professional criticism on archival practice of any era, especially our own, given how close we are to it and how immersed we are in the culture that archives operate within.

The connection of museums to history and historians is a common theme throughout the essays. The essay by Julia Adeney Thomas on how some Japanese photographic museums had separated themselves from their nation's history leads to some interesting speculation about the role of archival finding aids. Thomas writes, "Curators can release images to function historically as points of reference for the viewers' engagement with the past, or they can highlight the qualities of these images in such a way that the photographs fail to intersect with any dialectic between past and present. In other words, photography curators create histories not from necessity but from desire and from aesthetic, social, and political commitments. If this desire is not present, the photographs will not by themselves emerge as resources for public recollection."[98] If the museum curator's intervention in labeling exhibitions is so explicit, what are the implications for how archivists describe archival records in finding aids? Paula Findlen's essay on Renaissance collecting notes how portraits became a popular form of commemoration, with collectors even placing their own images in their collections. Is the role of the archival collector so obvious in archival collections or in guides (such as finding aids) to these holdings? If we can study Renaissance collecting because of explicit clues left by the collectors about themselves, will future generations of scholars be able to understand who archivists were and how they made decisions about what went into archives in the twentieth century?

Other essays in Crane's collection also pose interesting questions for archivists. Diana Drake Wilson's essay on her experience of taking American Indians into three museums exhibiting on their culture and history raises some points about how archivists see visiting researchers and vice versa. Wilson concludes:

For some American Indians, things exhibited in museums *are* events that took place in the past and are still taking place; they are artifacts that carry the material traces of events of the past into the present. Many Euro-Americans read exhibits like texts, a series of discrete signs having an arbitrary but shared meaning.[99]

Native Americans read the exhibits very differently. What does this suggest about the variety of people who come and use archives? What are the implications for how archivists use finding aids, exhibitions, and websites to explain what archives are and how they might be used? What are the audiences archivists seek to engage, and are they successful with the use of devices as diverse as registers and inventories and Web pages? Visitors to archives (both bricks-and-mortar and online) might view archival records not as inert holdings but as living collections, with present significance to their lives. Tamara Hamlisch's discussion of the formation and preservation of the Chinese imperial collections poses similar issues. In considering what has happened to these collections, she writes: "For centuries, the Chinese imperial collections had symbolized both political and moral authority. Throughout Chinese history, dynastic succession was marked, in part, by the appropriation of the imperial palace and its collection of art and antiquities. Thus the state's appropriation of the imperial collection legitimated its political power and authority."[100] Such an assessment raises issues about the symbolic power of archives and certainly the role such power plays in how archivists appraise, acquire, and depict archival records. These are matters also raised in Crane's study of early German collecting, and there is certainly contemporary relevance in how governments, institutions, and particular societal groups identify, care for, and generally relate to records related to them.

Howard Mansfield's *The Same Ax, Twice* is not a scholarly tome (unlike the other two books reviewed here) but a series of homilies about individuals who have labored to restore or save older things. Mansfield, a journalist and freelance writer who has written other books on similar themes,[101] says that his "book looks at the impulse to preserve and restore, an impulse we share with the farmer who keeps changing the handle and head of an old ax in an attempt to have the same ax. This impulse leads us into the contradictions of time and history (and some of the folly and silliness)."[102] *The Same Ax, Twice* is not only an effort to understand the impulse but an effort to understand ourselves, and, as a result, it is almost a religious text: "What I am looking for is the trick of having the same ax twice, for a restoration that renews the spirit, for work that transforms the worker. We may talk of saving antique linens, species, or languages; but whatever we are intent on saving, when a restoration succeeds, we rescue ourselves."[103] Mansfield is quite explicit about the religious aspect of restoration in his last paragraph in the book: "Ours is an age of broken connections, lost connections between heart and work, soul and politics, community and the self. Restoration is renewal—and effort to mend the world—or else it is not worth doing. Good restoration is a prayer, an offering. It's praise, attention paid; it revels in the glory and spirit of this life."[104] There is a New Age religious tone to such sentiments, but they are precisely what confront archivists in their efforts to appraise, knowing they must destroy more than they save. Although Mansfield acknowledges such a process of decay and loss as very natural and inevitable, it is a process that is nevertheless difficult to describe in an understandable fashion to those who look at archives and libraries from the outside.

Mansfield gives us a series of vignettes about restoration efforts. Included are descriptions of restoring and maintaining old ships, old houses, old airplanes, old technologies, old furniture, landscape, place, historic sites, and other things; running house museums; participating in reenactments of historic events; finding quiet places; and carrying on old techniques. Each story focuses on an individual and recounts the individual's reflections on what he or she is doing. Scattered through all the stories are reflections on the meaning of such work:

Each time we renew the meetinghouse steeple, replant a forest, heal an injured animal, teach someone to read, each time we do this we are restoring the life, the best in us, as well. Mending the world, rebuilding it daily, we discover our better angels. We are on the side of life.[105]

Or,

As our society has become more ordered and corporate, there is a greater desire for pageantry, for myth, a hunger to touch something of a grand scale, if only for a weekend. Pageants restage the grand movement of time. They put us, the nine-to-five workers, on the stage of great moments. One has extended one's life, taken a timeline and shot it like an arrow into the air.[106]

And,

> There is something hopeful and American about never finishing your house, like Jefferson at Monticello. There was an optimism, a buoyancy, in all the fashionable remodeling and destruction. There was a belief in new beginnings.[107]

If one is looking for an understanding of how Americans think about their past, there are more sophisticated studies to draw upon.[108] The value of Mansfield's writing is how he captures the more personal feel of the past, something archivists need to bear in mind as they work with the public, donors, the media, and researchers. As archivists appraise or reappraise, they need to keep in mind how the public will react to their decisions to destroy certain documents. In describing what goes on in some museums, Mansfield reflects, "Curators have an impossible mandate: First, find the truth about the past, and then communicate that truth to visitors. They are supposed to make objects, documents, and artifacts speak."[109] Making records speak is a task archivists must mull over when they know that there is a general lack of understanding about how archives are formed and for what purposes. Archival appraisal is difficult because it is about *selection*. As Mansfield writes about the restoration of historic structures:

> To restore is to choose. To restore is to create, to compose a new picture out of the pieces we find. Every large restored cultural monument is surrounded by a passionate debate about its authenticity. Each age creates willfully, or by accident, the ruins it likes.[110]

Mansfield's latest book is part of the growing chorus of concern about the impact of technology on our society. When he writes about maintaining place, Mansfield muses, "What we may really lack is place. We are not at home in any one place. We are here in these small towns, but not here. We are uplinked, downloaded, commuting, encapsulated by shell after shell of our clever devices."[111] Mansfield delves into the "hidden meanings" of things because they represent continuity versus the unprecedented change of modern society. This is how he describes someone acquiring an old rocking chair at an auction:

> People bid and you have to guess about hidden meanings. A rocker may be just a rocker, but to one person it may represent the home they lost, the unrecoverable past, and to another, the home they hope to create. Each auction is a story of greed and desire, loss and gain.[112]

These seem to be the sentiments supporting the bidding on eBay, and as archivists we must be prepared for the fact, no matter how uncomfortable it is, that what we recognize as debris may be valuable to others for a variety of reasons.

What we find in the writings of the authors represented here are challenges to what we do. I must admit that they do not make me feel any easier about the already difficult process that is archival appraisal. So I will keep reading and looking for answers.

CONCLUSION

A few final comments about how archivists should consider collecting are in order, most importantly that they have devoted too little attention to the real history and value of collecting as a pursuit in the context of the broader professional mission of the archivist. Are archivists here to fill repositories with all sorts of stuff, or do they have a mission to protect crucial evidence to provide a foundation for matters such as accountability and corporate and public memory, and is there a difference? Archivists have tended to compile a spotty record about the legacy of nineteenth-century collecting while not critically considering the twentieth-century counterpart at all. Archivists have also not considered the relevance of collecting in an age that is embracing electronic record-keeping systems. Can we even still collect? Have older collecting efforts even been successful? More critical, scholarly inquiry about the nature, results, and value of and issues generated by collecting needs to be done by archivists.

It is also necessary for archivists to devote as much attention to understanding the nature of their records holdings as to mastering the subject or informational value of these holdings or even administering them. In fact, I would argue that more attention needs to be devoted to the evidence issues, to comprehending the record-keeping systems and to seeing that "collections"—in the true sense of the term—be understood through their formation and subsequent preservation and management. Susan Pearce, in the introduction to her recent anthology, wrote:

> It is . . . incumbent upon the investigator to try to find ways in which, first, the social meanings of individual objects can be unravelled; second, the significance of the museum as a cultural institution can be understood; and third, the processes through which objects become component parts of collections, and collections themselves acquire collective significance, can be appreciated.[113]

Looking at this assessment from archivists' disciplinary vantage, it seems apparent that the lack of scholarship about the history of American archives as well as fundamental principles and activities of archival practice could derive from a lack of critical perspective on the records held in our repositories.

Understanding our records means adopting some new approaches. It still seems that most descriptions of archives dote on the subject content. There have been persuasive arguments for transforming description to emphasize functions and activities. Looking at collecting, as I have tried to do in this chapter, suggests something else. The descriptions of "collections" acquired by archives and manuscripts repositories should focus more on the collectors' activities and objectives than on the potential subject use by subsequent researchers; after all, the evidence of these records can be and often is compromised by collecting that pulls them from their context. Eilean Hooper-Greenhill, in her history of museums, wrote that the "collection of things by donation [in the early formation of European museums] meant that items were presented that seemed appropriate from the point of view of the donor."[114] This seems to be a continuing truth about most donations, artifacts or archives, suggesting that the descriptions might be more useful if they tried to reveal the donor's view—why they were both collected and then donated. While the museum curator, in organizing or exhibiting objects, is creating an understanding of the object,[115] the archivist's role should not be to impose a new order but to reflect the purposes, organic nature, and activities of the creator of the records system.

Archivists must reflect, as well, on why they collect. Oscar Handlin, more than two decades ago, made a reference to the collecting and publishing of sources in the mid-nineteenth century by Jared Sparks. As Handlin suggested, the "assumption that history was the sum of the biographies of a limited number of dominant individuals came easily to an age which conceived the hero as the center of society."[116] In a similar fashion, archivists seem prone to justify collecting all sorts of materials because every individual and every culture has become the center of our society. Archivists need to understand their motivations. Archivists know full well that they cannot preserve all records with archival value. At the least, they can describe and otherwise deal with the records they have with full honesty about the fact that they represent serendipitous acquiring by collectors and acquisition for reasons other then the evidential and informational values they have learned to use for justifying such collecting. Descriptions of archival records and manuscripts collections need to be devoted as much to the origins of the acquisition as to any other matter.

Finally, although archivists need to understand the symbolic and cultural value of archives, archivists also need to struggle with the impact of collecting as a means to this end. Ken Burns, producer of the acclaimed documentary *The Civil War*, stated that most people are captivated by history through "story, memory, anecdote, feeling. These emotional connections become a kind of glue which makes the most complex of past events stick in our minds and our hearts, permanently a part of who each of us is now." The producer also noted that the source of these emotional connections was the archives documenting the war, so rich that an original plan for a five-hour documentary was scrapped in favor of the eleven-hour series.[117] This value of archives and historical manuscripts is also one of the reasons their collecting is such an obsession of many archivists as well as a wide array of the public. However, just as we cannot overlook the weaknesses of the use of archives and historical manuscripts by a documentary producer like Burns, archivists must not turn a blind eye to the many problems caused by a focus on collecting. Recent scholarship on collecting reveals, at least, the potential for study and reflection by archivists about this activity.

NOTES

1. "Telling Objects: A Narrative Perspective on Collecting," in *The Cultures of Collecting*, ed. John Elsner and Roger Cardinal, (Cambridge, Mass.:

Harvard University Press, 1994), 99. In the interest of trying to keep this chapter manageable, I did not include this book in the body of the review. However, I certainly recommend it, with its insightful essays on the psychology and motivations of collectors, the history of particular museums, and related essays attempting to understand how collections come to be formed.

2. Lester J. Cappon, "The Archivist as Collector," *American Archivist* 39 (October 1976): 433.

3. Christopher Lasch, *The Revolt of the Elites and the Betrayal of Democracy* (New York: W. W. Norton, 1995), 97.

4. The quote is from Todd Gitlin, *The Twilight of Common Dreams: Why America Is Wracked by Culture Wars* (New York: Metropolitan Books, 1995), 197.

5. The quotation is from Lawrence Weschler, *Mr. Wilson's Cabinet of Wonder* (New York: Pantheon Books, 1995), 61. Weschler's book is a description of the Museum of Jurassic Technology located in Los Angeles. Weschler writes that this "museum affords this marvelous field for projection and transference. It's like a museum, a critique of museums, and a celebration of museums—all rolled into one" (40). There is a sense, of course, that the rapid transformations in our society have brought about an increased sense of interest in acquiring old objects, like relics, similar to the collecting going on in the first decades of the nineteenth century by the historical and antiquarian societies. For an example of this, refer to the extremely uneven *Lucy's Bones, Sacred Stones, and Einstein's Brain: The Remarkable Stories behind the Great Objects and Artifacts of History, from Antiquity to the Modern Era*, by Harvey Rachlin (New York: Henry Holt, 1996).

6. Cullen Murphy, "Backlogs of History," *Atlantic Monthly* 277 (May 1996): 20, 22.

7. Richard C. Berner, "Archival Management and Librarianship: An Exploration of Prospects for Their Integration," in vol. 14 of *Advances in Librarianship*, ed. Wesley Simonton (Orlando, Fla.: Academic Press, Inc., 1986), 262. Berner saw that each state had "two or more major repositories and a state archives" forming a "veritable archival network of national and even international scope. With proper leadership these efforts could be concerted deliberately and help assure more comprehensive documentary coverage in the process." Such networks have not been developed.

8. Werner Muensterberger, *Collecting: An Unruly Passion; Psychological Perspectives* (Princeton: Princeton University Press, 1994).

9. Muensterberger, *Collecting*, 11.

10. Muensterberger, *Collecting*, 48.

11. Muensterberger, *Collecting*, 256.

12. Muensterberger, *Collecting*, 4.

13. Muensterberger, *Collecting*, 107.

14. Muensterberger, *Collecting*, 9.

15. Muensterberger, *Collecting*, 56.

16. Muensterberger, *Collecting*, 7.

17. Muensterberger, *Collecting*, 15. A more entertaining way to consider the psychology of collecting, with an uncanny similarity to many of the features profiled by Muensterberger, is to read Susan Sontag's *The Volcano Lover: A Romance* (New York: Farrar Straus Giroux, 1992). The novel, set in late eighteenth-century Naples, follows the flawed career of the Cavaliere, a diplomat and collector. The novel is an exploration into the interplay between one's personal and professional lives and the impulse to collect. Consider some examples of Sontag's commentary: "The true collector is in the grip not of what is collected but of collecting" (24); "To collect is to rescue things, valuable things, from neglect, from oblivion, or simply from the ignoble destiny of being in someone else's collection rather than one's own" (25); "The great collections are vast, not complete. Incomplete: motivated by the desire for completeness" (72); "A collector is happy to be known, mainly known, as the proprietor of what—through so much effort—has been collected" (138); and "Collecting is a form of union. The collector is acknowledging. He is adding. He is learning. He is noting" (157). Sontag places the Cavaliere in a world wracked by social and political change, and describes one of the great impulses of collecting and collectors, to nail down a spot in the universe or to make some meaning of it all: "To collect is by definition to collect the past—while to make a revolution is to condemn what is now called the past. And the past is very heavy, as well as large" (268).

18. Russell W. Belk, *Collecting in a Consumer Society* (New York: Routledge, 1995), 65.

19. Belk, *Collecting in a Consumer Society*, 81.

20. Belk, *Collecting in a Consumer Society*, 124.

21. Susan M. Pearce, *On Collecting: An Investigation into Collecting in the European Tradition* (New York: Routledge, 1995).

22. Pearce, *On Collecting*, 411.

23. Pearce, *On Collecting*, 4.

24. Many of the sources from other professional literatures have been included in her valuable anthology *Interpreting Objects and Collections* (New York: Routledge, 1994), a volume including a number of essays on the nature of collecting by Pearce, Pomian, Schulz, Baekeland, Belk, and others, those usually cited in the recent scholarship on collecting. Again the emphasis is on museum objects and artifacts.

25. Pearce, *On Collecting*, 23.

26. Pearce, *On Collecting*, 24.

27. Pearce, *On Collecting*, 96–97.

28. Pearce, *On Collecting*, 235–236.

29. Pearce, *On Collecting*, 249.

30. Pearce, *On Collecting*, 142.

31. Pearce, *On Collecting*, 279.

32. Pearce, *On Collecting*, 166.

33. Pearce, *On Collecting*, 301.

34. Phyllis Mauch Messenger, ed., *The Ethics of Collecting Cultural Property: Whose Culture? Whose Property?* (Albuquerque: University of New Mexico Press, 1989).

35. Messenger, *The Ethics of Collecting Cultural Property*, 64.

36. Messenger, *The Ethics of Collecting Cultural Property*, 97–98.

37. Messenger, *The Ethics of Collecting Cultural Property*, 149.

38. Dan Hofstadter, *Goldberg's Angel: An Adventure in the Antiquities Trade* (New York: Farrar, Straus, Giroux, 1994).

39. Hofstadter, *Goldberg's Angel*, 143.

40. Thatcher Freund, *Objects of Desire: The Lives of Antiques and Those Who Pursue Them* (New York: Pantheon Books, 1993).

41. Freund, *Objects of Desire*, 153–154.

42. Lynn H. Nicholas, *The Rape of Europa: The Fate of Europe's Treasures in the Third Reich and the Second World War* (New York: Vintage Books, 1994).

43. Nicholas, *The Rape of Europa*, 97.

44. Nicholas, *The Rape of Europa*, 444.

45. Kenneth W. Rendell, *History Comes to Life: Collecting Historical Letters and Documents* (Norman: University of Oklahoma Press, 1995).

46. Compare, for example, to Hamilton's *Collecting Autographs and Manuscripts* (Norman: University of Oklahoma Press, 1961, 1970).

47. Rendell, *History Comes to Life*, iii.

48. Rendell, *History Comes to Life*, 1.

49. Rendell, *History Comes to Life*, 7.

50. Rendell, *History Comes to Life*, 5.

51. Rendell, *History Comes to Life*, 8.

52. Even in Rendell's interesting and useful book on forgeries, *Forging History: The Detection of Fake Letters and Documents* (Norman: University of Oklahoma, 1994), there is no assessment of why forgeries occur. Could they occur at least partly because the autograph market drives up prices, which invites people to try to cash in?

53. Kevin M. Guthrie, *The New-York Historical Society: Lessons from One Nonprofit's Long Struggle for Survival* (San Francisco: Jossey-Bass, 1996).

54. Guthrie, *The New-York Historical Society*, 4.

55. Guthrie, *The New-York Historical Society*, 153.

56. Guthrie, *The New-York Historical Society*, 166.

57. Guthrie, *The New-York Historical Society*, 31.

58. Guthrie, *The New-York Historical Society*, 31.

59. Guthrie, *The New-York Historical Society*, 154.

60. Guthrie, *The New-York Historical Society*, 36, 74, 135.

61. Guthrie, *The New-York Historical Society*, 111.

62. Guthrie, *The New-York Historical Society*, 24.

63. Guthrie, *The New-York Historical Society*, 140.

64. Guthrie, *The New-York Historical Society*, 73.

65. Guthrie, *The New-York Historical Society*, 127.

66. Nicholas A. Basbanes, *A Gentle Madness: Bibliophiles, Bibliomanes, and the Eternal Passion for Books* (New York: Henry Holt and Co., 1995).

67. Basbanes, *A Gentle Madness*, 3.

68. Basbanes, *A Gentle Madness*, 438.

69. The failure of this book is also seen when reading a brief article by Dana Gioia, "The Hand of the Poet: The Magical Value of Manuscripts," *Hudson Review* 49 (Spring 1996): 9–29. Gioia gets to the heart of why manuscripts, even those with questionable or unknown value, are acquired by institutions. The author dismisses the market's setting values, examines what insights literary manuscripts can provide into the work of a particular author, and then contends that such materials are being collected because of reasons having to do with their symbolic value in a technocratic age. As Gioia states:

> An institution of learning seeks significant manuscripts because they possess qualities that scholarship cannot entirely reproduce—an authentic, holistic connection with the great writers of the past. It is not the intellectual content of the manuscript that is important but its material presence—ink spots, tobacco stains, pinworm holes, and foxing included (22).

Whether you agree with this assessment or not (and I do not agree with it completely), the point is that his twenty-page article is much more insightful than a book thirty times longer.

70. In its May 2001 newsletter, the National Archives of Australia announced its intention to reappraise its records:

> Over the years we have collected hundreds of thousands of shelf metres of records created by government. To house them, we have needed huge repositories in every State and Territory. It is part of sound archival practice to review the collection to make sure that we are keeping the right records, in the right places, and in the best way for all Australians to have access to them.

This institution argued:

> We've discovered that many of the records deposited with us in the past have no archival value. In Australia we have collected far more records than other national archival institutions, especially when you consider the size of our pop-

ulation and the fact that the Commonwealth government has existed for only 100 years.

Because "the buildings holding these records are getting older and more expensive to maintain," the National Archives:

> needed to reduce the size of the haystack to make the needle easier to find, without throwing out the needles with the hay. To do this we are reviewing our collection to ensure we have kept the right records, and we are using new approaches to appraisal to make sure we collect the right records in the future.

See "Archives on the Move," *Memento*, no. 17 (May 2001), available at http://www.naa.gov.au/publications/memento/ISSUE_17/html/feature_three.htm and accessed June 13, 2001.

71. Bruce Craig, on behalf of the National Coordinating Committee for the Promotion of History, summarized the case in this fashion:

> On June 7, 2001, the Organization of American Historians sent a letter to the Smithsonian Board of Regents stating its "full support" for the staff of the National Museum of American History in their efforts to uphold exhibit standards. The letter also requested "respectfully [that] the Regents review and reconsider their recent agreement with Catherine B. Reynolds respecting the establishment of a Hall of Fame for American Achievers." According to sources inside the Smithsonian, efforts are currently underway to create a separate "points of agreement" document necessary for implementing aspects of the Reynolds gift agreement. On June 12, under the signature of James Bruns (the Smithsonian Director of Operations), with copies being distributed throughout the historical community and to various members of Congress, the Smithsonian responded to the OAH letter. Bruns stated that in its letter the OAH relied on one-sided opinions and "distorted media accounts." "The visionary changes that the Institution's new Secretary has presented may indeed be unsettling to some staff," stated Bruns, and that staff is engaging in "a campaign of manipulation of facts and selective leaks to the press to delay or reverse such progress." The letter, for the first time, put in writing assurances that the "professional staff members on the achievement exhibition team will control all aspects of the exhibition's content and presentation[,] . . . that the control of the content for this exhibit will reside with the staff" and that the exhibitions standards adopted by the OAH and other groups, "will be among the guidelines that are used by staff in the creation of an accurate professional exhibition."

From NCC Washington Update, vol. 7, no. 24, June 15, 2001, available at http://www.h-net.msu.edu/~ncc and accessed June 16, 2001.

72. The book I am referring to is Nicholson Baker's *Double Fold: Libraries and the Assault on Paper* (New York: Random House, 2001). At the time of writing this review, I was in the midst of preparing a book-length response to this tome, building off of my earlier responses, "The Great Newspaper

Caper: Backlash in the Digital Age," *First Monday* 5 (December 4, 2000), available at http://firstmonday.org/issues/issue5_12/cox/, and "Don't Fold Up: Responding to Nicholson Baker's *Double Fold*," *Archival Outlook* (May/June 2001): 8–14, available at http://www.archivists.org/news/doublefold.html.

73. Archivists and records managers looking for a useful website for explaining records might consider The John Curtin Prime Ministerial Library at Curtin University of Technology's new site, "Understanding Society Through Its Records" at http://john.curtin.edu.au/society. The site endeavors to explain the "concepts and universal importance of record-keeping to personal life and to business and government." The site includes "explanations of the principles and concepts for managing all forms of purposefully recorded evidence for as long as required"; "a sensible and accessible framework for understanding record-keeping in most environments—offices and repositories, collecting and in-house, large and small, traditional and electronic"; "images, references and links to print and online readings selected from across the Australian, US, Canadian and International Council on Archives (ICA) literature"; and "summaries of the best of English-speaking practice and . . . Australian contributions to record-keeping knowledge and practice." The site was prepared by Kandy-Jane Henderson (Archivist, John Curtin Prime Ministerial Library) and Ann Pederson (Visiting Fellow in Record-keeping Studies in the School of Information Systems, Technology & Management at the University of New South Wales).

74. Susan A. Crane, *Collecting and Historical Consciousness in Early Nineteenth-Century Germany* (Ithaca: Cornell University Press, 2000).

75. Susan A. Crane, ed., *Museums and Memory* (Stanford: Stanford University Press, 2000).

76. Howard Mansfield, *The Same Ax, Twice: Restoration and Renewal in a Throwaway Age* (Hanover: University Press of New England, 2000).

77. Crane, *Collecting and Historical Consciousness*, 176.

78. Crane, *Collecting and Historical Consciousness*, xiii.

79. Crane, *Collecting and Historical Consciousness*, 21.

80. Crane, *Collecting and Historical Consciousness*, 26.

81. Crane, *Collecting and Historical Consciousness*, 28.

82. Crane, *Collecting and Historical Consciousness*, 81.

83. Read, for example, Ian Buruma, *The Wages of Guilt: Memories of War in Germany and Japan* (New York: Meridian, 1994); Jeffrey Herf, *Divided Memory: The Nazi Past in the Two Germanys* (Cambridge: Harvard University Press, 1997); Jane Kramer, *The Politics of Memory: Looking for Germany in the New Germany* (New York: Random House, 1996); and, especially, Rudy Koshar, *Germany's Transient Pasts: Preservation and National Memory in the Twentieth Century* (Chapel Hill: University of North Carolina Press, 1998).

84. Crane, *Collecting and Historical Consciousness*, 106.
85. Crane, *Collecting and Historical Consciousness*, 109.
86. Crane, *Collecting and Historical Consciousness*, 111.
87. Crane, *Collecting and Historical Consciousness*, 139.
88. See, for example, Hans Booms, "Society and the Formation of a Documentary Heritage," *Archivaria* 24 (Summer 1987): 69–107.
89. Crane, *Collecting and Historical Consciousness*, 118.
90. Crane, *Collecting and Historical Consciousness*, 123.
91. David D. Van Tassel [*Recording America's Past: An Interpretation of the Development of Historical Societies in America 1607–1884* (Chicago: University of Chicago Press, 1960)] is the coiner of the phrase. See also George H. Callcott, *History in the United States 1800–1860: Its Practice and Purpose* (Baltimore: Johns Hopkins University Press, 1970) for another analysis emphasizing the fixation with documentary sources in this period.
92. Crane, *Collecting and Historical Consciousness*, 176–177.
93. Crane, *Museums and Memory*, 1.
94. Crane, *Museums and Memory*, 3.
95. Jacques Derrida, *Archive Fever: A Freudian Impression* (Chicago: University of Chicago Press, 1996) and Thomas Richards, *The Imperial Archive: Knowledge and the Fantasy of Empire* (London: Verso, 1993) are two recent examples. No matter what insights these works provide (and they provide many), one must still work hard to capture the precise meaning of archive or archives as utilized by these authors.
96. Crane, *Museums and Memory*, 46.
97. Crane, *Museums and Memory*, 70.
98. Crane, *Museums and Memory*, 113.
99. Crane, *Museums and Memory*, 120.
100. Crane, *Museums and Memory*, 150.
101. Most notably, Howard Mansfield, *In the Memory House* (Golden, Colorado: Fulcrum Publishing, 1993), describing the work of historical societies.
102. Mansfield, *The Same Ax, Twice*, xiii.
103. Mansfield, *The Same Ax, Twice*, xii.
104. Mansfield, *The Same Ax, Twice*, 276.
105. Mansfield, *The Same Ax, Twice*, 10.
106. Mansfield, *The Same Ax, Twice*, 44.
107. Mansfield, *The Same Ax, Twice*, 150.
108. Especially Roy Rosenzweig and David Thelen, *The Presence of the Past: Popular Uses of History in American Life* (New York: Columbia University Press, 1998).
109. Mansfield, *The Same Ax, Twice*, 62.
110. Mansfield, *The Same Ax, Twice*, 70.
111. Mansfield, *The Same Ax, Twice*, 171.
112. Mansfield, *The Same Ax, Twice*, 203.

113. Susan Pearce, ed., *Interpreting Objects and Collections* (New York: Routledge, 1994), 1.

114. Eilean Hooper-Greenwell, *Museums and the Shaping of Knowledge* (New York: Routledge, 1992), 160.

115. See Kevin Walsh, *The Representation of the Past: Museums and Heritage in the Post-Modern World* (New York: Routledge, 1992).

116. Oscar Handlin, *Truth in History* (Cambridge, Mass.: Belknap Press, 1979), 267.

117. Ken Burns, "Four O'Clock in the Morning Courage," in *Ken Burns's The Civil War: Historians Respond*, ed. Robert Brent Toplin (New York: Oxford University Press, 1996), 160.

4

The Traditional Archival and Historical Records Program in the Digital Age: A Cautionary Tale

Throughout the world, records by the billions are regularly created. While many are traditional paper documents, an increasing number are complex digital records. Since the eighteenth century, the primary means of managing these records has meant their physical collecting, often long after their creation and primary use. In the United States, for the better part of two centuries, the historical society or a descendant form of archival program—such as the university special collections—has played the pivotal role in archival collecting and documentation. Throughout America, these venerable institutions dot the landscape, from small town to major urban center.

Even institutional archives and records programs, such as in governments or corporations, have adopted the mode of archival collector. Armed with collection policies of varying sophistication, archival programs identify, acquire, and make accessible historical records—following such functions with a museum-like gathering of records as physical artifacts. Records management programs might lack collection or acquisition policies (although they should have these), but they often use records retention schedules in a similar fashion—identifying what records would or should come to the records center and/or archives. What looms ahead of us, however, is the uncertain future of the collecting repository stressing the record as artifact while records and their supporting systems migrate to digital applications or are born digitally with no paper surrogates. Does the traditional archival repository have a role to play in the future? What is the future of the records center? Can this role be expanded or refined into a twenty-first-century institutional paradigm? What is the evidence of this shift from a repository to some other kind of program?

The historical society, the prototype of the traditional archival repository and the precursor of any modern records repository, stems from its origins as a cultural enclave, often mixed with religious, political, social, and economic agendas. Such institutions usually adopted a broad historical and educational mission, such as to acquire and preserve the records and artifacts of American or even world history. For most of these institutions, donations of manuscripts, organizational records, and even governmental records rolled in at a regular but often undisciplined rate. Through the nineteenth and well into the twentieth century, the historical society served as the lone bulwark against the destruction of the materials of our documentary heritage. By the mid-twentieth century, the historical society was surrounded by other historical manuscripts and archival programs, and it survived either by adopting a competitive stance or by refining its mission to focus on very specific collecting agendas (including sometimes the acquisition of older paper documents). By the dawn of the twenty-first century, the traditional archives typified by the historical society held to a questionable agenda as electronic records replaced or transformed many of the kinds of documents that it had formerly collected (the manuscript letter is now e-mail and the literary manuscript is now a pile of 3.5-inch diskettes or CD-ROMs). This is *not* to argue that there is no need to acquire, protect, and make available older records in traditional, original formats. There are, indeed, symbolic and cultural reasons we would do this. However, my suspicion is that too much attention is being paid to the traditional records and too little (in a practical sense at least—the writings on this subject are now immense) to records in digital form.

Either the repository tightened even more its acquisition regimen to stress early traditional sources or it needed to adopt a more expansive, cooperative approach to its documentary function. By now the stresses and strains felt by the historical society were also being experienced by other institutional and governmental records operations. The corporate records management program has faced, for example, similar stresses and strains. Despite the very different institutional focus, corporate and governmental records management programs often have operated like older historical societies. That is, they "collected" older institutional and governmental records. Many, especially university archives, have struggled to do more than collect older records in a haphazard fashion while being less than successful in establishing systematic records retention schedules and other venues for administering the voluminous current records. The American practical approach to collecting, often with marked successes, has been the hallmark of most records programs. Looking more closely at the nature of contemporary historical societies reveals deep fissures and cracks in these approaches.

A number of archivists and records managers have questioned whether electronic records can be collected and managed like other documents. Much of the argument of these records professionals has rested on the nature of these new and emerging records systems, and, while there is an internal debate within the ranks of archivists and records managers about the veracity of this perspective, it is just as obvious that the old means of collecting have never been as sound and foolproof as we have assumed. And this state of affairs extends to both archival programs like historical societies and institutional records management programs. The notion of seeking out archival records and bringing them into a repository is one that has always been somewhat problematic. Evaluating the American historical society a bit more closely points out such problems. Although many fine archival and historical manuscripts collections—in universities, historical societies, or museums—connect to the pioneering work of individual collectors and the aggressive and creative work of archivists and manuscripts curators, the notion of acquiring records is a process in need of reevaluation. At the beginning of the twenty-first century, however, we need to question whether old acquisition models and patterns are still relevant.

FROM THE RESEARCHER'S PERSPECTIVE

The researcher walks out the door, armed with laptop computer and scratch paper for the miscellaneous note, heading off to discover what he or she can about the development of urban planning (we could pick any topic, but this seemed like a good one). The researcher encounters some immediate choices, primarily whether to work in libraries with printed materials or visit one of any number of archives in the city. Other choices are to be made. In the libraries, the researcher might discover caches of archival records, and in the archives the researcher will undoubtedly encounter quantities of published reports and printed ephemera. The way in which a researcher makes choices will undoubtedly depend upon the nature of the question, the extent of information needed, his or her own academic background and training, and the purpose of gathering the information. Upon further thought, the researcher might turn around and go back to the telephone or computer to make inquiries about what it is he or she wants to know and where the answers to the research questions may be found.

The researcher also faces a set of immense philosophical or conceptual problems no matter what choice he or she makes or what purpose is in mind. These problems might not be immediately obvious, but they will emerge, in some form, sooner or later. If they are not considered, then the validity of the research conducted can be questioned. What remains of the original documentary universe related to urban planning? How can the researcher determine what the remnants of this archival documentation represent—is this documentary universe the result of an accidental or natural selection formed by natural disasters or the product of careful, predetermined selection for some purpose, perhaps preserved precisely for the kind of research being embarked on? How can you evaluate the evidence a researcher might uncover and hold in hand if the researcher cannot understand the context of this evidence?

This leads to reflecting about what an archives is and, given this research, what an urban or regional archives is (or should be). The answers seem too deceptively easy because we often have the wrong models in our vision. Archivists, records managers, and their colleagues need to reconsider what they are doing, not to be too self-critical but in order to develop clear and precise visions that enable them to answer the most basic questions any researcher can ask—

what does this record represent and what does it mean if I can discover no (or little) evidence about a particular event or issue? They also need to reflect on the currency or relevancy of the information in the archival evidence.

If records professionals cannot provide a satisfactory answer to these questions, the possibility of discovering the evidence any researcher needs becomes more conjectural than factual. We enter into the world of television docudrama or Disney theme park instead of the universe of real historical event or trend. We long for the ability of the creator of Jurassic Park to recreate the past before us so that these other problems can be resolved. Or perhaps we decide to try our hand at historical fiction. Or we opt to sit back and watch society bungle its decisions because it lacks the necessary information and the sense of the past's relevance to the present. In other words, archivists, records managers, and their colleagues need to ask questions about anything they and their repositories do, including even their most precious assumptions, because their mission is so fundamental to the well-being of any society. Records are maintained because of their importance for accountability, evidence, and social or organizational memory—and these important values can be achieved only through careful appraisal and acquisition.

FUNDAMENTAL QUESTIONS AND ISSUES

What are archives? An archives is generally assumed to be the repository for archival (some would say *historical,* some would say *old*) records. The notion of a repository, one location in which related (in terms of either creation or unifying theme) records can be housed, is an old concept that goes back at least 2,000 years. The ancient Sumerians, Greeks, and Romans had such a vision of archives. The monasteries provided this sort of role after the end of the Roman Empire by acquiring, preserving, and copying old manuscripts (both books and records) and by accumulating chronicles of their orders, rulers, and events. The archival notion reemerged in Medieval Europe as writing and literacy spread and the importance of records and record keeping increased. In the Renaissance, archives were joined by museums and libraries as repositories for collecting records and artifacts of interest to scholars and antiquarians. The nineteenth-century historical society movement in the United States was but another manifestation of the aim to provide homes for manuscripts, archives, books, and artifacts.

Examining the archival landscape from a historical perspective is important. The present college and university archives and special collections, local public library history rooms, historical societies, and research rooms in records centers are little different in conception from the archival repositories of 2,000 years ago. The furniture might be different and computers might be there instead of scrolls, but the general tasks and attitudes might not be very different. We need to ask more questions. Archives are a place, a repository for the records documenting our past. But what are these repositories housing? Are these repositories housing the right stuff? Are they successful in their mission to document society?

What are archival records? We seem to have different answers. They are records saved because of some potential value for historical research, states one scholar. Archives are records maintained because they have continuing utility to the creating organization and to the broader society, suggests another, probably an administrator. Can we reconcile these views? The latter definition of archives as the records possessing continuing value to their original creator does not minimize in any fashion the potential of those records' being of use to the individual wishing to use them for scholarly purposes. Archival theorists have termed this the difference between primary and secondary, or of evidential and informational, values. The rub comes with the way we have generally sought to preserve our archives. Traditionally, we have established repositories and purposely sought those materials of use to historians and other scholars seeking to study the past, subverting a definition of records (and archives) as having value to their creator. Is it more valuable and more utilitarian for society or for the records creator to value archives?

THE MODERN HISTORICAL SOCIETY

Consider the nature of archives in any American city as a case in point when considering such questions. Most cities have at least two major archival programs. Typically, one, the oldest, will have been established in the late nineteenth century or will be a later version of such an organization. The historical society was modeled on the private historical societies of the East Coast that had started appearing nearly a century before and which flourished in every state and nearly every major urban area. These institutions had many purposes beyond providing the means to preserve historical documents and other materials, but they have continued to be collecting organizations that swept up nearly anything of value for understanding or representing the past. Recent evaluations of institutions such as these suggest that these acquisition efforts often supported building a "cohesive and positive image" of the group or groups they supported, implying that some of the seeming randomness might not be "politically" or "culturally neutral."[1] Regardless of motivations, corporate records as well as personal and family papers were brought into this society. Although the society has in the past decade transformed its mission from its previously elitist vision to one that has tried to represent the pasts of many ethic, racial, and socioeconomic groups, the historical society has remained first and foremost a collector of the records and material remains of the past.

Another typical dominant archival program in any city would be the university, probably establishing a collecting program in the early 1960s, the result of historians who wanted to ensure that they had access to records related to the industries and ethnic and other groups that had made up the area's industrial formation. When this archives was founded, the historical society was heavily focused on the first families and had little concern for Eastern Europeans, racial minorities, or the other groups making up the population mosaic. The university now looms as a competitor of sorts to the historical society. As it turns out, thinking of these programs as competitors is ludicrous for those interested in preserving the archival records in this region.

Often other archives are in the city, of course, but they all possess a much lower public profile than the two briefly described. There are institutional archives, such as those of the Catholic diocese and the county government, and those of various colleges and universities. Museums and historic sites have established programs to administer their archival records. Even local professional associations have created archival operations. Yet, despite the fact that they are lesser known than the historical society and the university, these kinds of programs provide an indispensable role in the protection of the city's documentary heritage. Actually, they represent the future of archives in the region, as well as nationally and even internationally.

Since the nineteenth century in this country, and earlier in Europe, society fostered the development of institutions that possessed a mandate to acquire in a single repository all the records of historical value to the society. As societies became larger and more complex, the number of collecting archives and historical records repositories expanded. The recognition of a more diverse, multicultural society led some traditional archives to redefine their roles in a major fashion. Just as prevalent has been the creation of new subject- or theme-oriented archival repositories to accommodate the acquisition of the records of seemingly neglected, underrepresented social groups. One question remains in all this expansion, however: Have we been successful in adequately documenting our society so that we can understand its present? Or, stated in another way, can we be confident that the records that currently exist provide the best representation and evidence on whatever aspect of our society we are interested in examining? Are these records the result of some sort of unfortunate disjunction from what they are supposed to document? One could ask similar questions within an organization if one were focused on records management. Have we documented the organization? Have we ensured that records needed to make the organization compliant are protected? Do we have the right records to retain the appropriate corporate memory?

Have those responsible for preserving the essential archival records of our society, or our region or organization, experienced some lapses before fulfilling their responsibilities? In other words, can we sit back and say, without hesitation, that the archival documentation preserved in any city's (or other region's) repositories is meaningful? Is it representative? Is it comprehensive? Is it selective in some fashion that can be defined? Is it meeting the needs of researchers interested in the history (or some aspect of the history) of the city? Is it relevant to current concerns and needs in our rapidly changing society? I posit that we cannot, unfortunately, answer most of these questions, because these questions have generally not been asked in any sustained fashion (even though archivists have been debating these issues for twenty years). We need to be able to do so. Archivists and other records professionals need to be able to articulate what their holdings represent. If the records professionals do not do this, who else will (except historians and cultural commentators who might look at such matters historically)?

What we can state is that there is a considerable quantity of historical or archival records housed safely in a considerable array of repositories and organizations in the city and the surrounding region. This is not satisfactory, for a number of reasons I have already hinted at. It is like saying I have a lot of money in different banks and other financial institutions, without knowing precise amounts or account numbers. Maybe I will be able to use it, maybe not. But I know I cannot responsibly conduct my affairs with such fuzzy information about my assets. Archivists, manuscripts curators, and records managers encounter the same challenge.

This sort of situation does not enable the researcher to be able to place his or her evidence in its context of time, place, actors, institutions, and other records. This lack lessens the value of the evidence as evidence. Just as importantly, the lack of such information weakens the ability to make adequate preservation decisions because there is a firm principle (as a result of limited resources) that to expend resources on preserving one set of records destroys by necessity another set (actually, probably many other groups) of records. Therefore, we must know whether the records we contemplate preserving are worthy of such expenditures or, in fact, are what we believe they are—the best evidence for documenting some event, movement, or ongoing function (or something else). Finally, archivists, manuscripts curators, and other records professionals cannot meet user needs if they cannot comprehend what the universe of documentation represents. If it is completely the result of chance, they can only hand the researcher a list of repositories and advise trying them all. They can only help a researcher to obtain a ballpark answer to his or her question. Is there any way in which the researcher can feel secure that he or she has obtained reliable information from the archival research?

REDEFINING THE HISTORICAL SOCIETY (OR OTHER TRADITIONAL RECORDS PROGRAM)

Is it possible to improve this picture? It is, and the solution is not a costly one or one that requires anything more than a different working paradigm and some creativity by archivists and their administrators. All it requires is a fundamental redefinition of archives and leadership, *and* some coordination. Some might argue that the solution might also require considerable imagination and creativity, but I do not believe that even these qualities are needed in large doses. It does mean that archivists must abandon one crucial aspect of historical knowledge, its dependence on a posteriori reasoning in favor of a broader vision of documentation and documentary goals. Whether we can move to a better version of such a vision might be another question, but it is one that can be answered only if an effort is expended in responding to such questions.

We must begin with redefining the purpose of an archival repository. It is clear that by using the word repository, we are continuing to believe that an archive holds or houses archival records—that records "repose" there. However, and this is a big however, archives must become the repository of last resort and not the housing of first choice. In other words, we must cease the incessant interest in collecting and move to another paradigm, that of mostly accepting only records possessing continuing value that are endangered. This is not to imply that there is no need for centralized repositories (there obviously is), but they are not the only, or always the best, means for such a purpose.

Some would argue that what I am proposing is precisely what we are doing now; I would argue we are doing the opposite. What do I mean by this? I believe archivists overemphasize the acquisition and centralization of records at the expense of endorsing, encouraging, and nurturing the growth of institutional archives. By this misplaced emphasis, archivists doom themselves to failure, no matter how they conceptualize the archival mission—unless it is to preserve a miscellany of interesting stuff. That is not, of course, a mission.

This challenge to transform what archivists do (and think) is best illustrated by some examples. Let's return to where we started, urban planning, for our initial case study. Urban planning is an ongoing activity evident in most American cities for the past century. It has been lauded, by Lewis Mumford, and it has been attacked, notably by Jane Jacobs' *Life and Death of American Cities*.[2] It has been dissected and analyzed, by Kevin Lynch in his *What Time Is This Place?*[3] It has been satirized and made fun of by many social critics, such as James Howard Kunstler.[4] Regardless, planning has been a prominent aspect of life in American cities throughout this century. Its prominence is obvious if for no other reason than because of the many volumes devoted to it by both critics and supporters. One cannot understand the last century of urban life without understanding the impulse, scale, purpose, success, and failure of planning.

For the individual seeking to understand planning and the archivist wanting to document it, planning is complex. It is complex because it happens as a result of many actors—government agencies, civic organizations, architects, prominent citizens, historic preservationists, the media, and major corporations and financial investors. What this means is that urban planning cannot be documented without taking into consideration the records and related documentation of all these individuals, groups, organizations, and institutions.

Documenting an ongoing function such as urban planning cannot occur with just modest coordination and cooperation. It needs both recognition and adoption of a new way of going about the business of archives. Adequate documentation of such a socially important function requires, minimally, that some attitudes, practices, and particular kinds of programs be in place guiding archival appraisal (and acquisition). Local governments must have viable records management and archives programs, with provision for open access, that are sensitive to being influenced by external articulations of documentary preservation priorities. Local government archives cannot be acquired in a piecemeal fashion by historical records repositories. A piecemeal approach destroys fundamental aspects of the records' context, structure, and content. In other words, the value of such records for evidence and information is considerably weakened. Historical records programs can serve as the official repositories for local government archives only if the local government has a satisfactory records management program, the repository agrees to serve as the home for all such records with archival value, and there is a contract detailing all requirements (such as access and preservation) for the management of these records. Local government records are not "collected"—they are naturally acquired in an orderly fashion befiting their organic nature and inherent structure. Collecting is a destruction of some of their evidence, no matter how well intentioned (and even if done as an act of desperation in the face of a complete abdication of responsibilities by the government).

Historical records repositories must exist to serve as a place for archival records that are homeless or threatened with immediate destruction. The role of these repositories is not to acquire such records in an aggressive manner, however, lest the prospects for institutional archives be undermined. These repositories should first provide leadership in promoting the development of key or essential institutional archives through educational venues and coordinated actions. Records that are endangered could be temporarily housed in these repositories so they can be evaluated (appraised, to use archival terminology) for permanent retention. Ideally, careful documentation analysis before such crises could provide useful criteria for determining whether such records should be saved even before they are transferred to some repository. All records have potential value, but not all records can be saved. Decisions to save records minimize the chances of preserving other records, and this predicament means archivists need to make the best choices they can.

Corporations and other institutions must establish institutional archives to care for their own records because archival records are first and foremost useful to their creators for corporate memory, accountability, and evidence rather than to a small handful of scholars and other researchers (although it is important that corporations and other institutions open up their records for bona fide, external researchers as well—within the bounds of appropriate private and proprietary considerations). This approach also recognizes that as organizations increasingly become digital and their record-keeping systems become electronic, multimedia, and networked, the most viable approach to maintaining such records is for the creating institution to take responsibility for the records and the systems. The old approaches for acquiring electronic or machine-readable records does not work for the new electronic record-keeping systems, which are far more complex in nature. While issues of access need to be worked out, they are minor problems compared to the loss of archival records now caused by a reliance on collecting archival programs. Without institutional archives, any chance of achieving balanced, representative, or comprehensive societal documentation is doomed to fail. Historical records repositories do not have sufficient space and other resources, or expertise, to care for and manage all these records.

Experts knowledgeable beyond archival and records management concerns must be involved in documentation analysis and planning. Although archivists possess subject knowledge, the broad nature of the potential disciplines and other topics they encounter requires a process that enables individuals with specialized expertise to assist in analyzing records and advising on appraisal decisions. Records managers should be most proficient in understanding the nature of record-keeping systems and the legal, fiscal, and administrative values of records. Archivists should be most proficient in evaluating the integrity of the records' evidence. The process of determining the value of records for documenting a particular topic, function, activity, or the like must be assisted by individuals with expertise in the relevant topic, function, or activity. The purpose of this assistance is not to determine whether the records might have some potential value (all records have such potential) but to help identify the small portion of records that must be maintained as archival records.

Community and civic associations and their leaders must understand the nature and importance of archival records, an area where much misunderstanding persists. Although it is perhaps not necessary for the public to have any detailed knowledge about what an archival record might look like, it is absolutely necessary that there be a broader appreciation of the purpose of archives in society. National debates over the appointment of the United States Archivist, standards for world history, federal government funding for cultural activities, and the declassification of and access to public records have generally revealed the wrong purpose of archives. Archives are seen as the province of the scholarly historian, not the general citizen. Archives are discussed as quaint, old records for the individual interested in curiosities and old things (garage sales and flea markets come to mind). Such perceptions are often the fault of what the archivist has portrayed. Instead of stressing evidence, archivists have tended to play up the soft, fuzzy, and feel-good concepts of history and interest in the past. Instead of emphasizing the value of accountability in government and other societal institutions, archivists have singled out only the few scholars using archives to write monographs that often reach a very narrow part of society. Instead of stressing the corporate memory that genealogists and others can find in these records, archivists long for the spectacular, attention-grabbing uses. Of course there are some individual exceptions, but in general, archivists seem to have reflected such attitudes or failed to correct popular stereotypes about themselves.

Archivists must adopt a mind-over-matter approach to analyzing archival documentation. This concept, coined by Terry Cook while at the National Archives of Canada and also called *macroappraisal,* basically suggests that archivists and their colleagues have defined what needs to be documented and preserved before they examine records.[5] It means that they can be strategic in navigating through the immense amount of records being rapidly created by society. It is also a very different paradigm from the one archivists have normally used. Normally, archivists, manuscripts curators, and records managers have first examined records and then determined their value, the hallmark of the kinds of collecting programs represented by historical societies and university and college special collections—attesting to the fact that many records managers also really collect as well. This model presupposes that there are enough archivists to examine all the records with potential value; there are not. It presupposes that all records with potential value will be made available for examination; they will not. The traditional approach of records managers working with records creators in more strategic ways, beyond only physical inspection, has some validity (although some legal cases—such as the well-known PROFS and FBI case files cases—suggest there are exceptions).

If there is a lead archival or historical records program in the geographic area, that institution must recognize that it cannot document the region by itself in any comprehensive manner. It probably cannot even fully document any one aspect of life in the region. It can acquire a considerable quantity of materials related to the region's history, and it can use these materials to serve some researchers, develop exhibitions about the region's history, and support the interpretation of the past to the general public. Although such a program can virtually independently take the lead in educating the public about the region's past, it cannot be as independent in acquiring the historical and archival sources (or in documenting the region), for the reasons already discussed. So, then, what should it be doing?

The formerly traditional repository should be a leader and facilitator in documenting the region's history, a mission that certainly fits with the current objectives of this institution. Its archives and other staff should be engaged in the following activities:

1. Creating an ongoing, sustained forum for considering, identifying, and planning for broad-based documentation projects concerning the region.
2. Fostering, through public relations and educational venues, the creation of key institutional archives in the region.
3. Serving as a clearinghouse to place immediately endangered archival records in appropriate repositories.
4. Functioning as a repository of last resort for endangered records for which there is no appropriate repository.
5. Making acquisition a secondary objective except to support its educational mission or to protect significant archival records threatened with loss.
6. Developing expertise to advise on records issues, ranging from legal matters (such as privacy and access) to technological issues (most notably, electronic records management and other digitization issues).

These activities transform archives as a repository (a place) into archives as an activity (a function). More importantly, the change provides a structure with some hope for success rather than an approach doomed to fail from the beginning (which is the reality of any collecting program with a broad mission). The role of the archives is not to preserve interesting stuff, however much fun and joy that might bring. It possesses the responsibility for protecting records with continuing value to society for memory, evidence, and accountability. This responsibility, a noble one as well as important, can be met only through a new cooperative and leadership approach. There is no other way.

BACKLASHES TO NEW PARADIGMS

Whenever an old program, such as a historical society, seeks to jettison its traditional approaches, there will be reactions (some good, some bad). One way of thinking about this is to imagine pains associated with growth spurts, a better scenario than the discomforts associated with dying. But such gloomy reactions are becoming much more common, possibly because the business of collecting old stuff is a hedge against the many phobias associated with the emerging digital age. Writer Nicholson Baker's diatribes against the destruction of old library card catalogs in favor of automated databases and, more recently, his attack on the destruction of original newspapers after microfilming are typical of the kinds of backlashes we must be prepared to deal with if we change our accustomed approaches. Baker's book *Double Fold: Libraries and the Assault on Paper* is typical of what we will be seeing and, in a sense, reflects the local battles that have already occurred.[6]

Not too many years ago, after having finished a leisurely walk through the British Museum, I came across a curious sight. Pausing in the museum shop, I noted that paper pads conveniently displayed for testing various pens for sale had been filled with messages demanding the return of the Elgin Marbles to Greece. When I was younger, we would have written "Richard loves Lynn" or, perhaps, something obscene. Now we visit the museum and question the legality or morality of its collections, if not the very reason for the museum's existence.

Such is the state of our cultural institutions today. While admittedly some of the world's greatest repositories of art, artifacts, books, and manuscripts are the result of violent looting from previous centuries of wars, social disturbances, and zealous collecting, until the past decade most had long since come to accept these institutions as places of quiet reflection, study, and even refuge. No more. They are attacked by patriotic and ethnic groups about what seem to be less than politically correct exhibits, hounded by the media who see in their once-quiet halls stories and exposés as powerful as any unfolding in government chambers or corporate boardrooms, and even policed by academics and scholars who before saw them as little more than custodians of study materials. Regardless of the origins of these institutions' collections, today they are also the target of thieves, organizational downsizing, and other challenges. Miles Harvey's compelling book about a map thief provides ample evidence that the custodians of rare and valuable materials need to do better in caring for their collections.[7]

The shame of all this scrutiny, in some cases long overdue, is that even some cultural institutions trying to do the right thing in managing their collections are caught up, sometimes unfairly, by the self-appointed guardians of the remnants of the past. Many of these guardians are the academic scholars, as we have seen in a wide range of cases from protests about the Smithsonian's withdrawal of its *Enola Gay* exhibition to threats to the funding of the documentary editions of the Founding Fathers' papers. But not all protests from the scholars are equal in importance or deserve much support, as can be seen in recent years in one case in Philadelphia. It is a tough time for American history museums, research repositories, and other institutions traditionally responsible for collecting and preserving the archives and artifacts documenting this nation's past. In recent years, these organizations have been buffeted by declining financial resources, growing financial responsibilities, changing public interests in the past, eroding support from foundations and government, and stinging debates about American history and its meaning. Hard and courageous decisions have been called for by the leaders of historical societies, history museums, and historic sites. Yet, seemingly, there is a price to be paid when such decisions are made and become public, as one historical society, founded in the early nineteenth century, discovered.

A few years ago, reports that an old historical society was planning to deaccession and sell some of its collections made the news. An article in the local newspaper reported that the organization had legal permission to dispose of some of its objects, ranging from portraits and statues of historical figures to personal objects owned by Thomas Jefferson and other famous individuals. Subsequent reports revealed that proceeds from sales of the artifacts would be used for maintaining the institution's research library and archives, and in fact the institution's leadership stated that the deaccessioning and sales were based on the realization that it could not continue to function as *both* research library and museum. The institution's president argued that the financial condition of the organization was "stable" and characterized the recent decisions as a rethinking of the organization's mission and activities. Although sometimes such public pronouncements try to divert attention from the real substance of a crisis, these decisions probably do have as much to do with missions as with money; it would be naive to think that financial considerations are not involved, but they do not lessen the importance of the organization's grappling with its mission.

Reactions were negative, as might be expected. Well-known historians were quoted deploring the dispersal of important treasures across the country like a flea market and declaring the sale a loss for scholars and the public. Former board members referred to the situation as a mess. Scholars and others seemed to view the institution's decisions as dismantling, even destroying, an important resource for studying American history and for educating the public about the past.

None of these critics commented on a multimillion-dollar building renovation program then starting that would improve environmental storage and security, a rare initiative for a private historical agency. Outside commentators need to focus instead on the institution's efforts to provide better care for what it has identified as part of its primary mission and in the knowledge on how these collections were formed in the first place. This is especially needed because the story is far from over. Although the historical society announced a few months into the fray that it had decided against getting rid of part of its collections—trying to stem the public controversy—I am confident that the organization (and others like it) will ultimately do what it started to do.

Although negative and emotional reactions might be called for given the continuing traumas faced by similar institutions, most publicly the New-York Historical Society, criticized for poor management and especially for its efforts of the past decade to sell collections to pay basic operating expenses—these fevered reactions might also be unwarranted given the historical development of these cultural repositories.[8] The Philadelphia-based institution's rationale for the deaccessioning might be a long-overdue response to a legacy that has shackled these organizations' ability to operate today.

The Historical Society publicly announced that the reason for its decision was its inability to financially support both museum and research facilities and that it was opting to focus on its collections of rare books and pamphlets, newspapers, graphic items, and manuscripts and archives. These are certainly important treasures, and the intention seems to be to better care for them by refocusing its mission. This is not an unprecedented decision. The American Antiquarian Society made a similar decision in 1909 about its historic twin roles as museum and research library, opting for the latter. That organization also recognized that it could not do both functions well. It also understood that it had been burdened by unbridled collecting for generations. At a 1964 conference, Clifford Shipton commented that the 1909 case was a "clear example of the fact that indecision in formulating a collecting policy, failure to adhere to policy, and failure to see one's policy in relation to the policies and resources of others can waste generations of work."[9] The actions of other historical societies need to be scrutinized in this manner, not with hysteria because some or even *many* objects will be deaccessioned and sold, traded, or transferred. A cursory glance suggests that the actions of the Historical Society are extremely similar to those of the American Antiquarian Society and, from a management perspective, might be the best means of preserving the most important collections. Statements about the need to keep together the collections of these kinds of institutions and descriptions referring to the treasures reflect a remarkable ignorance of what such collections actually represent.

Shipton's commentary on the American Antiquarian Society leads one to wonder what these historical societies and museums were about as they proliferated across the American landscape from the early nineteenth century to their peak at the nation's bicentennial. Created long before the establishment of government-supported archives, historical societies, history museums, and historic sites, these private organizations played an important role in saving historical manuscripts and other rare materials that most certainly would have been lost without their intervention. However, these institutions also collected everything and anything, from artifacts to archives to natural history specimens and relics of dubious quality and relevance to their organizational missions. Many of these institutions held collections as suitable for a circus or carnival as for a repository supporting serious study. The only reason to maintain these collections in perpetuity would be to create a museum about nineteenth-century antiquarian societies, and there are certainly other ways to document their legacy in the formation of our national heritage.

Even in the early days of these organizations, concerns were expressed about the breadth of acquisition. In the mid-nineteenth century, some scientists argued that natural history collections were out of place in the historical societies, and in the early twentieth century, others lamented that historical societies seemed to think stuffed birds as good as newspaper or rare imprints. The issues now being faced by organizations like historical societies have been considered before, and decisions about deaccessioning and refocusing might be long overdue; if we wish to criticize, perhaps the main point would be that it has taken this organization nearly two centuries to get to this point in its management (although it is ahead of others in trying to wrestle with such hard decisions). It could well be that if more of these societies had made such decisions fifty or a hundred years ago, their collections would have been better cared for, and many of the present financial challenges could have been avoided.

There are other issues. The legacy of excessively gathering the basic materials of American history has become more difficult to sustain as old endowments stagnate and thin financial resources dwindle further. Walter Muir Whitehill, in a massive study about the financial condition of these kinds of repositories nearly forty years ago, wrote that the financial resources of the independent historical societies are almost universally less than needed.[10] Too often such studies have not prescribed the kinds of radical thinking needed to make these historical organizations capable of meeting their missions. Whitehill's work was a loving tribute to these organizations. A study two decades later by the American Association for State and Local History resulted in a pessimistic profile of societies, sites, and other organizations needing professional and dynamic leadership while lacking the resources to acquire it.[11] None of this shortfall, however, is just a matter of money.

Because institutions like historical societies were filling voids in repositories available for gathering the records and material remains of American history, they were aggressive in accepting anything offered to them. These organizations were formed prior to the establishment of professional disciplines represented by historians, museum curators, archivists, and records managers, and the antiquarians and amateurs leading the societies did their best in acquiring what they thought was important to understanding the American past. Mistakes, some silly, were made about what should be collected or preserved (I once visited a local history museum holding as part of its collection the reputed testicle of a horse burned seventy-five years before in a famous conflagration). The complaints or fears raised by historians and other scholars need to be considered, but their commentaries also need to be understood in light of strong, focused missions, optimum professional practices, and the many and conflicting priorities set by researchers, policymakers, and the public for historical repositories.

Obviously, the times have changed. Professional principles and methods are available for helping these organizations to make better and more judicious decisions about what they will accept. There are more repositories now than ever, and cooperation is an alternative to the vacuum cleaner approach, pulling in all that is available for documenting the past. And the increasing use of electronic records and information technologies by both organizations and individuals is changing how we conceptualize collecting and physical custody of records deemed to have continuing value. Not all can be collected. Not all should be collected. A single institution cannot deem itself a self-sufficient repository to gather under one roof all archives, printed ephemera, decorative arts, and material culture. This did not work two hundred years ago. It certainly cannot work now. Because virtually any object or record can be deemed to have value for some purpose, it is not surprising that announcements of acquisition policy changes and deaccessioning by older institutions will be seen by some as a betrayal of public trust, as Nicholson Baker has argued in his essay about the destruction of newspapers. And the interdisciplinary needs of many scholars studying the past—with a strong desire to use historical manuscripts and archives along with decorative arts, printed documents, material culture, and archaeological remains in new and creative ways—have doubtless encouraged these scholars to lament the dispersal of collections. But who really believes that *one* repository can serve such a purpose? Can there be one repository gathering up all the *treasures* of even one city?

The true betrayal of public trust might result if historical societies did not make such decisions but instead steered along the same course they have followed since their founding nearly two centuries before. The 1996 study by Kevin M. Guthrie of the management of the New-York Historical Society, founded in 1804, repeatedly targets that organization's emphasis on acquisition of collections as the source of most of its financial and managerial problems. As more collections were added, cataloging backlogs grew and preservation problems increased even as financial resources declined. Hard decisions were not made for a very long time. The result was nearly the loss of the collections anyway. As Guthrie concluded in his study, the Society's board was composed of collectors who focused on collecting rather than managing.

None of this is to suggest that venerable institutions such as our historical societies should be allowed to jettison, with little supervision, their collections. However, a historical society's deaccessioning actions are hardly to be deprecated if done well and responsibly. I have observed, over a quarter of a century of work in archives and

records management, too many organizations making poor decisions to acquire when they could not justify why they should possess a particular item or collection or when they were limited in
professional expertise and other resources necessary to care for the
collections they already possessed.

Here is my advice for the leadership of traditional archival programs facing change:

1. Proceed cautiously and conservatively.
2. Follow professional principles for the deaccessioning of such
   collections.
3. Develop a precisely focused policy for collection development
   and ensure that it will be adhered to in succeeding generations.
4. Try to transfer the collections to other repositories instead of
   selling them (the marketplace for antiques and antiquities is in
   its own right a quagmire of ethical compromises and ought not
   to be encouraged).
5. Develop a thick skin for criticism because it will come.

But, then again, all such momentous decisions bring criticism and
consternation because such decisions are about change. American
historical societies have long been in need of change. Perhaps such
change is now starting.

Whatever change might have started with historical societies and
other traditional records programs seems to have been momentarily
derailed by the cultural schisms and tensions of the 1990s and
beyond, popularly referred to as the era of the "culture wars." Every
element or faction in society seemed determined to hold on to its
own unique values and even, at times, to foist its views onto others.
Historical societies were created in a different time, and they often
possessed a conservative perspective of building harmony or accent-
uating common views. The archivists and records professionals
who lay the foundation for appraisal values and approaches, from
collecting policies to retention schedules, emanated from a much
quieter period, when consensus seemed to prevail about documentary evidence, the essence of being an American citizen, and the connection of records to organizational functions and norms. With
everything now seemingly in flux, the old motives for collecting
archival records or managing organizational records do not seem
nearly as clear or clean as they once did. Add to this the obvious

questions inserted by technology and the failures to collect in coherent and meaningful fashion, and we have a much more problematic foundation for the role of records programs and professionals.

Some will charge me with wanting to destroy what repositories such as historical societies have taken more than a century, even two, to accumulate. I reject this, of course. We could start by elaborating on what we think these institutions *have done*, but I prefer not to follow on with such a negative thread of discourse. We need to consider, instead, a *new*, but not radically new, *documentary* mission for these repositories. Leadership, cooperation, mission, vision, and other attributes, such as creativity, all seem to assume a much more important role in the new century than ever before—except perhaps at the dawn of the historical society movement in the early nineteenth century and the creation of the modern records management profession a century and a half later.

CONCLUSION

Institutions like historical societies need to be held accountable for their actions. But shouldn't we hold them accountable for trying to take bold, perhaps risky, steps to manage what they consider to be the core of their research collections? Yet, perhaps the greater problem is that these repositories have taken so long to take chances that might lead to more innovative practices in appraising and administering the results of such appraising?

These are not a grandparent's attic of potential "treasures." They are important, serious-minded repositories for documenting American history and memory and taking some *extra-ordinary* measures to manage their most important collections more effectively. If historians cannot understand this, it is likely that they do not understand the historic role of these institutions in the fabric of this nation's memory. Perhaps *this* is what all the fuss should be about. Or, perhaps, the fuss should be about those older, traditional programs that make *no* effort to change or to deal with the changing nature of archival record. Archivists and records managers need to reevaluate the effectiveness of their operations. Archivists engaged in traditional collecting programs might face a tough challenge in trying both to gain support for radical new approaches and to accommodate new electronic records systems in their documentary efforts.

Records managers also face difficult tasks when dealing with new technologies and wrestling with institutional interests that resist centralizing either records or even supposedly proven functions such as retention schedules.

Although historical societies have existed for over two centuries and institutional records management programs for sixty years, the longevity of their traditional approaches needs to be reconsidered. A study of organizational longevity recently concluded that organizations have to consider the following kinds of actions:

1. "Put in place a system for understanding the interaction between the organization and the environment. This includes the anticipation of environmental demands for change and constant diagnosis of discrepancies between environmental needs and organizational actions/strategies. The latter should spur action plans for strategy design, development, and implementation. Essential is the continuous monitoring of environmental response to these strategic changes."

2. "Alter the organization's culture such that the engagement in ongoing change becomes second nature to ensure organizational learning. Given that we define organization development as planned change, the true key to successful change is employee involvement. A major element in planned change is organizational culture: feelings, norms, member behavior. . . . [The] learning organization depends heavily on a culture of involvement and empowerment. To this end, there must be available to all employees the information, support, and resources they need to instill in them the value of organizational learning."

3. "Enmesh in this modified culture a mechanism for the development and support of conceptually complex leaders. The previous two steps fall under the purview of organizational renewal, a process of continuous improvement, which holds a significant place in the vision of the organization. To ensure this renewal, there must be a conceptually complex leader who fosters involvement by empowering others to create strategic change as necessary. In cases where no such leader appears to be a part of the organization, development efforts must be undertaken. The cognitive behaviors associated with conceptual complexity can be developed."[12]

Here we see it all. Understanding the changing environment, altering organizational culture, and nurturing new leadership are the necessary ingredients for breathing new life into old institutions, ideas, and professional objectives. The importance of the archival record remains a constant, but the constantly transforming technology of the record and expectations of what archival records programs (and all records management programs) will look like and what purpose they will serve suggests the need for renewed vigor and experimentation.

Although historical records collecting or archives programs have been around much longer than records management programs, the latter also must put themselves through some self-scrutiny and consider whether they remain relevant to their organizations. The potential changing roles of traditional archival operations give records managers much to mull over. Here are some basic areas that records managers might reflect on:

How are records and record-keeping systems changing, and what are the implications of these changes for records management programs?

What are a program's accumulated records intended to represent or support? Do they support legal, administrative, and research needs?

How does the mission of the records management program support or reflect the mission of its parent organization?

What kind of image does the records management program have, and is it the appropriate image?

What are the changing means of access to records, and what are the implications of these changes to the records management program?

Do the present uses and users of records in the records management program represent the kinds of uses and users that the program is intended to support? Are there other uses or users not represented that should be present?

Are there cooperative means (with other organizations and records programs) of meeting the objectives of the records management program that are not being utilized?

Does the current staffing (meaning professional background, experience, and education) of the records management program support the program's mandate or potential future directions?

By asking and answering such questions through planning processes, use of outside consultants, and other means, modern records management programs can avoid seeing their role wither within organizations. Because records are important to every organization and to society because of their evidence and information and the roles they play in providing corporate memory and accountability, some organizational unit or leader will assume responsibility for the administration of records. A continuous process of self-evaluation by considering the fate of other records programs will help maintain a fresh and vital records management program.

NOTES

1. Elisabeth Kaplan, "We Are What We Collect, We Collect What We Are: Archives and the Construction of Identity," *American Archivist* 63 (Spring/Summer 2000): 130, 147.

2. Jane Jacobs, *The Death and Life of American Cities* (New York: Vintage Books, 1993).

3. Kevin Lynch, *What Time Is This Place?* (Cambridge, Mass.: MIT Press, 1976).

4. James Howard Kunstler, *Home from Nowhere: Remaking Our Everyday World for the Twenty-First Century* (New York: Simon and Schuster, 1996).

5. Terry Cook, "Mind Over Matter: Towards a New Theory of Archival Appraisal," in *The Archival Imagination: Essays in Honour of Hugh A. Taylor*, ed. Barbara L. Craig (Ottawa: Association of Canadian Archivists, 1992), 38–70.

6. Nicholson Baker, *Double Fold: Libraries and the Assault on Paper* (New York: Random House, 2001).

7. Miles Harvey, *The Island of Lost Maps: A True Story of Cartographic Crime* (New York: Random House, 2000).

8. Kevin M. Guthrie, *The New-York Historical Society: Lessons from One Nonprofit's Long Struggle for Survival* (San Francisco: Jossey-Bass, 1996).

9. Clifford K. Shipton, "The Museum of the American Antiquarian Society," in *A Cabinet of Curiosities: Five Episodes in the Evolution of American Museums* (Charlottesville: University Press of Virginia, 1967), 48.

10. Walter Muir Whitehill, *Independent Historical Societies: An Enquiry into Their Research and Publication Functions and Their Financial Future* (Boston: Boston Athenaeum, 1962).

11. Charles Phillips and Patricia Hogan, *The Wages of History: The AASLH Employment Trends and Salary Survey* (Nashville: American Association for State and Local History, 1984) and *A Culture at Risk: Who Cares for America's Heritage?* (Nashville: American Association for State and Local History, 1984).

12. L. A. Montuori, "Organizational Longevity: Integrating Systems Thinking, Learning and Conceptual Complexity," *Journal of Organizational Change* 13, no. 1 (2000): 71.

5

The Archivist and Collecting: A View from the Inside

Archival collecting—the acquisition of organizational records and personal papers for housing, management, and use in archival and historical records repositories—has a long and tangled history.[1] In many cases, archivists equate appraisal, the identification of records with continuing or enduring value, with collecting (and vice versa). Some archivists believe that records do not become archives without the blessing of archivists through an appraisal process, or, at the least, the physical housing (by whatever means) within archives and historical manuscripts repositories. Others place records on a continuum, and they designate a record as archival based on a continuing value because of the importance of the warrant or function generating the record. In the midst of this comes the much older idea of collecting, bringing records into centralized repositories for convenience of research use.

These complicated matters cut into cultural, political, professional, and personal concerns. There are differences with archival collecting within American, European, and other nations. Europeans, operating within a more centralized and controlled regime, tend not to think about collecting in the way North Americans approach this matter. In the younger nation of Australia, the collec-

tion of personal and private papers has not been a primary emphasis, at least when compared with the focus on institutional and
governmental records.[2] Many archivists on both continents adhere
to a view of appraisal advocated more than half a century ago by
Hilary Jenkinson, who believed that the creators of records made
selection decisions and that this ensured an objectivity impossible
to achieve by any other means.[3] American archivists have focused,
however, on a serendipitous collecting as well as more systematic
appraisal approaches, reflecting their less regimented national
archival system.[4] Some would argue that the greatest emphasis,
both practical and theoretical, on *collecting* has come from North
Americans, and as a result, this chapter concentrates on the topic of
the archivist and collecting from a distinctly North American perspective.

BASIC DEFINITIONS

Some observers have connected the ability to document the past
with the strength of the archival and historical manuscripts repositories that have been formed. In an assessment of how well America
was caring for its historical records, Gerald George (then Director of
the National Historical Publications and Records Commission, the
national funding arm of the U.S. National Archives) wrote:

> In the ongoing struggle with capricious fortune, the nation's collective
> success in documenting its history is directly connected to the strength
> of archival and historical institutions, the security of their facilities, the
> scope of their holdings, their ability to provide access, and the aggres-
> siveness of their collecting—or their ability to persuade others to pre-
> serve materials accessible to historians.[5]

The issue of collecting is what this chapter is about, but the degree
of aggression or activity George emphasizes seems to me to be far
from the main issue to be worried about. Collecting has played an
important role in forming what archivists do, but it has also played
havoc with systematic or standardized approaches to the management of archival records.

For the past century, the nature of archives and historical manuscripts programs in the United States that might collect records has

remained fairly constant. Forty years ago, one archivist provided a typology of collecting programs in this fashion:

> Basically there are four types of collecting agencies: (1) the private collector; (2) historical agencies devoted to the preservation of research materials—including manuscripts—primarily for cultural or historical purposes; (3) archival agencies serving their own governments, businesses, or organizations; and (4) agencies that combine both manuscript-collecting and archival functions.[6]

This aptly describes the nature of archival programs today. Although such programs are more diverse and greater in number today, they still fall largely within these four categories. And just as they did a century ago, there are tensions caused by the existence of these various collecting groups.

In the United States, the development of archives and historical records programs has been connected to two distinct traditions, built around the manner in which they acquire records. The historical manuscripts tradition relates to collecting repositories like historical societies and colleges and universities. The public archives tradition is connected to the local, state, and federal archives, in which records are acquired primarily through regular transfers, usually as part of a records management program.[7] Even public archives have "collected," generally in their formative years as they discover older records, deal with the recovery of older records found by agencies, and evaluate records delivered to them unannounced and without any relationship to formal records retention and disposition schedules.[8] Many state governments worked in the early nineteenth century to copy records related to their colonial past in the archives of Europe, constituting a primitive kind of archival collecting.[9] In addition, most states labored to gather, copy, and preserve their oldest records.[10] Although one cannot find a formal definition of archival "collecting" within the main professional glossary, it is still the case that the physical acquisition of records is what most archivists have their sights set on.[11]

PIONEER COLLECTORS AND COLLECTING

The collecting emphasis in the American archival profession stems substantially from nineteenth-century historical societies. These historical societies were part of a desire by Americans to develop a usable past for their young nation, a new interest that developed in tandem with historical novels, museums, autograph collecting, and other such activities and trends. One historian even characterized this period as one beset by "documania."[12] The historical societies were also modeled after English and European organizations established in the Renaissance, generally with antiquarian and nationalistic motives similar to those of their American descendants.[13] The equating of archives with their collecting has long been associated with nationalism, as in some nations where war memorials included not just the erection of monuments but the collecting of records related to the conflict.[14]

It is not accidental, therefore, that the earliest historical societies were established in the first years of the American republic. The Massachusetts Historical Society, formed in 1791, was the first American historical society, and it was followed by a few other societies in the subsequent decades. Between 1820 and 1860, historical societies were established in nearly every hamlet and major urban center and certainly every state. By the end of the nineteenth century, hundreds of these repositories existed, each generally subscribing to a "collect everything" mission. As many have pointed out, these were the main protectors of America's historical records before the advent of government, institutional, and university and college archives. Historical societies often collected primarily to reflect the interests of their board members, and they often acquired items in a highly competitive way. Admittedly these institutions operated long before there was an archival profession, professional standards, and distinctions between the business of libraries and that of archives. But their highly charged desire to collect everything and anything set a tone that still permeates large sections of the modern archival profession. Although we can discern some narrowing of collecting foci by these institutions as they ran out of space, faced increasing competition from other repositories, identified particular constituencies, and hired more professionally trained staff, there is still no question that by any standard their acquisition desires remained broad and sometimes quite eclectic.[15] In some ways, the general American's intense interest in the past, including collecting, continues today, and it serves as a reminder that archivists, despite training and vocational choice, are part of the general populace as well.[16]

One of the devices used by these historical societies was the issuance of wanted lists, circulated to individuals and communities in order to advise them of important and valuable archival records and historical manuscripts. The practice continued well into the twentieth century, when historical pageants organizers often put out calls for historical documents and artifacts.[17] Beyond such pageants, modern historical societies, such as the Minnesota Historical Society, effectively did the same. A pamphlet issued by the society in 1951 carried an age-old sentiment:

> Between the records and those who would destroy stands the collector. He knows that it is impractical or impossible to save everything, for only a fraction of all the records that have been created have enough historical value to warrant the investment of time and money necessary to preserve them. But, out of the mass, the collector must select the essentials, the manuscripts that will insure remembrance of our past.[18]

In this statement, the "collector" was the state or local repository; a century ago it would have been *both* institution and individual.

The historical societies served many roles, but it was primarily as a collecting agency—even if somewhat unfocused—that these organizations made their most important contributions to the development of a documentary heritage. For example, long before government archives were established in the early twentieth century, historical societies often acquired public records that might have otherwise been lost because of neglect or willful destruction.[19] Still, it is also obvious that these organizations at times inflicted damage on public records by removing them from their records context, treating them as isolated personal papers rather than organizational records, and removing the responsibility from governments to care for their archives. In this way, they reflected the activities of earlier English and European collectors who gathered up stray public records, personal papers, artifacts, and other materials in the pursuit of documenting the past for present use while arguing for their more systematic care.[20]

One of the roles of these historical societies was to acquire printed ephemera and nontraditional record sources. Over a century ago, it was likely that ephemeral material would be swept up just as eagerly as more substantial records. Many of the most valuable ephemera collections reside in these older institutions. Now, archivists are developing methodologies to help them identify criteria for dealing with ephemera and other nontraditional records.[21] Sometimes, what seem to be fairly routine business records take on more useful importance in repositories and societies, where their research value is recognized beyond their business utility. The obsolete files of publishers and literary agents, for example, have become sought after because of what they reveal about particular writers as well as the publishing industry.[22] Archival collecting can become messy and undisciplined when missions are set so broadly, even when individual researchers attest to the potential and actual value of such collections. Without some criteria or parameters, the older antiquarian tradition of collecting for collecting's sake becomes the guiding principle.

COLLECTING AND THE FORMATION OF THE EARLY MODERN PROFESSION

Acquisition, collecting, appraisal, and selection have long been thought to be crucial functions of the modern archival profession (usually considered to have started in the late nineteenth century in Europe and in the early twentieth century in North America).[23] German archivist Karl Otto Muller, working as the American archival profession was forming, is considered by some to be the first to state that selection was the primary matter for archivists to resolve, and he argued that "What is not worth preserving, should never be allowed into an archive." In the years since then, archivists worldwide have developed a variety of models, methods, and mandates for guiding archival appraisal and acquisition, ranging from allowing the records creator to make the decision to elaborate planning approaches.[24] Always working against the systematic approach to appraisal and selection have been the more romantic stories of the great collectors, the pursuit of important collections, and the defying of odds in saving significant records and sources. Such stories often play a major role in inspiring individuals to become professional archivists and manuscripts curators.[25]

The romance of collecting fits well with what occurred during World War II. The obsession that is collecting can be seen most dramatically in tragic events where one people's misfortunes become an opportunity for another's collecting. For centuries, conquering nations have carried off the archives of other nations (when they haven't destroyed them), although the reasons are often complicated; motives such as destroying a people's identity are often stronger than making a profit or acquiring an object.[26] World War II was particularly disturbing in this regard in that the Nazis carted off art and historical treasures, including many historical manuscripts. These documents and objects came onto the market, and many wound up in the hands of private collectors or public repositories. In the 1980s and 1990s, as records of the warring nations were declassified and the generation of Holocaust survivors began to die off, the looting of Europe became more well-known and controversial.[27] The end of the Cold War also has brought new attention to matters like these, especially calls for the return of displaced archival treasures.[28] The increased public scrutiny on the events of World War II also shone more intense light on the troublesome aspects of an international trade in collecting antiquities, art, and archives.

SHIFTING NOTIONS OF
ARCHIVAL COLLECTING

There have been noteworthy changes in archival collecting in the past half century in the United States and around the world, some caused by societal developments and others generated within the profession itself. Philip Mason, a leading labor archivist and archival educator, sees a substantial change after 1950, when "emphasis on elite groups continued to dominate the collecting priorities of established archival institutions but increasingly attention was devoted to new areas." As Mason sees it:

> The major change in the focus of archives came about through the efforts of the newly established archival programs, especially those affiliated with colleges and universities. Unfettered by traditional collecting practices and free from conservative governing boards, the new archives branched out into new subject fields. Some chose a geographical area or region as their focal point of collecting, whereas others selected a subject theme around which to develop an archives.[29]

In fact, the origins of many nationally and internationally known repositories developed because of perceived gaps in collecting or the need to locate archives and records closer to the researchers.[30] This is a very different emphasis from what propelled pioneers like Jeremy Belknap (founder of the Massachusetts Historical Society) in the early years of the historical societies—when there were few repositories, researchers resorted to building their own collections, and crucial records were viewed as "monuments" in claiming a past for the young nation.[31]

After a century of wide-scale founding of state and local historical societies, the twentieth century became a period of more focused collecting by repositories either to document specific groups or to support the research of scholars.[32] Those programs that did not refocus their collecting efforts often discovered that the financial burden of collecting had become substantial, requiring them to either rethink their mission or face escalating costs threatening to put them out of business.[33] Nonetheless, archivists persistently have collected virtually every type of record representing every discipline, topic, and trend—such as science,[34] publishing,[35] law,[36] ethnic groups,[37] and labor.[38] Most of these collecting areas developed because historians and other scholars identified gaps in the holdings of repositories where they conducted their research. Although these efforts have often had noteworthy results, they have also contributed to the general randomness of collecting and often sidelined rigorous standards for appraisal in favor of a "just in case" or "might be of use someday" stance. Such views are particularly vulnerable as the future brings immense changes in records technology, the use of records, and how society understands and approaches fundamental matters like evidence and information.[39]

THE FUTURE OF COLLECTING

If anyone wonders where archival collecting might lead, a reading of Thomas Mallon's fictional article about the National Archives in the year 2099 will inspire thoughts. Archives II, the newer building of the National Archives in College Park, Maryland, has been turned into condos because all the records have been digitized and the space is no longer needed. The National Archives collects artifacts or, as one of the characters in the short story mutters, "Junk is the Archives' business."[40] Indeed, "archival" collecting was driven by the desire to acquire almost anything or to serve the needs of researchers, although public records staff have begun to shift to more critical matters such as accountability. Some have argued that such matters are also relevant for collecting repositories, such as in gathering materials for supporting environmental issues or in ensuring political freedom.[41] Despite two centuries of collecting and continued reflection on what it means to acquire records for archives, archivists and their predecessors have spent little time gathering data about why people donate records to repositories. This is a fruitful area for research,[42] as is almost any aspect of archival appraisal and collecting.[43]

Although the emphasis of collecting in the nineteenth century was on the papers of individuals and families rather than institutions (and when institutional records were acquired, they were treated as personal papers), many today believe the emphasis has shifted too far toward collecting government records, especially electronic records. Some have even argued that the archivists who collect personal papers have been victims of "marginalization."[44] Some of these commentators have stressed that the changing record-keeping technologies require that both collecting and organizational repositories cooperate as well as develop similar approaches to appraising records.[45] Other archivists have gone even further with this concern, worrying that the shift to electronic records management will have archivists forget about the artifacts of record keeping. One archivist contends that archives do not store information but rather hold "artifacts in which information inheres." Archives are, according to such a perspective, like a "documents museum."[46] Tension has also been increasing between archivists who seem to emphasize responsibility for organizational records and researchers (especially historians) who worry about where privately created records are being acquired.[47] Such debates indicate that archivists are worried about both what they will be able to collect and whether their facilities will be relegated to lesser roles as places to store old and obsolete documents.

COLLECTING INSTITUTIONS AND INDIVIDUAL COLLECTORS

The idea of professional collecting does butt up against the avocation of collecting by private individuals. Despite the connection of

collecting to various stages in the history of the archival profession
and the formation of a genuine documentary heritage, in the past
few decades tension has been increasing between private collectors
(individuals, not institutions) and repositories, from government
archives to collecting programs in universities and historical societies. One case involved the state government of North Carolina seeking legal action against an autograph dealer who offered in his
catalog records that had been in the state government's hands a long
time before.[48] A famous incident in the 1950s concerned a question
of ownership of the records of the Lewis and Clark expedition to the
Pacific Ocean in the early nineteenth century. Were the manuscripts
the property of the federal government, which commissioned the
expedition, or of descendants of the explorers?[49] Another replevin
case occurred in the early 1980s when one repository, the Western
Reserve Historical Society, deaccessioned a group of surveyor's
drawings and notes related to Louisiana and adjacent states and put
the records up for auction. Pursued by the Historic New Orleans
Collection, a private repository, and the Louisiana State Museum, a
public agency, the Louisiana state government ultimately attempted
to seize a portion of the records as having belonged to the government.

Although the contention that these were public records appeared
a bit specious, the various parties managed to reach a compromise
whereby the entire collection was acquired by the Historic New
Orleans Collection.[50] From the archivist's viewpoint, the concept is
generally very clear: "The archives and institutional collections that
are now established have taken the place of the private collector as
the major agent for the preservation of our documentary heritage."
Or, "Replevin actions for public archival estrays sustain a historical
view and belief that official records belong to the *people* as represented by their governments."[51] Private individual collectors have,
of course, a very different take on this matter. Although private collectors had played a crucial role in the nineteenth century, they are
now seen by the multitude of established programs as threats to
security, access, and other matters.[52]

The tension between private collectors and archival repositories
should not be surprising. In many cases, individuals and institutions compete for the same items. Sometimes, collectors use institutions, such as libraries, as ways of building their own private
holdings (as libraries unsuspectingly weed out rare and valuable

materials).[53] Just as often, archival programs collect the collections of private collectors.[54] In more rare, but important, cases, private collectors establish important repositories for their collections, blurring the distinction between personal and institutional collecting as professional staffs become involved in the new institutions.[55] At the least, many archivists, manuscripts curators, and special collections librarians relished collecting with the same passion as private collectors. University librarian Lawrence Thompson noted that "Strict objectivity, total indifference to partisan issues on the site of collecting, and an unmitigated passion for identifying the truth are the hallmarks of the collector's trade."[56] The collector was identified as both individuals *and* institutions.

The problems represented in this aspect of collecting are caused by how popular the autograph trade has become as an investment hedge, important enough to be featured in magazines such as *Forbes*.[57] The continuing interest in personal autograph collecting can be seen in the ongoing proliferation of "how-to" books on the subject.[58] Despite this fascination with autographs, we do not yet have a good social history of such collecting, but rather we possess isolated studies of particular collectors,[59] autograph albums as genres,[60] and the autograph business.[61] The rising monetary value of manuscripts also contributes to other problem activities, such as forgery, although the history of forgery is also connected to other developments in record keeping (such as the transition to written records as the primary form of evidence and changing trends in scholarship).[62] Some forgery cases, such as the Hitler diaries debacle or the celebrated case concerning the forgeries of Mormon documents in the 1980s, have become international events and leave no doubt that the primary motive was to make money.[63]

Even today, conflict between the appraisal of government records and the collecting of records exists, as evidenced by litigation concerning the U.S. National Archives appraisal of FBI records and the ongoing case regarding the maintenance of electronic mail concerning the Iran-Contra affair.[64] Such cases are less problematic than ethical aspects of collecting. The Society of American Archivists Code of Ethics suggests that an archives or historical manuscripts repository ought to have a collecting policy, provide adequate resources for maintaining the records acquired, work against excessive donor restrictions, use legal documents in making acquisitions, and seek acquisitions in a fair manner.[65] Most repositories do have these ele-

ments in collecting or acquisition policies, but the specter of theft
and other problems haunts these repositories and the profession.
Again, the more human aspects of collecting often overwhelm the
mundane but necessary elements of maintaining archives. Thoughts
of publicity or of beating another repository in acquiring a particular
collection can mute the influence of ethics.

Despite the intense discussion and development of new appraisal
methods during the past two decades, many collecting programs
still acquire the collections of private collectors. Many of the holdings of historical manuscripts programs are actually former private
collections. The stress between private and institutional collectors is
somewhat modified by this relationship. Private collectors often create trends in collecting or have the financial resources to build collections; it is often up to institutional repositories to house them and
make them available for researchers.[66] It is precisely at this intersection between private collector and institutional repository that the
most dramatic aspects of the psychological nature of collecting are
seen.

THE PSYCHOLOGY OF COLLECTING AND
THE COLLECTING IMPULSE

In some cases, archivists have exhibited some of the most blatant
desires for collecting as a human and competitive instinct. Howard
Gotlieb, a long-time archivist at Boston University and the chaser
of records of celebrities and other noteworthies, was described as
collecting:

> to preserve a moment in time; thus, he pleads that each member of his
> ever-growing "family" save every scrap of paper upon which a little
> or just one single word has been written or typed. He claims that each
> manuscript or typescript piece of paper is like an irreplaceable paint-
> ing as it is the only one extant. Gotlieb is so persnickety about this mat-
> ter that he, on occasion, sends empty boxes to collectees to use as
> receptacles for any paper discards that they may have. "We want
> everything," explains Gotlieb.[67]

Such sentiments are supported by the many volumes of memoirs of
collectors and dealers who describe the thrill of the chase, ecstasy
in finding treasures in dunghills, and the pleasures associated with

outdoing individual and institutional competitors.[68] This is a far cry from those archivists who struggle to understand whether systematic analysis of organizational records can lead to the type of documentation needed for purposes of organizational memory and future research use.[69]

Collecting has been connected to all sorts of human instincts and interests, from the personal[70] to societal consumerism.[71] A significant challenge to the archivist and to collecting is the archivist's impulse to collect. Most archivists remain fearful that if they do not step in to save records, something important will be lost.[72] Bruce Montgomery, writing about the more than 1,000 human rights organizations in North America, stated that the lack of research about human rights "stems largely from the paucity of archival evidence in research universities and other educational institutions, and illustrates the danger to the historical record when significant materials on leading worldwide social and political movements remain uncollected."[73] Although some collecting stems from personal and psychological impulses, some of it also extends from the importance of assembling archives in new areas. As an archivist of dance writes:

> The emergence of new archives can only offer greater nourishment and benefit to any tradition. . . . It is also a fact that the growth of an archive has a direct impact on a community and a country's sense of self or their personal self-esteem. It is a force which guards its heritage, while at the same time providing educational materials on traditions of the past and customs of the present for its members.[74]

A part of coming to terms with the psychological dimensions of collecting has been a substantial rethinking of archival appraisal and collecting in the past two decades.

RETHINKING ARCHIVAL
APPRAISAL AND COLLECTING

In the 1970s and 1980s, concerns about effective collecting led to efforts to systematize the development of archival collecting policies. Here is where archival appraisal and collecting approaches have melded, both hindered by a sense that the records (and other materials) archivists and manuscripts curators were gathering were inadequate for a full or balanced documentation of society.[75] There was some borrowing from librarians experienced in the development of collecting policies, who stressed planning, selecting, evaluation, and cooperative activities.[76] The fullest articulation of what goes into a collecting policy for manuscripts was also developed in this time period and emphasized a statement of purpose, types of programs supported by the collection, clientele served by the collection, priorities and limitations of the collection, cooperative agreements affecting the policy, resource sharing, deaccessioning, procedures for supporting the collecting policy, and procedures for monitoring the development of the collection.[77] By the early 1990s, archivists like Barbara Craig were stating this about appraisal (and, by implication, acquisition and collecting): "We do not create the past like an artist creates a work of art; rather, we aim to control the past, or more accurately, to control the documentation of the past, like a systems methodizer, balancing aims, objectives, resources and demand."[78]

In some ways the opening salvo in this reconsideration of collecting by archivists was fired by F. Gerald Ham in his 1974 presidential address to the Society of American Archivists. Ham, then state archivist for Wisconsin, lamented that archivists and manuscripts collectors seemed to be casualties of the constantly changing vogues in research trends and practices. Ham argued that archivists needed to take the lead by acquiring records that would support current research but that would also open new avenues for historical research.[79] Ham's eloquent message brought both short-term and long-term responses. Typical of the short-term response was that of Lester Cappon, drawing on fifty years' experience, who argued:

> On the archival edge the archivist as collector is confronted with certain dilemmas, not inherently new in the twentieth century, that are insoluble, to some degree, but open to accommodation. On the one hand, the quantity of certain records demands drastic measures, wisely to save and to destroy; on the other hand, the paucity or lack of certain records, attributable to telephone communication, tempts him to fill the void by creating records for the service of scholarship.[80]

The challenges facing archivists in collecting and appraising are, of course, difficult and complicated.

Because of dissatisfaction with what has long seemed to be random or skewed collecting, the decades of the 1970s and 1980s became a time when archivists devoted considerable attention to developing a system for acquisition. Archivists began to question the usual approaches by which they sought to appraise records, and this ultimately affected the standard means by which archivists collected. Some efforts sought to develop a more objective appraisal process, although the development of models and the use of models varied wildly.[81] Archival documentation strategies emerged as a model of such an approach, promising to bring together archivists, records creators, and the users of archives in a forum that would support clearer planning and literal collecting.[82] Archival macroappraisal approaches, stressing functions of records creation, also emerged in this period, although it has been more directed to government and corporations.[83] Since these professional discussions, some contentious debate erupted over the foundation of archival appraisal and acquisition, generally revolving about notions of archival science versus historical approaches to appraising and collecting.[84] The documentation strategy model or concept (it has been termed various things) was attractive enough that it was discussed as a foundation for documenting certain aspects of society, such as adult education,[85] higher education,[86] medicine and health care,[87] and geographic regions.[88]

This transformation of thinking about appraisal and collecting led to a consideration of more standardized approaches and reevaluation of cherished ideas and values. For a long time, the assumption and practice of collecting records has been to focus on their informational value (that is, their value beyond the immediate uses to the creators of the records—the evidential value). Some case studies are suggesting that such distinctions are quite artificial.[89] On the other hand, some archivists have come to see the degree of use as the only means by which appraisal or acquisition can be effectively evaluated.[90] At the least, there is some room for connecting archival appraisal, records management scheduling, and the more systematic collecting approaches.[91]

The most recent move to reconsider archival appraisal generally stemmed from the realization that records were voluminous and increasing in volume, leading to more calls for discipline, restraint, and intelligence in collecting.[92] As some might argue, as the nature and breadth of records systems increased, appraisal (and collecting) simply become *more* difficult.[93] However, the challenge of volume has been commented on by every archival thinker or theoretician for the past century. There must be other motives for such reevaluation. Although government records have become subject to reappraisal[94] (the systematic reevaluation of records acquired by archival programs), for example, the records and manuscripts acquired by collecting repositories have not been the target of such reexamination. Since the notion of reappraisal or deaccessioning surfaced twenty years ago, there seems to have been little effort to apply this approach in repositories.[95] Collection analysis (closely related to reappraisal), the systematic reevaluation of holdings against perceived or assumed collecting objectives, has had a mildly better history, with some intense case studies and follow-up examinations.[96] The lack of attention to such analysis suggests the importance of carefully developing collecting criteria in the first place; it also suggests that systematic approaches still have not reinvented appraisal or collecting practice. It might be other factors that transform the basic archival attitudes toward collecting.

BARRIERS TO COLLECTING

Many problems persist in modern collecting of personal papers, such as privacy of those still living.[97] In fact, personal privacy has become so significant an issue that popular novels have focused on the role of archivists and manuscript collectors in preserving manuscripts that reveal the private lives of public figures.[98] And life imitates art, as the daughter of writer Bernard Malamud laments concerning access to her late father's papers; she wonders whether such personal papers might be better off destroyed.[99] Some of these problems have persisted for a long time, such as the recognition of the complicated and laborious relationship between repositories and the donors of archives and manuscripts.[100] Such challenges extend beyond the nature of the materials and require asking hard questions, such as why many archives and historical manuscripts programs have shied away from confronting (and collecting in) controversial areas.[101]

Those programs that have tried to deal with controversial topics, by acquiring the records of organizations like the Ku Klux Klan, for example, have found public reaction and media attention difficult to contend with.[102] Indeed, we could ask today whether it is possible to collect *at all* and avoid controversy. Nearly every aspect of history, historical interpretation, and historical sources has been caught up in controversies, ranging from national history standards in education to exhibitions in major museums.[103] The American archival profession seems timid in dealing with such issues, suggesting that records posing the slightest problems may be bypassed in favor of less contested and, often, older materials. Although there are continuing challenges to access to government records, it is difficult to find evidence of a dynamic archival profession arguing for more liberal interpretation of classification regulations.[104]

The records of American businesses have presented a particularly difficult aspect of collecting, as archivists realized that the businesses themselves were rarely establishing institutional archives and that the records were voluminous in comparison with other types of records.[105] Archival programs with a national scope in documenting businesses often had to reevaluate just how they were conducting their mission. Harvard University's Baker Library shifted from a national scope to one focused on the New England region and, even then it had to develop aggressive criteria for reducing the size of its holdings—at a time long before the archival profession began to develop theoretical foundations for such work.[106] In the mid-1990s a national conference on the appraisal of American business records tried to deal with the myriad challenges posed by corporate records, but whether it really drew any closer to workable solutions is unclear. The American archival profession still sees itself as collectors of such records, while the quantity and complexity (especially the uses of electronic information technology) of these records defy the possibilities of acquisition.[107] Calls for the profession to work on establishing institutional or corporate archives have gone largely unheeded.[108]

Cooperation has also been recognized as a crucial, but elusive, element in collecting and appraising. Government archivists pushed for cooperation, especially in the sharing of scheduling information, so as to bring control to the housing of voluminous quantities of records. In 1988 the Intergovernmental Records Project, uniting in 1990 with Research Libraries Information Network's (RLIN) Government Records Project to share descriptive information, started as a pioneering step toward some sort of joint appraisal effort.[109] But cooperation has not been a general success, even though it is obviously needed in the archival community. When surveys accumulate data about collecting practice, interest in and activity supporting cooperative approaches generally come up as the weakest link.[110] Some would contest this conclusion. Philip Mason, in the early 1980s, said this about labor archives:

> The issue of competition between labor archives is no longer the problem that it was twenty or thirty years ago when the "scarcity" theory of collecting dominated the field. Archivists now recognize that not only are there enough important and valuable collections for all archives to share, but indeed, the existing programs cannot begin to collect and preserve the available union sources. Cooperation has replaced competition among labor archivists.[111]

If this is the case, such cooperation is a rarity.

In other documented instances, two or more repositories have worked together to deal with voluminous or complex records.[112] However, these have been either rare occurrences or rarely documented. The establishment of statewide regional networks in the late 1960s seems to be the apogee of such archival cooperation, but they have been well documented as being more effective in nurturing use than in coordinating collecting and acquisitions.[113] Thirty years ago archivists realized that they needed to be organized in some manner that would enable more focused collecting and that would reduce competition. In the United States a number of states set up regional systems, usually under the direction of the state archives.[114] But there is another tension here. For generations archival repositories seemed to thrill in the competitive hunt for personal papers, family manuscripts, and similar materials. Increasingly the necessity of strong and able cooperation has been recognized.[115]

There have been other persistent barriers to collecting. Prior to such ideas as systematic analysis and collecting, archivists, convinced of the inability to assess the overall documentation universe, tended to focus on approaches promising flexibility and experimentation.[116] In the not-too-distant past, many archivists stressed more good public relations and cooperative efforts rather than a high degree of analysis that could be called appraisal.[117] The amazing growth in thematically oriented collecting programs also created new problems for institutions like colleges and universities. The fact that a single faculty member, with a diverse career and research interests, might be the target of two or more such programs generated the need for more cooperation between repositories.[118] This is a different problem from the business of trying to develop criteria such as tenure status, reputation, institutional service, and community role as the basis for collecting decisions.[119]

Some aspects of appraisal and collecting require multi-institutional partnerships, such as when working with moving image records, which somehow moves the process far beyond just a collecting function—although thousands of repositories worldwide probably acquire motion pictures when they are offered.[120] Still images, that is, photographs, have been even more problematic. They are generated in the millions by government, corporations, artists, commercial photographers, and private citizens, yet they are eagerly collected, often violating provenance, without much regard to rigorous standards (although such standards have been around for quite a while).[121] Some record materials, such as sound recordings, require so many accommodations for technical issues of maintenance and use that their collecting is very different from that of the normal or traditional paper-based records systems.[122]

One of the greatest challenges is the lack of a national system of appraising and acquiring records, leading to calls for better communication about appraisal decisions.[123] Many other countries have recognized problems with their lack of national policies to guide coordinated appraisal and collecting.[124] There have been some considerations of the legal implications of such problems, with the usual laments about weak national, regional, and local legislation supporting the acquisition and maintenance of records.[125]

As a result of such problems as these, some archivists have called for sensitivity in appraising large accumulations of government records, such as case files, for underdocumented elements of society.[126] This concern brings up the question of what the collecting mission of any archives should be. Canadian archivist Jim Burant, examining the collecting of Native American visual records, laments that too many archivists are "driven" to meet researchers' needs "rather than attempting to take a more all-embracing approach to documenting and reflecting society." Burant continues that "as an archivist, as a native Algonquin, and as a human being, I feel that public institutional archives must reflect as broadly as possible the nature, fabric, and conflicts of the society from which they spring."[127] Others have made similar pleas for a social sensitivity in appraising and collecting,[128] but the uninhibited nature of collecting works against any kind of uniform approach for dealing with such matters.

CONCLUSION

Archival collecting is not just a mindless exercise in sweeping up old records or sitting back and waiting for the important records to appear for maintenance by an archive. Rather, collecting is a process enmeshed with political, theoretical, psychological, and historical elements. More research is needed about the nature of archival collecting. As well, society needs a better understanding of how archives and historical manuscripts repositories are formed. The image of an archivist as an Indiana Jones–type character, adventurously hunting out the treasures of the past, is romantic but inaccurate. Rather, archivists are flawed humans trying to develop clear and reliable methods for identifying records that should be acquired by archives. Important appraisal work has been accomplished by archivists and manuscripts curators gathering records, but more reflection and experimentation are needed. It seems that the new archival hunters and gatherers will be using very different techniques to sleuth about in the sophisticated record-keeping technologies of the twenty-first century.

NOTES

1. The author appreciates the assistance of Judith Silva, his graduate assistant during the academic year 1999–2000, for help in searching for relevant writings on archival collecting.

2. Graeme Powell, "Collecting of Personal and Private Papers in Australia," *Archives and Manuscripts* 24 (May 1996): 62–77.

3. See, for example, Luciana Duranti, "The Concept of Appraisal and Archival Theory," *American Archivist* 57 (Spring 1994): 328–344. That American archivists have stressed more pragmatic ideas about collecting can be seen in a response to the Duranti essay by Frank Boles and Mark A. Greene, "Et Tu Schellenberg? Thoughts on the Dagger of American Appraisal Theory," *American Archivist* 59 (Summer 1996): 298–310.

4. The lack of a national system was explored by Richard J. Cox, "The Federal Government's Interest in Archives of the United States," in Oddo

Bucci, ed., *Archival Science on the Threshold of the Year 2000* (Macerata, Italy: University of Macerata, 1993), 207–241.

   5. Gerald George, *The State of the American Record: A Report on How Well Americans Are Documenting Their History* (Washington, D.C.: National Historical Publications and Records Commission, 1994), 8.

   6. David C. Duniway, "Conflicts in Collecting," *American Archivist* 24 (January 1961): 58.

   7. Richard C. Berner developed the concept of the two traditions in his writings in the 1970s; for the most extensive of his argument about these traditions, refer to his *Archival Theory and Practice in the United States: A Historical Analysis* (Seattle: University of Washington Press, 1983).

   8. A good description of this kind of collecting by a state government archives is David Duniway, "How Does One Collect Archives?—The Oregon Experience," *Indian Archives* 17 (1967–68): 50–57. The movement for the United States National Archives was largely focused on gathering and centralizing the archives of the nation; see Victor Gondos, Jr., *J. Franklin Jameson and the Birth of the National Archives 1906–1926* (Philadelphia: University of Pennsylvania Press, 1981); H. G. Jones, *The Records of a Nation: Their Management, Preservation, and Use* (New York: Atheneum, 1969); Donald R. McCoy, *The National Archives: America's Ministry of Documents 1934–1968* (Chapel Hill: University of North Carolina Press, 1978); and Timothy Walch, *Guardian of Heritage: Essays on the History of the National Archives* (Washington, D.C.: National Archives and Records Administration, 1985). For a good description from the Canadian perspective of the Canadian archives' role in acquiring related regional records and in establishing Canada's own national archives, see Paulette Dozois, "Beyond Ottawa's Reach: The Federal Acquisition of Regional Government Records," *Archivaria* 33 (Winter 1991–92): 57–65; and Donald MacLeod, "'Quaint Specimens of the Early Days': Priorities in Collecting the Ontario Archival Record, 1872–1935," *Archivaria* 22 (Summer 1986): 12–39.

   9. Lilla Mills Hawes and Albert S. Britt, Jr., eds., *The Search for Georgia's Colonial Records*, Georgia Historical Society Collections, vol. 18 (Savannah: Georgia Historical Society, 1976).

   10. H. G. Jones, *For History's Sake: The Preservation and Publication of North Carolina History 1663–1903* (Chapel Hill: University of North Carolina Press, 1966).

   11. There are definitions for "acquisition" and "acquisition policy," but there is no formal definition for the idea of collecting; see Lewis J. and Lynn Lady Bellardo, *A Glossary for Archivists, Manuscript Curators, and Records Managers* (Chicago: Society of American Archivists, 1992), 1. These definitions are remarkably lifeless when considering the dynamic processes of acquiring records, including the personal, psychological, cultural, economic, and other facets making up such processes.

12. George H. Callcott, *History in the United States 1800–1860: Its Practice and Purpose* (Baltimore, Md.: Johns Hopkins University Press, 1970); H. G. Jones, ed., *Historical Consciousness in the Early Republic: The Origins of State Historical Societies, Museums, and Collections, 1791–1861* (Chapel Hill: North Caroliniana Society, Inc., and North Carolina Collection, 1995); David D. Van Tassel, *Recording America's Past: An Interpretation of the Development of Historical Societies in America 1607–1884* (Chicago: University of Chicago Press, 1960); and Walter Muir Whitehill, *Independent Historical Societies: An Enquiry Into Their Research and Publication Functions and Their Financial Future* (Boston: Boston Athenaeum, 1962). Van Tassel is the historian who describes "documania."

13. Joan Evans, *A History of the Society of Antiquaries* (Oxford: University Press for the Society of Antiquaries, 1956).

14. Alistair Thomson, *Anzac Memories: Living with the Legend* (New York: Oxford University Press, 1994). It is also the case that the U.S. National Archives appealed to veterans' groups looking for a means to commemorate their service, especially as recounted in Victor Gondos's book on Jameson and the National Archives cited earlier.

15. Louis L. Tucker, "From Belknap to Riley: Building the Collection of the Massachusetts Historical Society," in *Witness to America's Past: Two Centuries of Collecting by the Massachusetts Historical Society* (Boston: Massachusetts Historical Society, 1991), 15–23; Louis Leonard Tucker, *Clio's Consort: Jeremy Belknap and the Founding of the Massachusetts Historical Society* (Boston: Massachusetts Historical Society, 1990).

16. Roy Rosenzweig and David Thelen, *The Presence of the Past: Popular Uses of History in American Life* (New York: Columbia University Press, 1998).

17. John Bodnar, *Remaking America: Public Memory, Commemoration, and Patriotism in the Twentieth Century* (Princeton: Princeton University Press, 1992).

18. Lucile M. Kane, *A Guide for Collectors of Manuscripts*, Service Bulletin Number One (St. Paul: Minnesota Historical Society, 1951), 1.

19. See, for example, Christopher P. Bickford, "Public Records and the Private Historical Society: A Connecticut Example," *Government Publications Review* 8A (1981): 311–320.

20. See, for example, C. J. Wright, ed., *Sir Robert Cotton as Collector: Essays on an Early Stuart Courtier and His Legacy* (London: The British Library, 1997).

21. J. Burant, "Ephemera, Archives, and Another View of History," *Archivaria* 40 (Fall 1995): 189–198.

22. Kenneth A. Lohf, "Treasures for Alma Mater: How Columbia University Acquired the Papers of Major New York Publishers and Literary Agents," *Manuscripts* 29 (Spring 1977): 103–109.

23. See Terry Cook, "What Is Past Is Prologue: A History of Archival Ideas since 1898, and the Future Paradigm Shift," *Archivaria* 43 (Spring 1997): 17–63.

24. This is discussed in Ole Kolsrud, "Developments in Archival Theory," *Encyclopedia of Library and Information Science* (New York: Marcel Dekker, 1998), 61: 94.

25. David Buchanan, *The Treasure of Auchinleck: The Story of the Boswell Papers* (New York: McGraw-Hill Book Co., 1974); Thomas Cahill, *How the Irish Saved Civilization: The Untold Story of Ireland's Heroic Role from the Fall of Rome to the Rise of Medieval Europe* (New York: Anchor Books, Doubleday, 1995).

26. James M. O'Toole, "The Symbolic Significance of Archives," *American Archivist* 56 (Spring 1993): 234–255, discusses such issues.

27. Hector Feliciano, *The Lost Museum: The Nazi Conspiracy to Steal the World's Greatest Works of Art* (New York: HarperBooks, 1997); William H. Honan, *Treasure Hunt: A New York Times Reporter Tracks the Quedlinburg Hoard* (New York: Fromm International Publishing Corporation, 1997); Lynn H. Nicholas, *The Rape of Europa: The Fate of Europe's Treasures in the Third Reich and the Second World War* (New York: Vintage Books, 1994); and Elizabeth Simpson, ed., *The Spoils of War: World War II and Its Aftermath; The Loss, Reappearance, and Recovery of Cultural Property* (New York: Harry N. Abrams, Inc., in association with the Bard Graduate Center for Studies in the Decorative Arts, 1997). The reason it took fifty years for some of these issues to become of sufficient interest to the public and media scrutiny is also complicated and has much to do with broader political, nationalistic, ethnic, and cultural events; see, for example, Peter Novick, *The Holocaust in American Life* (Boston: Houghton Mifflin Co., 1999).

28. Charles Kecskemeti, "Displaced European Archives: Is It Time for a Postwar Settlement," *American Archivist* 55 (Winter 1992): 132–138.

29. Philip P. Mason, "Labor Archives in the United States: Achievements and Prospects," *Labor History* 23 (Fall 1982): 487.

30. Lewis E. Atherton, "Western Historical Manuscripts Collection: A Case Study of a Collecting Program," *American Archivist* 26 (January 1963): 41–49; Lucile Kane, "Collecting Policies of the Minnesota Historical Society, 1849–1952," *American Archivist* 16 (April 1953): 127–136; and Edith M. Fox, "The Genesis of Cornell University's Collection of Regional History," *American Archivist* 14 (April 1951): 105–116.

31. Tucker, *Clio's Consort*, 83.

32. Jacqueline Goggin, "Carter G. Woodson and the Collection of Source Materials for Afro-American History," *American Archivist* 48 (Summer 1985): 261–271; Susan Grigg, "A World of Repositories, a World of Records: Redefining the Scope of a National Subject Collection," *American Archivist* 48 (Summer 1985): 286–295.

33. Kevin M. Guthrie, *The New-York Historical Society: Lessons from One Nonprofit's Long Struggle for Survival* (San Francisco: Jossey-Bass, 1996).

34. Paul G. Anderson, "Appraisal of the Papers of Biomedical Scientists and Physicians for Medical Archives," *Bulletin of the Medical Library Association*, 73 (October 1985): 338–344.

35. D. Pratt, "Kenneth A. Lohf: Collecting for Columbia," *Columbia Library Columns* 42 (November 1992): 2–12.

36. Marsha Trimble, "Archives and Manuscripts: New Collecting Areas for Law Libraries," *Law Library Journal* 83 (Summer 1991): 429–450.

37. Chang C. Lee, "Collecting, Organizing and Using Chinese-American Resources: An Archival Approach," *Journal of Library and Information Science* 16 (October 1990): 24–42; R. Joseph Anderson, "Building a Multi-Ethnic Collection: The Research Library of the Balch Institute for Ethnic Studies," *Ethnic Forum* 5 (1985): 7–19.

38. Philip P. Mason, "Labor Archives in the United States: Achievements and Prospects," *Labor History* 23 (Fall 1982): 487–497; and "The Archives of Labor and Urban Affairs, Walter P. Reuther Library, Wayne State University," *Labor History* 23 (Fall 1982): 534–545.

39. Within the archival profession, this can be seen in the massive recent writing on the nature of records and record-keeping. For citations to the extensive literature on this topic, refer to Richard J. Cox, "The Record: Is It Evolving?" *Records and Retrieval Report* 10 (March 1994): 1–16; "Archives as a Multi-faceted Term in the Information Professions," *Records and Retrieval Report* 11 (March 1995): 1–15; "The Record in the Manuscript Collection," *Archives and Manuscripts* 24 (May 1996): 46–61; and "The Importance of Records in the Information Age," *Records Management Quarterly* 32 (January 1998): 36–46, 48–49, 52.

40. Thomas Mallon, "Love Among the Records," *GQ* (November 1999): 336.

41. Michael Cook, "Appraisal and Access: We Should Expect Changes Driven by the Media and by Public Awareness," *Records Management Journal* 8 (April 1998): 3–9.

42. A good start is Lila Teresa Church, "What Motivates African Americans to Donate Personal Papers to Libraries and How Their Giving Decisions Affect the Quantity and Quality of Collections Procured for Archives," MSLS, University of North Carolina at Chapel Hill, April 1998.

43. For an example of the kind of basic, applied research needed, see Jennifer A. Marshall, "Documentation Strategies in the Twenty-First Century?: Rethinking Institutional Priorities and Professional Limitations," *Archival Issues* 23, no. 1 (1998): 59–74.

44. G. Powell, "The Collecting of Personal and Private Papers in Australia," *Archives and Manuscripts*, 24 (May 1996): 62–77; Adrian Cunningham, "Beyond the Pale? The 'Flinty' Relationship between Archivists Who Col-

lect the Private Records of Individuals and the Rest of the Archival Profession," *Archives and Manuscripts* 24 (May 1996): 20–26; Chris Hurley, "Beating the French," *Archives and Manuscripts* 24 (May 1996): 12–18.

45. Adrian Cunningham, "From Here to Eternity: Collecting Archives and the Need for a National Documentation Strategy," *LASIE* 29 (March 1998): 32–45.

46. Carolyn Heald, "Are We Collecting the 'Right Stuff'?" *Archivaria* 40 (Fall 1995): 187.

47. See this debate between a historian and archivist: Robert A. J. McDonald, "Acquiring and Preserving Private Records—A Debate. Who is Preserving Private Records?" *Archivaria* 38 (Fall 1994): 155–157; Christopher Hives, "Thinking Globally, Acting Locally," 157–161; and Robert A. J. McDonald, "Acquiring and Preserving Private Records: Cultural Versus Administrative Perspectives," 162–163.

48. William S. Price, Jr., "N. C. V. B. C. WEST, JR.," *American Archivist* 41 (Winter 1978): 21–24.

49. Paul Russell Cutright, *A History of the Lewis and Clark Journals* (Norman: University of Oklahoma Press, 1976).

50. Patricia Brady Scmit, "Compromise Resolves Fate of Documents; Replevin Avoided," *Manuscripts* 37 (Fall 1985): 275–282.

51. James E. O'Neil, "Replevin: A Public Archivist's Perspective," *College & Research Libraries* 40 (January 1979): 27.

52. Richard J. Cox, "Collectors and Archival, Manuscript, and Rare Book Security," *Focus on Security: The Magazine of Library, Archive, and Museum Security* 2 (April 1995): 19–27.

53. For an example of this, refer to John Swan, "Sound Archives: The Role of the Collector and the Library," *Wilson Library Bulletin* 54 (February 1980): 370–376.

54. This has been more documented in terms of literary collections, such as James G. Watson, "Carvel Collins's Faulkner: A Newly Opened Archives," *Library Chronicle of the University of Texas at Austin* 20, no. 4 (1990): 89–97.

55. Donald C. Dickinson, *Henry E. Huntington's Library of Libraries* (San Marino, California: Huntington Library, 1995).

56. Lawrence S. Thompson, "Incurable Mania," *Manuscripts* 18 (Summer 1966): 19.

57. Christie Brown, "Buyer Beware, Seller Too," *Forbes* 151 (March 1, 1993): 124; Joe Queenan and Manjeet Kripalani, "The Handwriting's Off the Wall," *Forbes* 144 (October 2, 1989): 186.

58. Notable publications on this topic include Edmund Berkeley, Jr., ed., Herbert E. Klingelhofer and Kenneth W. Rendell, co-eds., *Autographs and Manuscripts: A Collector's Manual* (New York: Scribner, 1978); Mary A. Benjamin, *Autographs: A Key to Collecting* (New York: Walter R. Benjamin Auto-

graphs, 1966); Charles Hamilton, *Collecting Autographs and Manuscripts*, rev. ed. (Santa Monica, Calif.: Modoc, 1993); and Kenneth W. Rendell, *History Comes to Life: Collecting Historical Letters and Documents* (Norman: University of Oklahoma Press, 1995).

59. There are no particularly scholarly studies of individual autograph collectors. The journal *Manuscripts*, the publication of the Manuscript Society, an organization dominated by individual collectors and dealers, contains many articles on individual autograph collectors.

60. Typical is Pamela Weston, "Vincent Novello's Autograph Album: Inventory and Commentary," *Music and Letters* 75 (August 1994): 365–380 (Novello was an early nineteenth-century collector of autographs of Mozart and people associated with Mozart), and Thomas A. Green and Lisa Devaney, "Linguistic Play in Autograph Book Inscriptions," *Western Folklore* 48 (January 1989): 51–58.

61. Lester J. Cappon, "Walter R. Benjamin and the Autograph Trade at the Turn of the Century," *Proceedings of the Massachusetts Historical Society* 78 (January–December 1966): 20–37.

62. Pat Bozeman, *Forged Documents: Proceedings of the 1989 Houston Conference; Organized by the University of Houston Libraries* (New Castle, Del.: Oak Knoll Books, 1990); Anthony Grafton, *Forgers and Critics: Creativity and Duplicity in Western Scholarship* (Princeton: Princeton University Press, 1990); and Charles Hamilton, *Great Forgers and Famous Fakes: The Manuscript Forgers of America and How They Duped the Experts* (New York: Crown Publishers, Inc., 1980).

63. Charles Hamilton, *The Hitler Diaries: Fakes That Fooled the World* (Lexington: University Press of Kentucky, 1991); Robert Harris, *Selling Hitler* (New York: Penguin Books, 1986); and Steven Naifeh and Gregory White Smith, *The Mormon Murders: A True Story of Greed, Forgery, Deceit, and Death* (New York: New American Library, 1988).

64. Susan D. Steinwall, "Appraisal of the FBI Files Case: For Whom Do Archivists Retain Records?" *American Archivist* 49 (Winter 1986): 52–63; David A. Wallace, "The Public's Use of Federal Record Keeping Statutes to Shape Federal Information Policy: A Study of the PROFS Case," Ph.D. dissertation, University of Pittsburgh, 1997.

65. For a good commentary on the Code of Ethics, refer to Thomas Wilsted, "Observations on the Ethics of Collecting Archives and Manuscripts," *Provenance* 11 (1993): 25–38.

66. A study that demonstrates this is Nicholas A. Basbanes, *A Gentle Madness: Bibliophiles, Bibliomanes, and the Eternal Passion for Books* (New York: Henry Holt and Co., 1995). Despite the title, the volume also discusses private manuscript collectors and collections.

67. Mel Yoken, "Collecting the Twentieth Century: Curator Howard Gotlieb," *Wilson Library Bulletin* 60 (April 1986): 25.

68. For some examples, see Charles P. Everitt, *The Adventures of a Treasure Hunter: A Rare Bookman in Search of American History* (Boston: Little, Brown and Co., 1952) and Robert Williams, *Adventures of an Autograph Collector* (New York: Exposition Press, 1952).

69. For example, Canadian archivists Bryan Corbett and Eldon Frost, "The Acquisition of Federal Government Records: A Report on Records Management and Archival Practice," *Archivaria* 17 (Winter 1983–84): 201–232, examine whether records retention/disposition schedules lead to fuller archival documentation of government agencies.

70. Werner Muensterberger, *Collecting: An Unruly Passion; Psychological Perspectives* (Princeton, N.J.: Princeton University Press, 1994).

71. Russell W. Belk, *Collecting in a Consumer Society* (New York: Routledge, 1995).

72. Timothy L. Ericson, "At the 'Rim of Creative Dissatisfaction': Archivists and Acquisition Development," *Archivaria* 33 (Winter 1991–92): 66–77.

73. Bruce P. Montgomery, "Collecting Human Rights Evidence: A Model for Archival Collection Development," *Encyclopedia of Library and Information Science* (New York: Marcel Dekker, 1999): 64: 52.

74. Genevieve Oswald, "One Approach to the Development of a Dance Archive: The Dance Collection in the Library and Museum of the Performing Arts (The New York Public Library at Lincoln Center)," in *Libraries, History, Diplomacy, and the Performing Arts: Essays in Honor of Carleton Sprague Smith*, ed. Israel J. Katz, Festschrift Series no. 9 (Stuyvesant, New York: Pendragon Press, in cooperation with the New York Public Library, 1999), 77–84.

75. See, for example, Linda J. Henry, "Collecting Policies of Special-Subject Repositories," *American Archivist* 43 (Winter 1980): 57–63.

76. Jutta Reed-Scott, "Collection Management Strategies for Archivists," *American Archivist* 47 (Winter 1984): 23–29.

77. Faye Phillips, "Developing Collecting Policies for Manuscript Collections," *American Archivist* 47 (Winter 1984): 30–42.

78. Barbara L. Craig, "The Acts of the Appraisers: The Context, the Plan, and the Record," *Archivaria* 34 (Summer 1992): 177.

79. F. Gerald Ham, "The Archival Edge," *American Archivist* 38 (January 1975): 5–13.

80. Lester J. Cappon, "The Archivist as Collector," *American Archivist* 39 (October 1976): 434.

81. One interesting effort to quantify the appraisal process was *Archival Appraisal*, by Frank Boles in association with Julia Marks Young (New York: Neal-Schuman Publishers, 1991).

82. Philip N. Alexander and Helen W. Samuels, "The Roots of 128: A Hypothetical Documentation Strategy," *American Archivist* 50 (Fall 1987): 518–531; Helen Samuels, "Improving our Disposition: Documentation Strategy," *Archivaria* 33 (Winter 1991–92): 125–140.

83. Catherine Bailey, "From the Top Down: The Practice of Macro-Appraisal," *Archivaria* 43 (Spring 1997): 89–128; Richard Brown, "Macro-Appraisal Theory and the Context of the Public Records Creator," *Archivaria* 40 (Fall 1995): 121–172; Richard Brown, "Records Acquisition Strategy and Its Theoretical Foundation: The Case for a Concept of Archival Hermeneutics," *Archivaria* 33 (Winter 1991–92): 34–56.

84. See, for example, Terry Cook, "'Another Brick in the Wall': Terry Eastwood's Masonry and Archival Walls, History and Archival Appraisal," *Archivaria* 37 (Spring 1994): 96–103; Terry Eastwood, "Nailing a Little Jelly to the Wall of Archival Studies," *Archivaria* 35 (Spring 1993): 232–252.

85. Terrance Keenan, *Documenting Adult Education: Toward a Cooperative Strategy*, Syracuse University Kellogg Project Technical Report Series, Report no. 2 (Syracuse, October 1989).

86. Helen W. Samuels, *Varsity Letters: Documenting Modern Colleges and Universities* (Metuchen, N.J.: Scarecrow Press, 1992).

87. Joan D. Krizack, ed., *Documentation Planning for the U.S. Health Care System* (Baltimore: Johns Hopkins University Press, 1994).

88. Richard J. Cox, *Documenting Localities: A Practical Model for American Archivists and Manuscripts Curators* (Lanham, Md.: Scarecrow Press, 1996).

89. R. C. Davis, "Getting the Lead Out: The Appraisal of Silver-Lead Mining Records at the University of Idaho," *American Archivist* 55 (Summer 1992): 454–463.

90. Mark Greene, "'The Surest Proof': A Utilitarian Approach to Appraisal," *Archivaria* 45 (Spring 1998): 127–169.

91. For an effort to make such connections, see Richard J. Cox, "Records Management Scheduling and Archival Appraisal," *Records and Information Management Report* 14 (April 1998): 1–16.

92. F. Gerald Ham, "Archival Choices: Managing the Historical Record in an Age of Abundance," *American Archivist* 47 (Winter 1984): 11–22.

93. Terry Eastwood, "How Goes It with Appraisal?" *Archivaria* 36 (Autumn 1993): 111–121. The best, and most dramatic, writing in which records volume is contrasted to appraisal approaches is David Bearman, *Archival Methods* (Pittsburgh: Archives and Museum Informatics, 1989).

94. Leonard Rapport, "No Grandfather Clause: Reappraising Accessioned Records," *American Archivist* 44 (Spring 1981): 143–150; Sheila Powell, "Archival Reappraisal: The Immigration Case Files," *Archivaria* 33 (Winter 1991–92): 104–116.

95. Little research has been done, but what has been done suggests reappraisal and deaccessioning are not being used. An example of such research is Andrew Hempe, "Deaccessioning Practices in Selected North Carolina Archives," MSLS, University of North Carolina at Chapel Hill, July 1996.

96. Judith E. Endelman, "Looking Backward to Plan for the Future: Collection Analysis for Manuscript Repositories," *American Archivist* 50 (Sum-

mer 1987): 340–355; Christine Weideman, "A New Map for Field Work: Impact of Collections Analysis on the Bentley Historical Library," *American Archivist* 54 (Winter 1991): 54–60.

97. Sara S. Hodson, "Private Lives: Confidentiality in Manuscripts Collections," *Rare Books and Manuscripts Librarianship* 6, no. 2 (1991): 108–118; Heather MacNeil, *Without Consent: The Ethics of Disclosing Personal Information in Public Archives* (Metuchen, N.J.: Society of American Archivists and the Scarecrow Press, Inc., 1992); Doug Whyte, "The Acquisition of Lawyers' Private Papers," *Archivaria* 18 (Summer 1984): 142–153.

98. A recent example of this is Martha Cooley, *The Archivist: A Novel* (Boston: Little, Brown and Co., 1998), telling the story of an archivist's decision to destroy very personal letters of T. S. Eliot housed in a repository.

99. Janna Malamud Smith, *Private Matters: In Defense of the Personal Life* (Reading, Mass.: Addison-Wesley Publishing Co., 1997).

100. Barbara J. Kaiser, "Problems with Donors of Contemporary Collections," *American Archivist* 32 (April 1969): 103–107. The most famous (or infamous) case was that of access to the Sigmund Freud Papers at the Library of Congress, placed on deposit and controlled by Freud disciples; see Janet Malcolm, *In the Freud Archives* (New York: Alfred A. Knopf, 1984).

101. Karen M. Lamoree, "Documenting the Difficult or Collecting the Controversial," *Archival Issues* 20:2 (1995): 149–154.

102. Frank Boles, " 'Just a Bunch of Bigots': A Case Study in the Acquisition of Controversial Material," *Archival Issues* 19:1 (1994): 53–65; Pam Hackbart-Dean, "A Hint of Scandal: Problems in Acquiring the Papers of Senator Herman E. Talmadge—A Case Study," *Provenance* 13 (1995): 65–80.

103. Gary B. Nash, Charlotte Crabtree, and Ross E. Dunn, *History on Trial: Culture Wars and the Teaching of the Past* (New York: Alfred B. Knopf, 1997), and Peter N. Stearns, *Meaning over Memory: Recasting the Teaching of Culture and History* (Chapel Hill: University of North Carolina Press, 1993). For a particular commentary on the problem with multiculturalism and archival acquisition, see Richard J. Cox, "Archival Anchorites: Building Public Memory in the Era of the Culture Wars," *Multicultural Review* 7 (June 1998): 52–60.

104. The best recent volume on the importance of records *and* the challenges of access to government records is Athan G. Theoharis, ed., *A Culture of Secrecy: The Government Versus the People's Right to Know* (Lawrence: University Press of Kansas, 1998). Compare this to Tom Blanton, ed., *White House E-Mail: The Top Secret Computer Messages the Reagan/Bush White House Tried to Destroy* (New York: New Press, 1995), showing a weakened archival profession not willing to try to enforce existing records legislation or to work for strengthened legislation.

105. Nicholas C. Burckel, "Business Archives in a University Setting: Status and Prospect," *College and Research Libraries* 41 (May 1980): 227–233.

106. Elizabeth C. Altman, "A History of Baker Library at the Harvard University Graduate School of Business Administration," *Harvard Library Bulletin* 39 (April 1981): 169–196; Florence Bartoshesky, "Business Records at the Harvard Business School," *Business History Review* 59 (Autumn 1985): 475–483; Florence Bartoshesky Lathrop, "Toward a National Collecting Policy for Business History: The View from Baker Library," *Business History Review* 62 (Spring 1988): 134–143.

107. James M. O'Toole, ed., *The Records of American Business* (Chicago: Society of American Archivists, 1997).

108. Richard J. Cox, *Managing Institutional Archives: Foundational Principles and Practices* (New York: Greenwood Press, 1992).

109. Marie B. Allen, "Intergovernmental Records in the United States: Experiments in Description and Appraisal," *Information Development* 8 (April 1992): 99–103.

110. See, for example, Roger Harris, "Bridges over Troubling Waters: Collection Development Patterns in Archival Holdings," MSLS, University of North Carolina Chapel Hill, July 1994.

111. Philip P. Mason, "Labor Archives in the United States: Achievements and Prospects," *Labor History* 23 (Fall 1982): 494.

112. Nena Couch, "Collection Division as an Acquisition Method: A Case Study," *Acquisitions Librarian* 8 (1992): 23–31.

113. See Richard A. Cameron, Timothy Ericson, and Anne R. Kenney, "Archival Cooperation: A Critical Look at Statewide Archival Networks," *American Archivist* 46 (Fall 1983): 414–432, for the most balanced assessment of these networks. Some have argued that the networks helped manuscript collecting, such as James E. Fogerty, "Manuscript Collecting in Archival Networks," *Midwestern Archivist* 6, no. 2 (1982): 130–141.

114. David E. Kyvig, "Documenting Urban Society: A Regional Approach," *Drexel Library Quarterly* 13 (October 1977): 76–91.

115. J. Cumming, "Beyond Intrinsic Value towards the Development of Acquisition Strategies in the Private Sector: The Experience of the Manuscript Division, National Archives of Canada," *Archivaria* 38 (Fall 1994): 232–239.

116. R. Joseph Anderson, "Managing Change and Chance: Collecting Policies in Social History Archives," *American Archivist* 48 (Summer 1985): 296–303.

117. John J. Grabowski, "Fragments or Components: Theme Collections in a Local Setting," *American Archivist* 48 (Summer 1985): 304–314.

118. Jane Wolff, "Faculty Papers and Special-Subject Repositories," *American Archivist* 44 (Fall 1981): 346–351.

119. Frederick L. Honhart, "The Solicitation, Appraisal, and Acquisition of Faculty Papers," *College & Research Libraries* 44 (May 1983): 236–241.

120. Sam Kula, *The Archival Appraisal of Moving Images: A RAMP Study with Guidelines*, PGI-83/WS/18 (Paris: UNESCO, 1983).

121. William H. Leary, *The Archival Appraisal of Photographs: A RAMP Study with Guidelines*, PGI-85/WS/10 (Paris: UNESCO, 1985).

122. See Helen Harrison, *The Archival Appraisal of Sound Recordings and Related Materials: A RAMP Study with Guidelines*, PGI-87/WS/1 (Paris: UNESCO, February 1987).

123. Max J. Evans, "The Visible Hand: Creating a Practical Mechanism for Cooperative Appraisal," *Midwestern Archivist* 11, no. 1 (1986): 7–13.

124. See C. Kitching and I. Hart, "Collection Policy Statements," *Journal of the Society of Archivists* 16 (Spring 1995): 7–14; P. D. A. Harvey, "Archives in Britain: Anarchy or Policy?," *American Archivist* 46 (Winter 1983): 22–30.

125. For a Canadian perspective, see Kathy Hall, "Archival Acquisitions: Legal Mandates and Methods," *Archivaria* 18 (Summer 1984): 58–69.

126. Terry Cook, " 'Many are called, but few are chosen': Appraisal Guidelines for Sampling and Selecting Case Files," *Archivaria* 32 (Summer 1991): 25–50.

127. Jim Burant, "The Acquisition of Visual Records Relating to Native Life in North America," *Provenance* 10 (1992): 21, 23.

128. Terry Cook, " 'Many are called but few are chosen', *Archivaria* 32 (Summer 1991): 25–50, and D. Laberge, "Information, Knowledge, and Rights: The Preservation of Archives as a Political and Social Issue," *Archivaria* 25 (Winter 1987–88): 44–49.

6

Metascheduling: Rethinking Archival Appraisal and Records Management Scheduling

Meta-[:] prefix . . . ; the principal notions which it expresses are: sharing, action in common; pursuit or quest; and, especially, change (of place, order, condition, or nature).

—*Oxford English Dictionary*, 2nd ed.

The prefix "meta" brings to the fore ideas about common actions, common objectives, and change. By "metascheduling" I suggest that we need to reevaluate the principles behind records scheduling and view it as a tool for both records managers and archivists. I also consider the records schedule as a mechanism or device that unites archivists and records managers, and because schedules are about records and their disposition, schedule creation is one of the strongest unifying actions for all records professionals. Finally, I will examine what changes new records technologies bring to an activity such as scheduling. In the past, archivists and records managers have discussed how responsibilities such as scheduling should unify archivists and records professionals.[1] Indeed, I am convinced that such a responsibility really points to a lack of distinction between archivists and records managers except as we can look at the professions historically. When it comes to records scheduling, we are all archivists and we are all records managers. Certainly, individuals outside the records community, including those people whom archivists and records managers work for, can hardly comprehend the differences—and with good reason. In advocating for the administration of records, we must not try to make fine distinctions between archivists and records managers but, instead, focus on the importance of records. Because records schedules involve many different individuals and professionals in organizations—in their analysis, approval, and use—they are a useful starting point for explaining why records must be managed.

In this chapter, I raise issues about the purpose and practice of records scheduling. This chapter is certainly more theoretical than based on current practice among archivists and records managers. However, practice is not always the best lens for viewing the core functions of records work. Theory, methodology, and practice clearly make up what constitutes archival and records management knowledge; the records schedule represents a practical tool but one built on an understanding of what records and record-keeping systems represent. This chapter is offered in that spirit and to stimulate additional discussion and advance our knowledge.

WHAT IS A RECORDS SCHEDULE?

What is the common view about the nature and purpose of a records schedule? In a standard records management textbook, we have this description:

> In simple terms a records retention schedule is a list of records for which predetermined destruction dates have been established. . . . Records scheduling has three broad objectives:
>
> 1. prompt disposal of records whose retention period has ended
> 2. storage of records which must be temporarily retained after they are no longer needed in current business
> 3. preservation of records which are of long-term value.[2]

Records retention or disposition schedules are well known to both archivists and records managers. In this fairly standard definition, we can perceive both the archival interest in identifying records with continuing value and the records management motivation to dispose of or efficiently store inactive records. Each schedule provides specific information on the records, the retention period, the ultimate disposition, and the basis for the decision (legislative, regulatory, administrative). Archivists, in their use of or contributions to retention schedules, will often draw on the traditional values of records, such as administrative, legal, fiscal, evidential, and informational. Within organizations, records schedules are the backbone of records programs, governing where records go, identifying what records systems exist, and coordinating or uniting archival and records management interests and objectives. They are the axis upon which the records program spins and gains direction.

The schedule captures information about the well-known concept of the life cycle of records. Records are created for a particular purpose, possess a period when they are particularly useful in the office generating them, have another period when they can be stored away from the office creating them, and then undergo their ultimate disposition: destruction or archives. In some ways, the records schedule creates the sense of such a life cycle by capturing information about these various phases; in other words, without the guiding schedule, we might not know that there is such a cycle. The real records cycle can be vague or faint, and the records schedule gives it form or substance. This is another clear example of the ridiculousness of separating archives and records management. Without an archives program, there can be no real cycle because there is then no real choice regarding disposition (records are held in records center purgatory or destroyed but never deemed to have continuing value and sent to an archive). Without a records management program, there is no way to govern the earlier stages of records or guide them to their ultimate fate; they could drift into the archives by accident or because someone does not know what to do with them. The records life cycle confirms the need for the records schedule, and the schedule confirms the need for both archives and records management, archivists and records managers. As we will see, this issue has become much more complicated.

There has long been a fixation in the archives and records management professions on whether something is theoretical or practical, usually with pejorative terms reserved for the former. This bias is probably endemic to any applied field, but sometimes archivists and records managers seem to squabble over whether something is a theory or methodology unnecessarily. This can be seen in the origins of the records schedule, which were nothing more than an effort to contend with the long period before it was appropriate to destroy records, the cumbersome procedures for making decisions about destruction, and the growing quantity of records in both government and the private sector. The early history of the records schedule suggests a period of trial and error until the concept of general and continuing schedules developed. The notion of the records schedule is more than a half century old, although changing records professions, record-keeping technologies, the evolving nature of records values, and a litigious society have all both supported and challenged the utility of the records schedule. The fact that the profession still looks to the National Archives and Records Administration's (NARA) general schedules, references such as Donald Skupsky's various guides to record-keeping requirements, and Cohasset Associates' legality publications (all offering specific guidelines for the amount of time that records should be maintained) attests to the importance of records schedules. However, this evidence doesn't reveal the *best* manner by which records schedules are formulated. In many cases, it appears that all anyone is interested in are the particulars of the time periods governing various records; this is a poor or inadequate use of the scheduling process.

Despite the differences between archivists and records managers, the records schedule represents some shared purposes. Both archivists and records managers seek to create and maintain records inventories, and these inventories traditionally have formed the basis for the records schedule. A crucial function of such inventories is to identify important records needing to be maintained in an ongoing fashion in order to protect the organization or some other group of people (such as the citizens in the case of the government). Establishing records schedules also allows unneeded records to be disposed of. Highlighting records with continuing value allows them to be retrieved efficiently when needed, and disposing of unneeded records seems to provide monetary benefits to an organization. Archivists and records managers might employ different terms (the records manager speaking of vital records and archivists of the moral defense of record), but something inherent in the records schedule seems to bind the two groups together. After all, careful analyses of records and records systems must be done before schedules are formulated. Yet some crucial issues and concerns pull the two groups apart and reveal some very different objectives for the use of records schedules.

ARCHIVISTS AND RECORDS MANAGERS VIEW SCHEDULES (OR, ARE THEY LOOKING AT THE SAME THING?)

Archivists see schedules as a tool for identifying records possessing archival value, and records managers view schedules as a tool to clear out records. This difference reveals the fundamental wall between archivists and records managers, one seeking to preserve and the other to destroy. Records managers want to provide both efficiency and economy by continually reducing records, but this approach can produce a false economy if records with continuing value to the organization are lost. Archivists want to zero in on those records with obvious research value, and they often do not want to be burdened with the other responsibilities of managing current records. This dichotomy is crucial because it masks the common interests of the two camps. Their common focus is the record. Their opposition suggests that two groups of records professionals with a common ancestry might have lost sight of *why* records need to be managed. Scheduling should be a product of records analysis, in which archival appraisal methods play a vital part; archival appraisal should never be guided only by existing records schedules. (That when asked to produce an appraisal report some organizational archives can produce only rudimentary records schedules indicates other, deeper problems in how records are being evaluated.)

These different professional views might also indicate another problem: Archivists and records managers—even when participating together in the creation of a records schedule—could have considerably different agendas and perspectives, a state of affairs that can undermine the preparation of realistic and useful schedules. For example, the traditional view of records values—administrative, legal, fiscal, and research—might have the records manager examining the first three and the archivist the last one. In such a case, it is difficult to imagine how practical records schedules can be created. The traditional views are too limited or, at the best, incomplete—

they fail to take into account, for example, that records possessing continuing value for purely administrative purposes are also the crucial records needing to be maintained for research uses. The evidential-informational distinction promoted by archival theorist T. R. Schellenberg, in which evidential indicates value to the records-generating organization and informational the value to researchers outside the organization, has always been too simplistic; more importantly, the informational-value idea is so open-ended as to be useless as a guide. I have always believed that informational value is one of the characteristics marking records with evidential value.

Records schedules often do not result in the identification and preservation of archival records. Records schedules do not always result in achieving records management economy and efficiency. Additional analysis, although it has been limited, has suggested that records schedules do not necessarily provide the benefits promised. Archivists have discussed the problems that in institutional settings the use of schedules does not always bring the crucial archival documents into the archives. Richard Brown, an archivist at the National Archives of Canada, writes:

> I think it is fair to say that the operation of traditional records "scheduling" for public institutions has produced mixed archival results and, in fact, many archives have benefited from fortuitous direct transfers of caches of important records. The institutional records and "collections" that archives are wont to highlight and advertise to users have not necessarily been acquired by virtue of an organized and rational disposition process.[3]

In one of the U.S. National Archives versions of its long-range plan, it was acknowledged that only 35–40 percent of government records are inventoried and scheduled within two years of their creation (an extraordinarily long period when considering electronic records) and only about a quarter of the records schedules are actively used. This problem caused the National Archives to stress the notion of "essential evidence":

> Only by assisting agencies with the management of their records from the time when those records are created can we ensure that essential documentation is available for the government itself, today's citizens, and future generations. Stressing the value of improved records management to all of us, NARA will work in active partnership with the

Administration, Federal officials, the Congress, and Federal courts to help them create, identify, appropriately schedule, and manage record material. Also, we will work with agencies and the courts nationwide to improve the effectiveness and timeliness of our processes for evaluating records and scheduling how long and where they should be retained for the benefit of users, so that essential evidence is not lost through internal inefficiencies or inadequate guidance.[4]

This suggests a serious failure in *both* archives and records management, but it suggests more that the mutual perspective on the purpose of schedules may be out of kilter. The strategic focus on essential evidence suggests as well (and this is positive) a renewed attention to the traditional purposes and uses of records schedules.

Although it is difficult to find similar statements or analyses from records managers about the use of schedules, one wonders whether schedules really have enabled them to position records programs to become key players in organizational information (and evidence) management or whether the schedules have become more ends in themselves. Has it been that some institutional records programs have not been driven by trying to use the schedules to push records along their life cycle rather than serving some broader mission? An aspect of this problem is evident in that schedules often miss the point of why and how records are created and why they need to be maintained. Again archivist Richard Brown has perceived this problem in the manner in which schedules rely on organizational charts, which are, at best, flawed pictures of how organizations really operate:

Employing a rudimentary signage, essentially consisting of an arrangement of labeled rectangles of administration outlined and connected by solid black lines against a white background, these diagrams typically model primary and internally concentrated mechanisms of formal bureaucratic structure. Consequently, [these] charts are either purposely or inevitably designed to ignore any operational entanglements that might compound or confuse primary-internal matters of jurisdiction and mandate. . . . Surrounding the official administrative "boxes" marked in black is merely a white and shapeless void. . . . The use of white *tableaux* as segmental surround not only creates an impression of infinite administrative stability, as if bureaucratic structures commonly exist in a wholly intransigent and immutable state; it also eliminates any hint of contextuality potentially offered by the situated character of their agency and interaction in time and space. [5]

The terror of this quotation is not the manner in which Brown describes the charts, a description that is admittedly obtuse at spots, but the fact that some archivists and records managers spend considerable time marking up organizational charts for appraising and scheduling as if these charts equaled the real world.

The same is true because we focus on records forms, especially in general schedules. The forms or genres of records tell us a lot about the nature of the records, but they do not always serve as accurate guidelines because of the manner in which we use them. One of the common problems with records schedules is that they seem to suggest that a particular form equals a particular value for the record, but this is simply not the case. "Correspondence" cannot be assigned a routine or generic retention period because the importance of correspondence depends on action and the creator or the warrant for the particular letter. "E-mail" or "fax" is a communications form, not a record form, and as a result, it is even more problematic as an item to be scheduled. Yet these very items appear on general records schedules, indicating a problem in the use of schedules—most notably a failure to understand that a schedule is a result of a sophisticated analytical process, not a simple form to be completed in order to expedite the disposition of records. Routine records as well can become extraordinarily important because of associations with crucial events or activities—exactly what the case of the Holocaust victims' assets (involving very routine banking accounts) indicates. But this goes far beyond just historic events or cases with extraordinary moral or ethical implications, resting instead on the crucial reasons, such as accountability, for which records are managed.

REDISCOVERING THE VALUE
OF RECORDS SCHEDULES

Step One: Why Records Are Important

Archivists and records managers have expended far too much energy on emphasizing disposal, litigation protection, preservation, and historical research. Here you can see why archivists and records managers have experienced a schism—these purposes seem to be anything but harmonious. Records professionals need to reconsider why records are important, and then proceed to use schedules to buttress these values; this is why the U.S. National Archives' notion of essential evidence is encouraging (in concept at least). Records hold the people who create them accountable for their actions, precisely the primary reason why records came into existence in the first place. Records enable the organization creating them to develop an organizational memory, supporting its ongoing work in a similar fashion to the way our own memories support our activities. Records constitute the evidence of transactions, from the most mundane to the most significant, and this evidence provides crucial information about the work of organizations and individuals. Finally, records provide a path to understanding our society and its culture; in other words, every records-generating organization has a place in the larger social or cultural landscape that must be considered when records are being analyzed. Too often, the records professional seems to be led to a belief that what he or she must do is protect an organization from being sued. However, as the Holocaust victims' assets and tobacco litigation cases suggest, there are ethical, moral, and historical reasons some records must be managed with an appreciation of more substantial cultural and social benefits. Nearly all of these aspects of why records are important connect back to larger organizational mandates, such as information resources management and, more recently, knowledge management. Thomas Davenport, a leading proponent of knowledge management, provides a clue to just such a problem when he writes about records professionals in this manner:

> This staff role first became established in the era of file folder-based customer information and has grown now to include both paper-based and electronic records. Records managers focus on creating, storing, retrieving, and using records without the loss of any vital data within those records. From a cultural standpoint, these managers are particularly concerned with preserving information, and are therefore less likely to enhance effective use of current information.

Records schedules, looking like grocery lists, must seem particularly unimportant to individuals such as Davenport. Yet, as a records manager suggests, "Knowledge resides in the people, not the technology, but it also survives where people have recorded their knowledge—in documents. And some of these documents are records."[7] If schedules can be made to support such concepts, then we are on to something.

Step Two: Understanding That Records and Organizations Have Changed

We need to remember that the concepts of records management and records schedules emerged in a time of the Industrial Age office, with its emphasis on paper records forms, assembly-line office procedures, and hierarchically structured decision making. This was also a time of simpler office technologies and a time when these technologies supported the need for control—of workers, processes, and products. The schedules—with their simplified schematics directing records from creation to disposition—reflected the orderly notions of organizational work.

Organizations and record-keeping systems have become extremely more complex in the past twenty years. Networked communications and multimedia records systems have pushed records managers and archivists in new directions, some of which are compatible with the traditional records schedule and some of which challenge this methodology. The records life cycle, the backbone for the records schedule, has begun to give way to the records continuum. Whereas in the older cycle, records professionals interceded further down the line in order to guide inactive records into the archives or the trash bin, in the newer continuum, records professionals work at the outset to assist in designing records systems that include establishing retention periods before the records are generated. A record with continuing or archival value is designed into the system at the beginning rather than left to be discovered months or years after its creation, then stored, and ultimately found needing to be disposed of or maintained. The motivations for the records schedule, either to dispose of records for economical purposes or to identify records as archival, have given way to identifying records with continuing value for the organization's knowledge. Organizations are more interested in knowledge management than in pushing paper records around in order to save costs in storage.

These changes can be seen in subtle ways, such as the way the U.S. National Archives has approached electronic records over the past thirty years. In the earliest years, the entire focus of the National Archives was on identifying electronic files with informational value based on subject matter and the quality of the data archives. This emphasis occurred, of course, because the federal government's main use of computers was in compiling statistical databases. With the shift to more complex online and networked electronic systems has come a decided move to deal with electronic records first as products of systems supporting business functions and then as evidence systems supporting the work of government and organizations and requiring that archivists ensure that systems are designed supporting the creation and management of records. These latter systems approaches suggest that disposition functions are moved within the systems and are to be done automatically. As part of this renewed interest in evidence, for example, we have statements from the U.K. Public Record Office, for instance, to the effect that the starting point is to ensure that all records are *captured*, they are *complete* (including metadata), and *links* to other records are maintained.[8] In all of this, records professionals can justify records being managed as investments in knowledge so that records represent both a source and an expression of the knowledge of its staff.

Step Three: Understanding That Records Professionals Have Changed

In the past, records managers ran records centers and archivists administered repositories. This is no longer true (at least, it is no longer true as the primary manner of doing business for the foreseeable future). Now the records professional (including both archivists and records managers) has a primary duty to keep the organization informed about the warrant for record-keeping—that is, to keep the organization aware of the regulatory, legal, and best-practices realms, governing when, how, and why records are created, maintained, and disposed. As part of this responsibility, and because of the nature of the newer and emerging electronic records technologies, records professionals will become less concerned with physical custody and more with governing records throughout the organization. Records professionals will provide advice to the records creators about the design of systems, provide policies and procedures for what records systems need to be maintained (and how they need to be maintained), and provide the gateway by which people get access to the crucial records.

Implicit in these comments are some important implications for appraisal and scheduling. Records appraisal could occur primarily when records systems have reached the point that they will be migrated or terminated. What mostly occurred with scheduling could happen when the records system is designed, incorporating disposition instructions. Records appraisal will stress, as it has to a considerable extent already, building on the records warrant. As part of this idea of the warrant, records professionals must become adept at following court cases involving records and perhaps even becoming parties to these cases; in the U.S. District Court's ruling concerning NARA's General Records Schedule 20—the one guiding disposition of electronic records—we find that the perspective on such schedules is that they are useful for housekeeping and certain other routine records but not for determining the importance of records connected to important events or activities or for records protecting citizens. Such cases are extremely important for helping records professionals redesign records schedules. What the records professional must bring anew to the records appraisal and scheduling process are *creative* approaches that ensure that the corporate memory and greater societal importance of records are supported by the identification of records with continuing value.

Step Four: Understanding That New Records Appraisal Approaches Are Crucial

Contrary to some more static notions of archival appraisal, there has been continuing debate about its theory, methodology, and practice concerning the way records should be analyzed to determine their continuing value. From the passive approach of relying on records creators to determine what records are maintained to the elaborate values approaches, we have now reached a period when records professionals are developing methods enabling the universe of records to be reduced, connecting records to essential business functions, and providing careful analysis of the records and record-keeping systems in their own right rather than as fodder for researchers or disposition exercises. The role of schedules is to reflect this analysis and to support the recommendations deriving from such analysis, in keeping with the notion of archivists and records managers being *experts* in records and record-keeping systems. Hence we come to the idea of "metascheduling."

The shifting emphases in archival appraisal provide a harbinger for a new concept for records scheduling. In the early decades of the twentieth century, the English archival theorist and practitioner Sir Hilary Jenkinson presented the idea that records creators are primarily responsible for determining what records go to the archives. This concept has held sway among many sectors of the archives community, and at the least, it has been a source of debate about appraisal. His American counterpart, T. R. Schellenberg, introduced the idea that there were primary and secondary values and that many records would be retained because of their specific value for historians and researchers—and this has caused a shift (focused on the notion of informational value) from the value of records for the creators of records to their value to others who might have reason to use them. The softer (more abstract, more open-ended) notion of informational value gained prominence as the American archives community became predominantly peopled by those working in *collecting* institutions (such as colleges and universities, historical societies, and even government archives). The practical emphasis shifted to acquiring as much as possible, almost mimicking the indiscriminate acquisition of nineteenth-century antiquarian organizations. Over the past twenty years, however, dissatisfaction with earlier and established appraisal practice has grown. This dissatisfaction is the source of newer approaches, such as metascheduling. The dissatisfaction arose because of far too much recorded documentation for older appraisal approaches to function appropriately, the need for methods to make this universe of documentation more manageable and, finally, the need for archival appraisal to focus on records that are relevant to records creators and established and potential records users (broadly defined, ranging from academics to journalists to community activists). This relevance includes the general public interested in issues such as accountability of organizations and public officials. The ideas of archival documentation strategies, functional analysis, and macroappraisal all are efforts to resolve the previous failings of archival appraisal approaches and to make records professionals more relevant and responsive to society and its organizations.

THE ELEMENTS OF METASCHEDULING

The recent archival appraisal approaches bring some significant ideas that should have a substantial impact on records management scheduling. First and foremost is the focus on records analysis, which reemphasizes that what makes an individual a records professional is his or her *expertise* about records and record-keeping systems. The archivist and records manager should be able to bring a substantial knowledge that includes the history of records systems, the manner in which current records systems are constructed, and the various regulations and practices that dictate what records and records systems are created and maintained. Every records professional thus comes to an activity such as scheduling not as a clerical exercise in making lists but as a professional enterprise in studying records systems as sources of evidence, information, and knowledge.

These newer archival appraisal approaches also imply some important concepts that beg for a tool such as a records schedule to be rethought. Although the analysis is, in my opinion, the most important contribution, we also see a push for the records professionals to fit into the organizational culture, relating the maintenance of records to crucial institutional activities. At the same time, these approaches stress more sensitivity to a wider range of groups, who might rely on records for informational, evidential, and even symbolic purposes. In other words, archivists and records managers do not labor in records appraisal and scheduling work in isolation, but they work in a complicated arena of rules, laws, issues, societal groups, and institutional needs. Archivists or records managers working in a corporation, for example, cannot operate as if their records have no relevance to larger societal needs. Records professionals in Swiss banks and American tobacco companies seem to have thought this, and their efforts have been critically evaluated on the front pages of newspapers all over the world (as they should have been).

Finally, these archival approaches bring out two quite important issues in records management scheduling. First, they should suggest a greater openness to experimentation and creativity in records analysis, appraisal, and disposition. It is no longer business as usual, with records professionals trying to quickly determine what and how records should be maintained; the rapidly changing records technologies suggest the need to adapt, try new ideas, and risk failures. We perceive that exactly this is happening as records professionals, especially archivists, have examined and reexamined theories and concepts from organizational and other experts as possible guides for analyzing records. As new records systems emerge, we need to go back and ask basic questions about established practices and methods to see if they remain relevant. We have already seen some of this concern expressed in the debates about whether records can be archives only if the archivist has physical custody.

Second, we see that these approaches suggest at least a rapprochement between archivists and records managers, perhaps even the emergence of a new records professional, which suggests that there are no distinctions between archivists and records managers. I have thought for a long time that the records life cycle supports this merging of professions, and the newer idea of the records continuum does, too. How such changes will occur given well-established professional associations such as the Society of American Archivists and the Association for Records Managers and Administrators is a matter I can't speculate much about. But the rapid transformation of graduate archival education certainly indicates that other aspects of the records professions may be the source of the changes.

Metascheduling could lead to schedules that look very different from the ones we presently possess. This change can be seen in the most elemental foundations for what I have been calling metascheduling. I have made repeated references to the newer notion of the records continuum. Without repeating myself, I want to stress that crucial to the notion of metascheduling is the idea that records professionals should spend more time building records systems than chasing after these systems and their particular products. This change has recently occurred in the major projects from some universities with wide funding support. Will we need to disseminate records schedules when we could be building them directly into the records systems themselves? Another way in which they might look different is that they will provide substantially more information not only about the records but about the process used to determine appraisal decisions and schedules. Where we have seen reasonably simple lists of records series with shorthand-like disposition instructions, it is likely we will now have schedules with fuller records descriptions, more specific notions of the warrant supporting the disposition instructions, and more information on the approach used by the records professional to arrive at the disposition decisions.

Most important, however, might not be the content of the schedules but how the schedules are used and what they represent. Most fundamentally, they will represent an end to a search for simplistic solutions in determining what records are to be maintained and for how long. There are no "magic bullet" solutions, just a lot of work, trial and error, and some mistakes. Almost as significant, the notion of metascheduling suggests a deemphasis on compiling records inventories in favor of more strategic methods. Macroappraisal and functional analysis are just those strategic approaches. We might have reached the point at which we develop methods, perhaps unique to particular corporate settings, that enable us to zero in on the most crucial records. Future records schedules might support this kind of work, and the emphasis could decidedly shift from general schedules to schedules targeted on crucial records.

CONCLUSION

If records managers are shifting to put disposition schedules *into* electronic records systems, if they are working with archivists and others to design records systems, and if the purpose of records disposition is dramatically shifting from just pushing records along for lower-level purposes such as destruction and cost savings, will we have records schedules in the future? Personally, I believe they will remain an important part of the profession, but they will serve much different roles and purposes than they have in the past.

NOTES

1. The literature on archival appraisal and records scheduling is extensive. Since this current paper is building on an earlier work about the relationship between appraisal and scheduling, I refer people to it for a check of references; see my "Records Management Scheduling and Archival Appraisal," *Records and Information Management Report* 14 (April 1998): 1–16. For references to the literature on archival appraisal, refer to my "The Archival Documentation Strategy and Its Implications for the Appraisal of Architectural Records," *American Archivist* 59 (Spring 1996): 144–154. In this chapter, I have documented only direct quotations.

2. Ira A. Penn, Gail B. Pennix, and Jim Coulson, *Records Management Handbook*, 2nd ed. (Brookfield, Vermont: Gower, 1994), 116.

3. Richard Brown, "Macro-Appraisal Theory and the Context of the Public Records Creator," *Archivaria* 40 (Fall 1995): 129.

4. This plan was available at http://www.nara.gov/nara/vision/nara plan.html

5. Brown, "Macro-Appraisal Theory," 139.

6. Thomas H. Davenport with Laurence Prusak, *Information Ecology: Mastering the Information and Knowledge Environment* (New York: Oxford University Press, 1997), 113.

7. Susan Myburgh, "Knowledge Management and Records Management: Is There a Difference?" *Records & Information Management Report* 14 (September 1998), 13.

8. Section 4.8, Public Record Office, *Management, Appraisal and Preservation of Electronic Records; Vol. 1: Principles* (Kew: Public Record Office, 2nd ed., 1999).

7

Evidence and Archives

Evidence has been a concept in American archival practice for a very long time. In the formative period of American archival theorizing, T. R. Schellenberg drew on the notion of evidence, along with that of information, to set up criteria for determining what records needed to be saved. His categorizing of records possessing evidential and informational values, based on his experiences in the National Archives, became commonplace thinking for most archivists, and this and other of his ideas are well known through most of the archival world. Whether one accepts Schellenberg's ideas or not, most research studies, opinion pieces, and new contributions to archival theory or methodology almost always start with or react to his approach to records.

The notion that Schellenberg summarized *all* archival theory in a timeless fashion seems to be a recent, peculiar idea emerging in debate about electronic records systems that he himself neither had the opportunity to observe nor could have predicted. In the most extreme defense of Schellenberg, Linda Henry contends that his work "foreshadowed writings of forty years later about electronic records" and mostly takes exception to the notion that newer definitions of record, developed from work with electronic records, "eliminates the concept of informational value." Henry sees many archival programs as continuing to rely on a "definition of a record that is similar to Schellenberg's."[1] Detecting similarities or even relating Schellenberg's concepts to everyday practice may be beside the point; we see instance after instance in which adherence to the older definition causes problems, partly because of the fuzziness of the definition and partly the manner in which the definition and related concepts of this archival pioneer are applied. (This misapplication is especially apparent in litigation such as the FBI case files and the PROFS case, in which archivists were pressed for specific definitions and procedures and where Schellenberg's concepts were questioned by outsiders.)[2]

Schellenberg himself might not have expected people to immortalize his work; in 1954, while in Australia and working on what became *Modern Archives*, he wrote in a letter that he was "tired of having an old fossil cited . . . as an authority in archival matters," referring then to Jenkinson's primer, which he also declared to be "unreadable."[3] Some of us refer so often to Schellenberg because he was a systematic, formative writer (perhaps also an archival thinker) in creating a working body of archival knowledge, but at times his writings also seem like an "old fossil." The concepts seem vague, more recited by archivists as justification for what they do and less as guides for their activities.

My own uneasiness with how Schellenberg is viewed derives partially from the fact that his achievement was to summarize working practice of several generations ago, providing a framework for how we view the intellectual foundations for archival work. These foundations may derive from the pragmatic tradition in American archival work, as Rand Jimerson contends it is, but I do not believe it is the chief attribute determining how successful archivists are or could be in their work. Jimerson writes:

> Rather than lament Americans' seeming lack of intellectual rigor or resistance to abstract truths, I think we should celebrate a national inclination toward meeting daily problems directly with a good dose of common sense. Archival theory will guide us in our approaches to meeting the needs of preserving the essential records of society and providing access to evidence that can assure accountability and protect rights of citizens. It will enable us to make correct choices among alternatives. But theory devoid of practical applications will stifle us and prevent us from completing our daily tasks as we fulfill our professional obligations. Theory is based on experience. Since the days of Schellenberg, this has been the distinctly American contribution to the world of archives. Theory and practice cannot be separated. They must work together to ensure the preservation of archival records and the

rights and guarantees that they protect. This recognition is what defines the American archivist.[4]

There is obviously a thread of such dialogue in the professional literature, as Mark Greene and Frank Boles seem to suggest:

> The American archival methodology articulated by Schellenberg is not a universal archival truth, but simply right and useful for its particular place and time. As American conditions change, so too should American archival theory evolve to reflect societal change.[5]

And it ought to change to reflect the use of records in court cases, the transformations in use of archives by researchers, and the dynamic nature of records and record-keeping systems technologies.

Although I agree with Jimerson's juxtaposition of theory and practice, it is his use of the word *celebrate* that worries me because, more often than not, practice is elevated to a much higher level of concern than are conceptual or methodological concerns, which can be crucial to helping us be wise and strategic in our work. Indeed, this practical orientation not only brings aversion to theory (writ broadly—a framework by which to approach work) but causes an inability to question or reevaluate present archival practice, to build new models, to adopt new ideas, and to play with new theories about records, record-keeping systems, and their management and use. I do not believe that evidence is the only manner in which to think about archives, I do not discount the cultural value of archives, I do not believe that knowledge about archival work is static or fixed, and I do not concur with the notion that pragmatism is the chief virtue or hallmark of the American archivist. But I do not intend to be defensive or critical but only to try to make the profession realize that because I see the complexities of archives and archival work (perhaps as a result of trying to teach people about archives and prepare them to work as archivists), my own views are in turn rather complex (and they should be that way for all of us). Some years ago, James O'Toole captured the changing notion of the concept of permanence, revealing a decided shift from permanent to continuing value.[6] With the advent of the pervasive use of and reliance on the Internet, we must stop and reflect on how we define the idea of continuing value.

My thesis for this chapter is that the debate over records as evidence and memory (or evidence and information or evidence and culture) is based on a false dichotomy. The real debate might be between those archivists and records managers who advocate careful articulation of records appraisal criteria and documentation of the process and those records professionals who possess weak criteria and uncertain missions and who collect or acquire with little careful thought as to the meaning or implications of what they are doing. Twenty years ago Gerry Ham argued, "I subscribe also to the notion that our work, and indeed our behavior as archivists, is determined by the nature of the material we deal with: we are what we accession and process."[7] I would turn this about and argue that we are what we do, and if we carry out our work in slapdash ways, then the results will also be suspect and poor—and the sense of an archival profession compromised.[8] The complexities of the volume and nature of modern documentation require us to adopt mechanisms that enable us to contend with these challenges, and these mechanisms require rigorous thinking, not just doing (or practice). We need to think *before* we do, not the other way around.

Adhering to an overall sense of some attribute of records and record keeping, such as evidence, provides a useful framework for meeting objectives while also revealing a consistent attribute of records and their creating/maintaining systems. "Evidence" also can have multiple meanings and be confusing if not carefully thought through by records professionals (in fact, the old evidential/informational notion of Schellenburg is vague, at least in its uses). A problem could be that the artifactual value often ascribed to paper documents is legitimate only if seen as a form of additional evidence generated from the records instead of the kind of passionate longing that is evident in the recent controversy about the preservation of books and newspapers.[9] It could be that the notion of intrinsic value views the physical aspects of the original form of the document as providing both information and evidence and, as a result, is a concept that links together evidence and information notions. Evidence takes on different meanings in systems not producing artifacts in the traditional sense. Do electronic records have intrinsic value, or can only their instrumentation—the screen, CPU, and keyboard—possess such value? As some have contended, the computer screen has become a metaphor for modern society,[10] and I must admit that there is some symbolism involved with computers and probably some of the records deriving from them as well. The warrant concept was derived from electronic records management work because of new demands on records professionals by the electronic systems. The record-keeping warrant becomes an overarching concept for records created and maintained in systems where evidence has less to do with physical objects and more to do with a record's structure, content, and context.[11] The warrant and the evidence found in or represented by records are aspects that all records and record-keeping systems universally share.

GETTING PERSONAL

As for myself, I never set out to write a systematic theology of archives or records, but I have been influenced by my very different professional positions, my professional activities, people I have come into contact with, and my own research and writing—especially since 1988 because of my teaching position. My writings have shifted about because of changing perceptions, although many of these perceptions overlap to a great degree. My current interests are (and have been for a very long time) archival appraisal, archival history, archives as a form of social and cultural memory, archival access and advocacy, records as a source of accountability, electronic records management, and the relationship of technologies to record keeping, professional standards, and archival education. In all these I see *evidence* as having a consistent value to understanding records and as being essential for other values of records, from the cultural to the organizational and managerial. I also see a unified concept of archives-records management, perhaps even in another umbrella concept (such as knowledge management),[12] linked together because of the life cycle or continuum concept (you can take your pick, because both require the functions and outlooks of archivists and records managers to be unified). Whether we are called *archivists* or something else is not as important as being responsible for an archival function and having the resources and influence to carry out the archival work.

The point in all this is quite simple. Viewed through the lens of my own professional career, my ideas—as well as knowledge—about my discipline and vocation (my calling) have and will continue to shift. For the initial stages of my career, I thought of myself as a historian (more a local historian), then I shifted more to an institutional archivist, then I became involved in professional leadership—when my self-identity as an archivist underwent its most drastic changes, and finally, over the past decade, my focus moved to why more than how as I became focused on educating individuals to become archivists. Through all this, other changes were evident. I became friends and colleagues with different people, some of whom had great influence on my career and my perceptions of what it meant to be an archivist. As I moved from practitioner to educator, I also saw the nature of the technologies supporting the creation and use of records and record-keeping systems. I came into the archives field before the advent of the personal computer, and I have lived in it right up to and through the World Wide Web.

Other archivists and records managers can close their eyes and reflect on all the ways they have changed their thinking in the course of their careers. What many might realize is that their motivations have been transformed, and that this is not at all bad. For myself, I have gained a much stronger and broader sense of why records are important to our society and culture. It does not mean that I dismiss the cultural or symbolic role of the archival record, but it also does not mean that I believe that this role is all that records are about. Before records or archives (in the aggregate) take on symbolic value, they exist as evidence of activity. Whatever symbolic or cultural value they assume is a kind of added-on value, not the sole explanation for their existence.

REEXAMINING WEAK LINKS

"A safe structure will be one whose weakest link is never overloaded by the greatest force to which the structure is subjected." So wrote that great communicator of engineering design and implementation, Henry Petroski.[13] Information value is, in my estimation, the weak link for archival work and practice. In general, information can have many definitions, most of which are quite vague and subject to highly variable, subjective, and idiosyncratic calls by archivists that can lead to poor and indefensible decisions. Declaring something worthy of being housed in an archive because of its informational value is often akin to assigning no value at all, save for the vague concept that the records might be used by someone at some point in the future (a scenario few archivists have the luxury of following). However, I believe that the more important reason for the weak link is the American archivist's emphasis on the information aspect of Schellenberg's configuration.

Some will argue, again, that the American archivist's immense practical emphasis or ability to innovate in pragmatic ways is the strength of our tradition. We have the ability to deal with rapidly changing conditions and to work out solutions without slavish adherence to theory, tradition, or tenet. Because the archivist was a spin-off from the historical discipline and most archivists saw their researchers as mostly historians, Schellenberg's concept of informational value seemed to make the most sense and was the easiest to contend with, even in the institutional setting. While all seemed comfortable with this notion and practice, the seeds of the present problem were being sown.

Mix in the notion of social history as it emerged in the 1960s, and its newer compatriot, cultural studies, of the past decade, and we should be able to see how complicated the situation has become. The idea of two information scientists, Jorge Reina Schement and Terry Curtis, that "though information fascinates many social, biological, and physical scientists, no interdisciplinary agreement on basic concepts seems likely, and no unified theory appears imminent," is really replicated in the humanities, where anything can have value and everything should be saved.[14] The great popular acclaim (thus far) for the Nicholson Baker book on library preservation is indicative of the dangerous ground archivists walk if they do not have more precise criteria for how they select or (just as important) if they fail to explain to the public that they are not merely warehousing everything but making careful and judicious selection. The burgeoning field of public or collective memory only complicates the matter more for archivists, in that it perhaps adds multiple new purposes and concerns to all the things archivists are already supposedly appraising and maintaining records to support. Individuals studying memory study anything—monuments, landscape, civic events, historic sites—opening up the door to the idea that any and every scrap of evidence or information is worth maintaining or, at the least, that the sources for study of public memory could lie well outside of traditional archives. Although the study of public memory can enrich the role and nature of archives in new ways, it might have other implications that undermine the ways archivists have viewed themselves and their missions.[15]

By another means we can examine the weak link of information in the archival panoply. When Schellenberg started musing about information and evidence in the 1940s, there was nothing like the networked digital environment we now reside and work in. But the Internet has cheapened information, both literally and figuratively, by providing so much of it to so many so fast.[16] We take information for granted, and many assume we can save most, if not all, of it because of the technology—indeed, the notion of "memory" has been expanded, or cheapened, depending on one's perspective.

There is something positive in this for archivists, however. Even if archivists are not discovering means by which they can harness the World Wide Web, computer scientists and other information professionals are discovering archival principles, concerns, and professionals. Computer scientist Su-Shing Chen starts off an article on preservation noting "Easy Internet access presumes that everyone can capture, access, and use the world's accumulated digital information." But there is a problem with this: "Unfortunately, we cannot guarantee the continued preservation and accessibility of digital information generated in this context of rapid technological advances." And this computer scientist laments what has been lost:

> To get a sense of what's at stake from a historical perspective, consider this cursory sampling of irretrievable information from the past 50 years: 50 percent (approximately 25,000) of the films produced in the 1940s, most TV interviews, the first e-mail sent in 1964, and many objects of intellectual and cultural heritage.[17]

Trying to define broadly something as nebulous as what "information" can be is both dangerous and impractical.

THE NOTION OF EVIDENCE

My emphasis on evidence exists because I think it is a bit "harder" to work with and closer to the reason records are created and maintained in the first place. Warrant—policies, procedures, best practices, legal, and other reasons for creation of records—leads to records that are evidence of activity (transactions), and it has long defined the reasons researchers from historians to journalists want and need information and the ways they search for evidence. The stress on evidence also opens up the other reasons records are kept: accountability, memory, and information. If records professionals focus on evidence and the needs for it, they will capture most, if not all, of the information needed. (Remember, because archivists cannot save everything, they need to have some means by which they apply strategies, probably in different ways and on different levels.) Does this mean that archivists occasionally and determine to keep some records specially for cultural or memory purposes? Of course. But this occasional exception does not mean that what archivists do is randomly accumulate materials and that this accumulation magically transforms into a cultural resource. (This transformation would happen only if others determine to study archives and archivists and their role in society rather than to study the records found in archives and historical manuscripts repositories.)

Now some will object that the notion of a records warrant (and, indeed, evidence) is something best reserved for organizational records and does not apply to personal papers. I do not believe this is the case at all. Personal papers—correspondence, checks, and photographs, among many forms—are a genre in which forms represent tradition, record-keeping systems, and other things that also reflect a warrant. Individuals maintain records because they have to (legal and regulatory mandates) or want to for individual and family memory and other purposes. (I think there is a kind of cultural or social warrant as well.) Again, personal papers are records because they possess a structure, content, and context, and also because these attributes emerge from the fact that records are (and have been for a long time) created for very specific purposes, reasons, and requirements. In fact, Schellenberg thought this was the case when he wrote his second and last major work, *The Management of Archives*.[18]

Records derive from a warrant—a purpose and authority for creation, resulting in transactions captured by records that must include content, structure, and context. So this is what we have when we think of a record and a record-keeping system. Archivists and records managers have long possessed a working definition of records, stressing the fact that they document a specific activity or transaction and that this documentation has a particular content (information), structure (form), and context (relationship to a creator, function, and other records). A record is a specific entity. Records are transaction oriented. They are evidence of activity (transaction), and that evidence can be preserved only if we maintain content, structure, and context. Structure is the record form. Context is the linkage of one record to other records. Content is the information, but content without structure and context cannot be information that is reliable. This is not a new definition; it goes back to the very origins of writing.[19] Writing was part of the very heart of organizations, record-keeping, and the varying information technologies. Now we are back to seeing a record not just as a bunch of data or information or even a physical object but as the consequence of a business event. Records thus encompass both personal and organizational transactions, and they are not merely a result of archival theory being superimposed on reality. I think of this view of records more as a means of understanding records and record-keeping systems and, perhaps just as importantly, of being strategic in trying to contend with all of the records.[20]

Archivists have been grappling with their professional mission for the better part of two decades. The 1980s, for example, was a period of immense emphasis on profession-wide planning, agenda setting, and self-evaluation. The Society of American Archivists (SAA) Committee on Goals and Priorities was but one example of an effort to carve out a working professional mission that was coherent. The 1980s also saw the start of statewide planning and assessment activities, debates about individual certification, and renewed efforts to define graduate archival education. Almost all of these activities tried to develop a concise professional mission statement that could be communicated to the public and policy makers and utilized in a variety of other functions and ways. The 1986 Committee on Goals and Priorities (CGAP) mission, "To identify, preserve, and make available for use records of enduring value," served us well for a time. It is concise, easy to remember, and engaging, but archivists have debated all of these functions, created new tools (especially for access), and even questioned whether they are in the enduring or continuing value business.[21]

So what is a better mission for archivists in light of all the changes in the profession, records, record keeping, society, and its use of information and information technologies? I am not going to try to write a succinct statement, but let me enumerate the elements of a better mission revolving around evidence. Records have continuing value, records professionals' responsibility is records and the information contained in them, the key to archival science (or whatever one wishes to call it) is understanding records and record-keeping systems, and records have importance to our institutions and society that far exceeds the traditional and too-limited constituencies of historians or some kind of definition that stresses only the cultural importance of records. The recent statement by the Australian Society of Archivists is a fuller description:

> Archivists ensure that records which have value as authentic evidence of administrative, corporate, cultural and intellectual activity are made, kept and used. The work of archivists is vital for ensuring organizational efficiency and accountability and for supporting understandings of . . . life through the management and retention of its personal, corporate and social memory.[22]

Here we can discern that evidence and information, evidence and culture, and evidence and societal memory are all interconnected, not in some hierarchical fashion but as different elements of the same general professional orientation (and certainly an orientation shared by many others when they think of records).

One of the reasons all these seemingly disparate notions fit or hang together is that records (including personal papers) reflect common characteristics such as compliance, legal mandates, best practices, traditional mechanisms for generating records, and genres or forms. Archivists and records managers share a trust in managing our documentary heritage; by this I mean they work with the records identified to have a continuing value to the records creators and to the broader society. Such records are maintained not just for a small clientele of academic historians or for only cultural purposes. Archivists manage records in order to ensure that the evidence of transactions supporting activities of organizations and individuals is captured and available as necessary for legal and related purposes. Records are created in order to provide a trail that would allow us to recreate a decision and a series of steps to carry out that decision. Archivists and records managers are concerned with records that enable an organization or an individual to be accountable. All organizations and all records professionals operate within a compliance environment. Records are essential when we believe that the public trust has been violated or an illegal action has been taken. Finally, archivists and records managers work to ensure that organizations possess a corporate memory or that society has a memory that cannot be easily manipulated or distorted to serve particular ends. That memory is a well of records (and other information) an individual or institution or society can reach into for a deeper understanding of the present or for planning for the future. The importance of records—both organizational records and personal papers—derives from the notion of what makes them records and not from merely some aspect of content. The diminution or loss of any one of the parts of a record undermines the "recordness" of a document because it minimizes its informational, cultural, or memory values.

We can easily discern many instances in which personal papers reflect structure and order, the same attributes individuals want to focus on when they consider organizational records. Scholarly studies of letter writing, diary writing, compilations of recipes, and other such documentary forms long associated with personal papers have discerned attributes that should make us understand that these are records. The award-winning study by Ulrich of Martha Ballard's diary of two centuries ago, just one example, reveals this quality:

> The structure of her diary derives from two workaday forms of record-keeping, the daybook and the interleaved almanac. In eighteenth-century New England, farmers, craftsmen, shopkeepers, ship's captains, and perhaps a very few housewives kept daybooks, running accounts of receipts and expenditures, sometimes combining economic entries with short notes on important family events and comments on work begun or completed. Other early diarists used the blank pages bound into printed almanacs to keep their own tally on the weather, adding brief entries on gardening, visits to and from neighbors, or public occurrences of both the institutional and the sensational sort.[23]

This brief glimpse makes us understand how this quintessential example of personal record keeping parallels the most systematic, bureaucratic, organizational record keeping. Ballard's diary is evidence of her activities, a quasi-official kind of public archive, and a symbolic artifact (albeit one that was long neglected—often typical of such items that eventually assume artifactual or symbolic value).

THE NOTION OF APPRAISAL

Appraisal also demands that you have something in view—a purpose, mission, mandate, or whatever one wants to call it. Nearly two decades ago, a group of archivists described appraisal in this fashion:

> The selection of records of enduring value is the archivist's first responsibility. All other archival activities hinge on the ability to select wisely. Two basic activities are required. . . . First, archivists must educate themselves about the records of contemporary society. . . . Second, archivists must educate records creators about the importance of retaining records of long-term importance and inform the general public about the essential work of the archival profession . . . .[24]

In other words, archivists need to be aware that all of the other activities they are engaged in depend on how well they appraise, another reason I believe a focus on evidence is not only useful, but imperative. Whatever purpose or perspective archivists have will affect, of course, appraisal and the nature of other archival activities and services. As Elizabeth Kaplan has suggested, archivists need to be aware of *us*, that is, the archivist's role in all these activities. Archivists shape, make decisions, make mistakes, and reflect their biases—but still they are in the records business, and records represent evidence. If archivists think they can randomly acquire or merely sit back and let "stuff" come to them, as if they were thereby providing some useful societal function, then I think they as a profession have some serious problems to sort out.[25]

What criteria archivists use for defining records, their mission, and appraisal are crucial to what they are and do. For me, the evidence/warrant notion makes sense as the primary lens by which archivists see themselves and their mission among all the means they can use to define records and archival appraisal. After all, archivists are appraising in an environment of huge amounts of records to contend with, in which technology is an increasing issue that has to be dealt with in new ways, and where postmodernism and cultural conflicts affect what and how they appraise and put them into a very contentious situation when they must justify their appraisal. The celebration of the so-called Information Age (leading to what many call "infomania") also lulls many into thinking that everything can be saved. What archivists use—a quest for representative documentation, documenting aspects of society in a strategic manner, using information or evidence, relying on the notion of a records warrant, pointing to a role for archives as part of societal or cultural memory, or whatever—needs to be defined, focused, used consistently, and documented so that people understand it. However, the means archivists use to justify appraisal—which after all most closely corresponds to how they see themselves, their mission, and their profession—can be muddied if they utilize terms that have become weaker, such as "information." Information in the Information Age has a thousand and one nebulous meanings, and it does not necessarily lead to precision or even strategic operations (both of which archivists need given the challenges of the documentary universe).[26]

All this suggests that society and its organizations (and people) are complicated and are becoming more complicated. Fran Blouin, in a recent essay on archives and social memory, muses on how the word "archives" has changed. Blouin notes that we have to be "clearer about the limits and boundaries of our work." More specifically, he suggests we need to be mindful that in a function like appraisal, "we may be pushed toward increased accountability for the processes we use."[27] Merely saying that what we have or want to collect is a monument to public memory or fulfills some other role is not enough if we are lax in documenting our own work, holding on to models-theories-knowledge as guides (we need them), and following some particular objectives or mandates.

One of the problems has been archivists' tendency to focus on records as *stuff* for historical and cultural purposes. Records make the news every day, as everyone recognizes, but the news concentrates predominantly on matters such as personal rights, accountability, secrecy and privacy, and the new notion of society[28] wrought by the Internet—which some have called the "transparent" society.[29] Records are essential for all these (and other) functions, mainly because of their role of providing evidence. Historians and other scholars can certainly argue and quibble about what is captured in a record or even turn their attention to other sources to fill in the silences left by the archives,[30] but evidence has a very different role and certainly a role with very different implications from what we find in the value of records for accountability and other purposes. The International Records Management Trust, working largely with Sub-Saharan nations, notes the "fundamental importance of records" as the "basis for formulating and evaluating policy, preserving the rule of law, managing finance and personnel, providing evidence for accountability and protecting the rights of individuals."[31] In stating this, the IRMT is not saying that records might not also possess cultural or symbolic value; rather, it is arguing that archivists have a much broader focus that could be best summarized as evidence.

Over time, many archivists naturally begin to gain a broader perspective. My teaching has evolved primarily from stressing archival functions (such as appraisal and arrangement/description) to emphasizing that archivists need to be scholars ("experts") in records and record-keeping systems. I do not mean that I am not considering the key archival or records management functions (I remain convinced of the significance of appraisal, as just one example) but that I am now building my teaching around why records systems are created, their continuing evolution, their historical continuity, and their value. Basic archival and records management functions are viewed through this broader perspective on records and record-keeping systems.

How is this perspective different from what archivists and records managers have been doing generally? For archivists, it means that they are not identifying and describing records for just historians (that hardy but definitely minor constituency) but for all potential users. This perspective moves records managers from the false gods of economy and efficiency to the use of the information in records for the institution's good and for its mission.

Archivists and records managers need to be experts about records, record-keeping systems, and how these systems are designed and intended and actually used. They must master an interdisciplinary knowledge base supporting an understanding of records and records systems, crossing the boundaries of such fields as anthropology, organizational theory, sociology, history, and political science, and supporting core principles of archival science and records management. All of these fields (and others) are concerned with some notion of evidence in records, and this curriculum does not necessarily have to transform what archivists think of themselves—provided they perceive themselves to be archivists. Some are more likely to describe themselves as curators, librarians, clerks, historians, or some other variation that may speak more to the historical antecedents of archivy or to the general problem of making people aware of what archivists are and what they do.[32]

Some have disparaged the focus on records or evidence as if the classic notion of archivist or archival work has been abandoned.

Some seem to think that archivists are like museum curators, but what kind of museum curator? Or from what period? Museums have been changing in many ways:

> Those institutions now called museums have family resemblances to one another, but they share neither a common history nor a common cause, not withstanding the emerging professionalism of museum work and the homogenizing discipline of museum studies.

The museum is "an institution in transition, influenced by change in physical resources and technology as well as by cultural sensibilities and ideology. The museum is a particularly sensitive barometer of such changes."[33]

WRESTLING WITH EVIDENCE

Although historians might be far less certain these days about the validity of evidence in records, most also struggle with the use of evidence in records. T. H. Breen's interesting memoir about serving as a resident humanist in East Hampton, New York, provides many useful allusions to the nature of such evidence. Breen notes, "Even the most elaborate, quantitative explanations of past behavior are really only plausible reconstructions based on the analysis of selected bits of surviving evidence." Because of the loss of church records, "We are doomed from the start to an unbalanced view of the past." So Breen is concerned about the availability of documentation, but he is also aware of its limitations. "Previous experience had taught me that official records are often less solid than they at first appear." As he looks at various records, he finds that they can "unravel, transforming themselves into little more than loose threads of competing fictions. They are products of an interpretive process that at the very best can generate only partial truths." Later Breen addresses the fact that colonists often did not record "routine acquisitions" in their documents, creating some awkward gaps. Breen also describes how we have to link our imagination to what we find in the records:

> Names that appear on ancient documents do not long remain abstractions. They are translated in our imaginations into real people. Words

in old records that seemingly have nothing at all to do with a person's appearance suggest for reasons that I do not fully understand an actual physical being. We know the men and women we study just as surely as if we possessed a photograph.

And finally Breen notes that he often has to deal with:

> abstractions, imagined pasts that I have glimpsed in the archives. . . . Like written documents, the things of material culture, by their very arrangement, their exclusion or juxtaposition, become highly charged texts that must be read and then contested.

Part of the reason for contesting records is that records reveal a:

> partial truth. It was a story told from records that just happened to have survived, that contained errors and omissions, that reflected the biases and special pleadings of those who had been entrusted to keep the village chronicles, that was silent about the founders' religious values, about their lives as fathers and mothers, as lovers, as people who for one reason or another had passed through East Hampton.[34]

What a historian like Breen is considering is the notion of the problem of historical knowledge and, for that matter, the problem of historical evidence as found in records (broadly defined). Indeed, despite whatever challenges are represented by archival and other records, historians still rely on the evidence found in the records as the basis for historical inquiry, as the recent controversy about Michael Bellesiles's book *Arming America: The Origins of a National Gun Culture*[35] and the David Irving trial about Holocaust denial suggest.[36] Archivists must cope with numerous matters:

the texture or the feel of the past,
memory and its various definitions,
the problems of accidental survivals and (sometimes quite deliberate) destruction,
social pressures for keeping more than we can really keep,
how to accommodate present values and some sort of objective approach to the records,
the different and often changing constituencies archivists serve (or think they serve),
and more.

The long-standing idea that archivists appraise for historians or work for historians is also complex because it presupposes many different ideas about history and records that must be dealt with.

Archivists and records managers need to be rethinking matters as fundamental as the evidence (or information) found in records because record-keeping technologies are constantly changing, because it forces them to rethink what or how well they are doing, and because the users of archives might have disparate views of what evidence constitutes. Historians, the traditional users of archives, have also described archival records as forms of evidence, and no one questioned the concept or even thought much about it. Everyone understood that a record was created as evidence of some action and that the action could be understood by using the documents generating it. Ah, the good old days. More recent technologies raised issues about evidence in records systems because matters of their reliability or authenticity seemed more problematic, especially in government and legal applications.[37]

Archivists need to remember that the renewed stress on records and evidence largely occurred because of the immense new varieties and implications of electronic information systems. Although some archivists seem to think that they can relax, sit back, and let others take care of the electronic records situation, the nature of electronic records management does not allow for such a perspective, whether it derives from conviction of the proper mission of the archivist or from complacency. In a wide-ranging discussion about evidence in rhetoric and communications studies, A. Cheree Carlson writes:

> Communication scholars who work from all perspectives need to stand toe to toe every now and then, and remind each other of what they are doing. We don't do it near enough. "Evidence" is one of those issues that we often take for granted; it needs to be revisited once in a while.

Carlson considers different perspectives on evidence, including external factors affecting the text, a focus on the text itself, and variables caused by the individual who is examining the text. Carlson also throws into the mix a political dimension, one that includes the politics within the discipline, including the availability of journals in which to publish.[38]

Those who perhaps believe that the recent focus on technology in archival work distracts archivists from the symbolic or cultural roles for archives need to bear in mind that technology itself is a product of societal elements. Arnold Pacey's brief book *The Culture of Technology* provides one of the most well-rounded efforts to demonstrate that technology does not operate on its own but is a product not only of technology but of cultural and organizational aspects. But I think archivists and records managers need to acknowledge that unless they step out of the box, there is still something missing. Seamus Ross reminds us:

> Digital information is a cultural product. As we think of physical products of culture as artifacts, so we should also be thinking of digital and electronic products as d-facts (or e-facts). These new products form an essential fragment of cultural record.[39]

Actually, many of those who have worked on the theoretical and practical implications of electronic records management have never forgotten this—but they had to start somewhere, and the focus on records as distinct entities with discernible attributes and specific purposes seemed to be the place to begin.

Some worry that with a seeming preoccupation with technology, archivists will lose something special in the future archives (although I see little evidence of such a preoccupation in the profession except that some of its most prolific writers seem engaged by it). Older manuscripts and books, especially printed books, are often the products of innovative (for their day) technologies, and as a result, they often require equally innovative technologies for copying or preserving them. Although some lash out against technology, such as Sven Birkerts (who defends print books) and Nicholson Baker (who defends print books and newspapers), praising the original artifact's preservation above all other responsibilities, these writers seem to be striking a blow against little more than the sterility of the digital age's excessive focus on information. Old books and paper archives seem to represent a stable, timeless form and structure when all else seems subject to constant, ever more rapid change. But they are still the products of technologies.

The conspiratorial tendencies of writers like Birkert or Baker (I like printed books and manuscript documents as much as they do) tap into another fine tradition, characterized by the work of Ned Lud and others who see evil in technology itself rather than in its

uses and implications. To deny using a personal computer in favor
of a typewriter is merely to exchange one set of technologies for
another and to cause us to miss the point that our archives—
whether a center for electronic records or one with eighteenth-
century letters, reports, and diaries—are comprised of records-generating technologies or, at the least, the end results of these technologies. The pencil, for example, is a device that is the result of
sophisticated technologies, designs, and trials and errors.[40] We
might come to appreciate archives in a new way, one that enables
us to enhance our sense of the importance of the building blocks of
archives—that is, records. Archives (at least in the traditional sense)
are comprised not of interesting old stuff or artifacts (although interesting old stuff and artifacts are certainly in archives) but records.
And records are created by both organizations and people—the distinctions between personal manuscripts and organizational records
are significant mostly in volume and particulars of origination, not
in being a record or something else. Again, Seamus Ross worries
that at present archivists are not preserving the "Web-based literature, net-based advertising, online databases, newsgroups, chat-
rooms, virtual communities, music recordings, websites (including
webcams), and digital images, which characterize the creations of
the several hundred million Internet users," or, in other words, the
evidence of a networked digital age. Although Ross acknowledges
that some of this evidence is an appraisal challenge, it is also a technical challenge.[41]

The change in technologies has certainly caused a proliferation in
records and the evidence found in them, something that should
remind archivists and records managers that the real issue in determining how they approach records is that they adopt strategies
enabling them to get a handle on a vast documentary universe.
Recently, as we witnessed a transition in presidential administrations, we also watched mounting concern that the information in
federal agency websites would be lost. Given that the handing of
the reins from the Clinton to the Bush administration encompassed
something new, the existence of the World Wide Web, it is possible
that our strategies for dealing with these materials were not developed enough. Just compiling snapshots of the federal agency websites was a project of immense proportions, entailing "21 terabytes
in all, enough to fill about 14 million floppy disks, or roughly twice
the amount of data contained in the books of the Library of Con-

gress." A report on this effort posed an interesting question: "In the process of creating a digital time capsule, the snapshot project is also spotlighting a problem that has been quietly nagging at archivists: How should agencies handle electronic records that exist only on the Internet?" Of course, copying everything on all the sites captured more than just records, suggesting that new strategies are needed. J. Timothy Sprehe, a federal information policy expert, captured the essence of the problem when he stated that the "Internet is increasing too fast for records management policies to keep up."[42] In the context of this chapter, the issue is that an archival focus on information is way too vague to be of much assistance in working with such challenges. However, the issue has to do with more than just technology. Thirty years ago, Hans Booms mused that "95 percent of all information lies beyond the capacity of any one individual to comprehend."[43]

Evidence provides at least a somewhat more manageable strategic mechanism for approaching records and for conceptualizing the roles of records professionals such as archivists and records managers. Although today we have a much wider range of criteria governing how we think of evidence, this growth might not be all that relevant to how archivists and records managers approach electronic records or any records. Legal authorities debate what constitutes evidence in a court of law, and it seems that little seems to fall outside the scope of evidence. Even this is not new, however, as Meyer Fishbein reminded us twenty years ago when he cited a 1838 case accepting notched sticks as evidence, although Fishbein believed that the archivist could use such legal precedents as a means for working with those designing and using electronic records systems.[44] Indeed, we must remember that every new technology generating and maintaining records has been greeted by debates, new regulations, and new laws, all while striving to protect evidence, accountability, and other issues related to the work of records professionals.[45] This occurred with microfilm, until the courts determined that it is legally admissible if it and the records were created in the normal course of business. The legal use of electronic mail as evidence is constantly under review, and it is dependent on the requirement that e-mail be shown to be a regulated part of an organization's record-keeping system (one reason why records professionals are often deposed or brought into court as witnesses to testify about the organization's policies and procedures concerning e-mail).[46] I am not arguing that records' value as evidence is restricted to the legal status of public records as a hearsay exception.[47]

Evidence in records encompasses legal parameters but also policies, best practices, and other disciplinary concepts. Organizational theorists attest to the importance of institutional memory, and they identify the memories of individual workers along with corporate myths, stories, symbols, reports, and transactional records as crucial to the evidence of an organization's functions. There are broad-based concepts of information documents—encompassing both traditional records (at least traditional to archivists) and an array of other documents, such as artifacts and even language. Even the once reliable historian, the mainstay of the archives, now either questions the veracity of the evidence found in records (and not just in a critical sense, but sometimes in a dismissive manner) and turns to other sources or uses his or her imagination to develop a sense of the past.

A MASS OF CONFLICTING VIEWS?

Considering all this, why is it that a group of archivists seems to have turned back to a concept of evidence? It is more tempting, perhaps, to throw up our hands, like the fictional sixteenth-century monk and cartographer Fra Mauro in James Cowan's novel *A Mapmaker's Dream.* Safely ensconced in his garret, Fra Mauro talks with travelers, consults archives brought to him, and converses with philosophers in an effort to create a map of the world, which he ultimately abandons as not having any meaning except for himself. Fra Mauro notes that his map was becoming a "mass of conflicting views," and then he comes to believe that his map is a "distortion," merely being how he understood his various sources. "I now realize that the world is not real save in the way each of us impresses upon it his own sensibility."[48] Some archivists might argue, as well, that the record is not real, and there are few if any reasons to develop systematic approaches to defining either a record or the means by which some records might be identified as having archival value. Records are flawed. Evidence is fuzzy. Archivists need to follow our instincts and collect what seems to be of value, even if that value is only of a symbolic nature.

But many recognize that documents are a primary means of

understanding information. Information scientist David Levy attests to this: "So what are documents? My answer is that they are bits of the material world—clay, stone, animal skin, plant fiber, sand—that we've imbued with the ability to speak." "What's useful about this perspective is the way it takes the focus off the technology per se. Any technologies or media that ensure repeatability will do." "Documents speak out, and by fixing their talk or otherwise making it repeatable, they make it possible for many people to hear what they have to say." "But documents not only support the social order, they themselves are part of it. They themselves need to be tended and taken care of, just like everything else in the world."[49] In a major treatise on the social life of information, something that should be comfortable for many archivists to consider, information scientists John Seely Brown and Paul Duguid argue that "Documents not only serve to make information but also to warrant it—to give it validity," and "Documents do not merely carry information, they help make it, structure it, and validate it."[50] Organization theorists view evidence through the lens of corporate memory, knowledge management, and strategic information resources management; information scientists now dote on "documents"; and historians mull over "texts."

Evidence is a concern for everyone, so why not archivists as well? In commenting on the shift from quantitative to qualitative approaches in the arena of communication studies, Philip K. Tompkins notes, the:

> burden will . . . be on "qualitative" or textual scholars . . . to do a better job for all of articulating the principles of rigor. The survival of our respective departments is dependent on our ability to spell out the *warrants* for our varied modes of knowing and reporting.[51]

Others within communication studies have commented in a similar fashion on the nature of evidence. Kristine L. Fitch writes, "Claims should be based on an adequate selection of the total corpus of data." She continues, "Data should come, at least partly, from particularly accessible observation records."

> Data and analysis should include consideration of inferences and interpretations, as well as concrete phenomena. I suggest this criterion based on an assumption that humans are social beings with memories,

motivations, plans, and sometimes shared history, and that all of these
are resources that they draw upon to make sense of immediately present events. Those resources can be deeply explored as part of the social
world through qualitative methods, and thus legitimately count as evidence.[52]

What such views should suggest is that not all evidence is legally
prescribed. We have "evidence-based" medicine or health care,
which stresses retrieval of information from literature, evaluation
and appraisal of the information, clinical research, biostatistics, and
other means to inform clinicians, health managers, and others.[53] In
this discipline, evidence brings together observed data (witnesses),
reported data (documents), and research data (scientific research),
in a manner that some believe is unique to this field because of its
well-developed terms, standards, and research norms.[54] Society's
grappling with all sorts of evidence can be detected in the growing
use of expert witnesses in the courtroom, with mixed results according to many commentators. The validity of expert witness testimony
has as much to do with the reputation of the particular witness or
the witness's discipline as with the relevance of the facts presented
by them in a particular case.[55] In fact, outside of formalistic disciplines and the law, people tend to think of evidence in softer ways,
taking more of an ad hoc approach with no hard and fast rules and
with considerable reliance on often very unreliable sources (such as
the mass media, popular magazines, and word of mouth).[56]

Philosophers and historians of science discuss the challenges of
"translating" evidence ("as translation involves the assignment of
meaning to a foreign or not understood text, so the history of science
involves the assignment of meaning to the foreign or not understood
actions and mental states of past actors"[57]), and communications
experts wrestle with expanding evidence to encompass various
communities and their audiences (if their research is to be compre-
hensible and relevant).[58] A recent proposal for dealing with electronic medical records notes that such records systems need to
provide for comprehensiveness, accessibility, interoperability, confidentiality, accountability, and flexibility. The authors of the proposal also provide this chilling assessment: "No computer system
has ever remained operational for the lifetime of a typical person;
hence we will need procedures to migrate records to new computer
systems and architectures."[59] Given that archivists are certainly

interested in documenting medical care, it seems imperative that they be involved in designing systems that enable the archival documentation of medical care to be identified and used. The question of evidence found in such systems, whether defined from a legal or some other perspective, seems to be an important means to reaching an end. Archivists, along with records managers and a whole host of other professionals, need to work to enable such records to be protected over the long term while respecting both personal privacy and institutional propriety concerns.

WHAT ABOUT SYMBOLIC
OR CULTURAL VALUE?

Does an emphasis on records, electronic technologies, evidence, and other such matters somehow minimize the symbolic value of archives? I do not think that it does. Even one of the great symbolic artifacts, in the archival sense, the original manuscript of the Declaration of Independence, is a record, evidence of an act, and the result of technologies. The particular nature of this act, its importance for the founding of the nation, is what imbues this document with its symbolic value.[60] Within the archival community, those reacting against the emphasis on records, evidence, and electronic technologies often seem to miss some basic points of those stressing these matters, contend that they are not technologists, and object to the obfuscation of the professional literature with new and different jargon. They contend that theirs is a cultural mission and that archivists are more like museum curators than software engineers. Because all records and record-keeping systems are technologies of some sort, all archivists must be technologists to a certain degree. Those reacting against electronic technology fail to understand that archival records are still evidence and that some records need to be kept primarily because of matters of accountability. If evidence, accountability, and other attributes of records can be comprehended as being strongly connected to the cultural importance of records, then I think we will be on the same page. To harp only on the cultural value of archival records seems to miss the point about what makes something a record to begin with. Some contend that society has invested in archives, just as in their museums, as cultural entities. This view fails to acknowledge, however, that society does not

really understand archives or archivists. They might have some perception of archives from watching the *Antiques Roadshow* or bidding
via eBay or reading Martha Cooley's novel *The Archivist*, but none
provide a very realistic concept of archives and the importance of
records or archivists. A recent "What is an archivist?" survey
revealed the standard lack of understanding; 90 percent of the archivists surveyed answered no to the question "When you tell a
stranger that you are an archivist, do they know what an archivist
is?"[61]

The present expanded view of the nature of evidence by historians also suggests that they too wonder what an archivist is. George
Lipsitz reminds us that "historical memories and historical evidence
can no longer be found solely in archives and libraries; they pervade
popular culture and public discourse as well."[62] Will researchers
still rely on archives? Will archivists collect everything or focus on
records and evidence? We have a pervasive diluted notion of both
evidence and culture. We know that there are such things as "cultural industries," which represent a "distinctive sector" of the
American economy: "The growing interest in creativity is a
response to the relentless pace of innovation in the Information
Age." This makes us worry that the "constant innovation can sever
our connections with the past and lead us to neglect our sources of
collective memory, values, and identity."[63] But are archives merely
"cultural" agencies?[64] Partly they are, but their vaults of evidence
are just as important as sources for noncultural functions such as
accountability.

The matter of the symbolic or cultural significance of archives versus their other values (such as evidence, accountability, or public or
corporate memory) is mostly an internal debate (that is, one occurring within the archival community) of marginal consequence to the
technologies supporting records and records systems. Regardless of
how archivists conceive of their mission or how they view the electronic technologies, they need to develop approaches enabling them
to manage technology effectively. Those who picked up on records
and evidence did so partly because of the historic dimensions of
these entities in the archival profession and its mission, but they also
did so because these systems require systematic, specific notions
identifying and capturing whatever information (let's call it "evidence") they contain that they and society deem to be important
enough to manage over time.

Someone might be studying the symbolic value of old computer disks, computer screens, CPUs, and computer manuals, but it seems to be a different kind of symbolism from what we have normally associated with printed books or handwritten manuscripts, which is a symbolism bordering on the same kind of Romanticism often associated with old ruins. Washington Irving, in his *Sketch Book*, thought "Europe was rich in the accumulated treasures of age. Her very ruins told the history of times gone by, and every mouldering stone was a chronicle," a place where he could "escape, in short, from the commonplace realities of the present, and lose myself among the shadowy grandeurs of the past."[65] Computers, supporting the Internet and World Wide Web, may allow other forms of escape, ones not so romantic as what Irving envisioned, but it is doubtful whether anyone is viewing old terminals and software as "mouldering" chronicles.

WHAT IS THE ARCHIVAL MISSION?

How archivists view evidence has to do with how they define their own professional mission. How or why records professionals use laws, regulations, and policies has more to do with how they define their own professional mission, and this might be the most important issue to consider in this debate. But how they define their professional mission might be questioned by employers and others who have to protect themselves by providing information about the "reliability and trustworthiness of the records,"[66] concepts similar to those being discussed by archivists and records managers. After all, the challenge is much bigger than a debate about records as evidence or information. Terry Cook and Tim Ericson give us a glimpse into the bigger issues. Cook notes, "The central dilemma for archivists is simply this: not all records having archival value can be kept."[67] Ericson muses:

> Our instinct is still to see ourselves in the role of a twentieth-century Horatius-at-the-Bridge: the last line of defense between preservation and oblivion. This causes us to make utterly ludicrous decisions regarding acquisition by cloaking ourselves in the virtue of maintaining culture: if I don't save it, who will?[68]

In my discussion about strategies and methods, I am not advocating that archivists toss out the baby with the bathwater. However, archivists need to be astute in how they conceptualize their mission, characterize their work, and consider their options and responsibilities. George Rawlins, contemplating the nature of our technocratic age, writes:

> Our legal, governmental, and social systems are still designed for a world without computers. Our sluggish social systems, intended for the languid bygone era of only a decade ago—an era filled with filing cabinets, paper documents, and five-day mail—haven't changed to keep up. And computer technology keeps changing so fast now that perhaps they never will.[69]

I am not suggesting that the reliance on evidence is only a byproduct of the growing use of computers, although I am arguing that the changing nature of records and record-keeping technologies requires archivists to adopt positions and postures that are broader than merely custodians of cultural memory.

The most depressing part of this debate may not be what individuals ascribe to the virtues of either position, the acrimonious nature of the debate, or the mischaracterizations of what the debate means. It is the fact that unlike other similar disciplinary debates, and there are many similar debates, the archival debate does not grab any real media attention (at least not in a manner that reflects the slightest understanding of archives or archivists). In the past, we have had such debates reflecting different perspectives of history (remember the wars between the cliometricians and other historians in the 1970s?), literary studies (the deconstructionists or postmodernists versus those who advocated the study of literary texts as literature), and multicultural interpretations (such as represented by the "culture wars" and Afro-centrist debates). All of these thoroughly professional and academic debates made the news and created books and articles that forced the public to rethink how these disciplines defined very basic notions of history, literature, and other matters. Most recently we have had debates between scientific and cultural anthropologists move from conference venues, academic journals, and faculty meetings to the newspapers, with one group characterized as searching for the "universal truths of man" and others as "an intellectual apprenticeship in the delicate art of getting to know other cultures without flattening them to the contours of your own."[70] Sadly, archivists' own debate, one seeming to get right to the heart of what constitutes an archival record, an archive, and an archivist—all matters we certainly deem to be important for society—does not make any newspapers or capture any public attention.

Archivists on both sides of this present debate need to look for common ground and consensus on our mission and mandate (perhaps a third group of synthesizers will need to bring this change about).[71] Archivists need to be able to think critically, radically, and differently, not merely buy into platitudes or accept the norms of the various records professions. Jane Jacobs speculates about societal discourse in this manner: "We're so brainwashed into thinking of dissent only in political or philosophical terms. But consider that every single improvement in efficiency of production or distribution requires dissent from the way things were previously done."[72] I have based much of my career on such dissent, hoping that it causes archivists and other records professionals to reconsider what it is that they are doing or at least to ask if their efforts are working. I think, write, and teach from the perspective that archivists cannot stand pat in how they work in modern society. They must be creative, energetic, vocal, and risk taking. Why? Because records (and archives) are often much more important to society than archivists seem willing to accept. Archivists need to get out, to think outside of the box, for that one reason.

NOTES

1. Linda Henry, "Schellenberg in Cyberspace," *American Archivist* 61 (Fall 1998): 310, 315, 316.

2. See David A. Wallace, "Electronic Records Management Defined by Court Case and Policy," *Information Management Journal* 35 (January 2001): 4–8, 10, 12, 14–15.

3. Jane F. Smith, "Theodore R. Schellenberg: Americanizer and Popularizer," *American Archivist* 44 (Fall 1981): 319.

4. Randall C. Jimerson, ed., *American Archival Studies: Readings in Theory and Practice* (Washington, D.C.: Society of American Archivists, 2000), 16–17.

5. Frank Boles and Mark A. Greene, "Et Tu Schellenberg? Thoughts on

the Dagger of American Appraisal Theory," *American Archivist* 59 (Summer 1996): 310.

6. James M. O'Toole, "On the Idea of Permanence," *American Archivist* 52 (Winter 1989): 10–25.

7. F. Gerald Ham, "Archival Strategies for the Post-Custodial Era," *American Archivist* 44 (Summer 1981): 207.

8. This has been a theme in my own writing, dating back to my "Professionalism and Archivists in the United States," *American Archivist* 49 (Summer 1986): 229–47.

9. This is a reference to the book by Nicholson Baker, *Double Fold: America's Libraries and the Assault on Paper* (New York: Random House, 2001), which, while making many good points about how and why reformatting has emerged as the dominant preservation mechanism, holds to the idea that all objects (such as books and newspapers) must be held in original form. For my primary response to this, see my *Vandals in the Stacks? A Response to Nicholson Baker's Assault on Libraries* (Westport, Conn.: Greenwood, 2002).

10. Sherry Turkle, *Life on the Screen: Identity in the Age of the Internet* (New York: Simon and Schuster, 1995) as one of many who consider the computer a symbol of modern life.

11. Wendy Duff, "Harnessing the Power of Warrant," *American Archivist* 61 (Spring 1998): 88–122.

12. The recent evolution of thinking is most evident in my two most recent books, *Closing an Era: Historical Perspectives on Modern Archives and Records Management* (New York: Greenwood Press, 2000) and *Records as Evidence and Information: Policy Issues* (New York: Quorum Books, 2001).

13. Henry Petroski, *To Engineer Is Human: The Role of Failure in Successful Design* (1985; reprint, New York: Vintage Books, 1992), 41.

14. Jorge Reina Schement and Terry Curtis, *Tendencies and Tensions of the Information Age: The Production and Distribution of Information in the United States* (New Brunswick, N.J.: Transaction Publishers, 1995), 3.

15. I first became interested in public memory more than a decade ago, as my "Concept of Public Memory and Its Impact on Archival Public Programming," *Archivaria* 36 (Autumn 1993): 122–135 suggests. There are so many innovative and interesting studies of memory as to make it foolish to try to describe them in a note. However, my own doctoral students have turned a considerable part of their attention to studying memory and archives, as was indicated at the 2001 Society of American Archivists meeting by papers as follows: "Some Thoughts on Reconciling Information, Memory, and Archives: Ideas for a Different Kind of Book Serving as a Session Introduction" by me; "House of Memory and Creation: Archives in an Artist's Colony," Jeannette Bastian, Simmons Graduate School of Library and Information Science; "An Accumulation of Truth: Museum Archives

and Institutional Memory," Bernadette Callery, Carnegie Museum of Natural History; "The Tuskegee Syphilis Study and the Politics of Memory," Tywanna Whorley, University of Pittsburgh; and "Archival Amnesia: Have Archivists Forgotten the Role of Archives in Constructing Collective Memory?" Jennifer Marshall, University of Pittsburgh.

16. The Internet has cheapened information in that it has been transformed into a commodity, the currency of business and all life (or so it seems). On the other hand, it takes a fairly sizable personal investment to buy and use the equipment to take advantage of the Internet and the World Wide Web and because the number of suppliers of information seems to be contracting in a manner suggesting an information monopoly. See Herbert Schiller, *Information Inequality: The Deepening Social Crisis in America* (New York: Routledge, 1996).

17. Su-Shing Chen, "The Paradox of Digital Preservation," *Computer* 34 (March 2001): 24.

18. T. R. Schellenberg, *The Management of Archives* (New York: Columbia University Press, 1965).

19. See Jack Goody, *The Logic of Writing and the Organization of Society* (Cambridge: Cambridge University Press, 1986).

20. Consider, for example, Christopher T. Baer, "Strategy, Structure, Detail, Function: Four Parameters for the Appraisal of Business Records," in James M. O'Toole, *The Records of American Business* (Chicago: Society of American Archivists, 1997), 75–135. Baer takes on the archival theorists directly, stating that "to attempt to fit the records of modern business into the world of theory as derived from traditional European archives is rather like being asked to shoehorn an automobile assembly line or particle accelerator into the Orangerie at Versailles" (117–118). Baer complains about being asked to follow a "simple catechism," and he argues for working it out in companies themselves. He believes it "all comes together in the expertise and experience of the archivist. This kind of expertise can only be acquired by doing, and experience can only be built through collaborative work, not pedagogy" (120). Baer continues:

> As a professional, the practicing archivist is like the lawyer or engineer, not a scientist who searches for abstract truths or constructs holistic frames of reference . . . but a technologist who must occasionally work in the absence of or in advance of theory and who must use a variety of tools to produce a useful product in response to conflicting and often irreconcilable demands. (121)

However, lawyers, engineers, and technologists work with principles and are strategic in how they work—all that constituting a focus on evidence or records (they are really one and the same).

21. I have tried to describe the nature of the debates and controversies in my *American Archival Analysis: The Recent Development of the Archival Profes-*

sion in the United States (Metuchen, N.J.: Scarecrow Press, 1990) and *Closing an Era: Historical Perspectives on Modern Archives and Records Management* (Westport, Conn: Greenwood Press, 2000).

22. You can find this on the website of the Australian Society of Archivists at http://www.archivists.org.au.

23. Laurel Thatcher Ulrich, *A Midwife's Tale: The Life of Martha Ballard, Based on Her Diary, 1785–1812* (New York: Vintage Books, 1990), 8.

24. Society of American Archivists, *Planning for the Archival Profession* (Chicago: Society of American Archivists, 1986), 8.

25. Elizabeth Kaplan, "Practicing Archives with a Postmodern Perspective," paper presented to "Archives, Documentation, and the Institution of Social Memory," University of Michigan, January 2001, and Helen W. Samuels, "Drinking from the Fire Hose: Documenting Education at MIT," *Archives and Manuscripts* 25 (May 1997): 36–49.

26. For a sampling of views about information, see Phil Agre, "The End of Information & the Future of Libraries," *Progressive Librarian* (1997) at http://www.libr.org/PL/12–13_Agre.html and "Institutional Circuitry: Thinking about the Forms and Uses of Information," *Information Technology and Libraries* 14, no. 4 (1995): 225–230 (also at http://dlis.gseis.ucla.edu/people/pagre/circuitry.html); Michael Buckland, *Information and Information Systems* (New York: Praeger, 1991), chapters one and two, and three online articles by Buckland: "Information as Thing," a preprint of an article published in the *Journal of the American Society of Information Science* 42:5 (June 1991): 351–360 (similar discussion occurs in the author's *Information and Information Systems*) and available at http://www.sims.berkeley.edu/~buckland/thing.html; "What Is A Document?" a preprint of an article published in the *Journal of the American Society of Information Science* 48, no. 9 (Sept. 1997): 804–809 and available at http://www.sims.berkeley.edu/~buckland/whatdoc.html; and "What Is a Digital Document?" a preprint of an article published in *Document Numérique* (Paris) 2, no. 2 (1998): 221–230 and available at http://www.sims.berkeley.edu/~buckland/digdoc.html; Norman D. Stevens, "The History of Information," *Advances in Librarianship*, ed. Wesley Simonton (New York: Academic Press, Inc., 1986), 14: 1–48; Noriko Kando, "Information Concepts Reexamined," *International Forum on Information and Documentation* 19, no. 2 (1994): 20–24; Joseph Nitecki, "The Concept of Information-Knowledge Continuum: Implications for Librarianship," *Journal of Library History, Philosophy and Comparative Librarianship* 20 (Fall 1985): 387–407; Erhard Oeser, "Information Superhighways for Knowledge Transfer and the Need for a Fundamental Theory of Information," *International Forum on Information and Documentation* 20, no. 1 (1995): 16–21; Zhang Yuexiao, "Definitions and Sciences of Information," *Information Processing & Management* 24, no. 4 (1988): 479–491; David Altheide, "The Culture of Information," *Journal of Education for Library and Information*

Science 31 (Fall 1990): 113–121; Cynthia J. Durance and Hugh Taylor, "Wisdom, Knowledge, Information and Data: Transformation and Convergence in Archives and Libraries of the Western World," *Alexandria* 4, no. 1 (1992): 37–61; and Robert Wright, *Three Scientists and Their Gods: Looking for Meaning in an Age of Information* (New York: Harper and Row, 1988).

27. Francis X. Blouin, Jr., "Archivists, Mediation, and Constructs of Social Memory," *Archival Issues* 24, no. 2 (1999): 110, 111.

28. The ways that records (and archives) make the news can be seen in a volume I coedited with David Wallace, *Archives and the Public Good: Records and Accountability in Modern Society* (Westport, Conn.: Quorum Books, 2002).

29. David Brin, *The Transparent Society: Will Technology Force Us to Choose between Privacy and Freedom?* (Reading, Mass.: Addison-Wesley, 1998).

30. Michel-Rolph Trouillot, *Silencing the Past: Power and the Production of History* (Boston: Beacon Press, 1995).

31. Kimberly Barata, Piers Cain, and Anne Thurston, "Building a Case for Evidence: Research at the International Records Management Trust, Rights and Records Institute," *Records Management Journal* 10, no. 1 (2000): 10.

32. For example, Mark A. Greene and Todd J. Daniels-Howell, "Documentation with an Attitude: A Pragmatist's Guide to the Selection and Acquisition of Modern Business Records," in *The Records of American Business*, ed. James M. O'Toole (Chicago: Society of American Archivists, 1997), 161–229, another defense of the pragmatic, antitheory perspective, uses "curators" partly because of its orientation to manuscript curators but also because of the authors' idea that archival appraisal is subjective and artful rather than driven by precepts and postulates. Obviously, I think we need to hold on to overarching objectives, principles, and the realization that we are not performing in a completely rational environment or carrying out merely a scholarly exercise.

33. Hilde S. Hein, *The Museum in Transition: A Philosophical Perspective* (Washington, D.C.: Smithsonian Institution Press, 2000), 18, 20.

34. T. H. Breen, *Imagining the Past: East Hampton Histories* (Reading, Mass.: Addison-Wesley Publishing Co., Inc., 1989), 14, 38, 39, 150, 191, 212–213, 215, 220.

35. Belleseiles was challenged about the manner in which he used probate and military records and other sources, sending historians scurrying off to check his cited sources.

36. Richard Evans, *Lying about Hitler: History, Holocaust, and the David Irving Trial* (New York: Basic Books, 2001).

37. J. Timothy Sprehe, "The Significance of 'Admissibility of Electronically Filed Federal Records as Evidence,'" *Government Information Quarterly* 9, no. 2 (1992): 153–154 and "Admissibility of Electronically Filed Federal Records as Evidence," *Government Information Quarterly* 9, no. 2 (1992): 155–167.

38. A. Cheree Carlson, "How One Uses Evidence Determines Its Value," *Western Journal of Communication* 58 (Winter 1994): 20.

39. Seamus Ross, *Changing Trains at Wigan: Digital Preservation and the Future of Scholarship*, NPO Preservation Guidance Occasional Papers (London: National Preservation Office, British Library, 2000), 3, available at http://www.bl.uk/services/preservation/occpaper.pdf40. Henry Petroski, *The Pencil: A History of Design and Circumstance* (New York: Alfred A. Knopf, 1990) provides ample evidence of these technologies.

40. Ross, Changing Trains at Wigan, 4.

41. Ross, *Changing Trains at Wigan*, 4.

42. William Matthews, "Preserving e-History for All; Efforts to Capture Web Snapshots Expose e-Records Dilemmas," *Federal Computer Week* 5 March 2001, available at http://fcw.com/fcw/articles/2001/0305/mgt-ehstry-03–05–01.asp.

43. Hans Booms, "Society and the Formation of a Documentary Heritage," *Archivaria* 24 (Summer 1987): 76.

44. Meyer H. Fishbein, "The Evidential Value of Nontextual Records: An Early Precedent," *American Archivist* 45 (Spring 1982): 189–190.

45. Sara J. Piasecki, "Legal Admissibility of Electronic Records as Evidence and Implications for Records Management," *American Archivist* 58 (Winter 1995): 54–64.

46. Robert L. Paddock, "Utilizing E-Mail as Business Records under the Texas Rules of Evidence," *The Review of Litigation* 19 (Winter 2000): 61–70.

47. Fred Warren Bennett, "Federal Rule of Evidence 803(8): The Use of Public Records in Civil and Criminal Cases," *American Journal of Trial Advocacy* 21 (Fall 1997): 229–267.

48. James Cowan, *A Mapmaker's Dream: The Meditations of Fra Mauro, Cartographer to the Court of Venice* (New York: Warner Books, 1996), 91, 132.

49. David M. Levy, "The Universe Is Expanding: Reflections on the Social (and Cosmic) Significance of Documents in a Digital Age," *Bulletin of the American Society for Information Science* (April/May 1999): 18, 19.

50. John Seely Brown and Paul Duguid, *The Social Life of Information* (Boston: Harvard Business School Press, 2000), 188, 189.

51. Philip K. Tompkins, "Principles of Rigor for Assessing Evidence in 'Qualitative' Communication Research," *Western Journal of Communication* 58 (Winter 1994): 46.

52. Kristine L. Fitch, "Criteria for Evidence in Qualitative Research," *Western Journal of Communication* 58 (Winter 1994): 36.

53. Judith Palmer, "Schooling and Skilling Health Librarians for an Evidence-Based Culture," *Advances in Librarianship* 23 (2000): 145–167.

54. Nigel Ford, Dave Miller, Andrew Booth, Alan O'Rourke, Jane Ralph, and Edward Turnock, "Information Retrieval for Evidence-Based Decision Making," *Journal of Documentation* 55 (September 1999): 385–401.

55. Howard Porter Belon, "Combat in the Courtroom: The Battle of the Experts, Reputation Bias, and Perceived Credibility," Ph.D. dissertation, University of Arizona, 1991.

56. Salomon Rettig, *The Discursive Social Psychology of Evidence: Symbolic Construction of Reality* (New York: Plenum Books, 1990).

57. Gary L. Hardcastle, "Accomplishing Translation: The Notion of Evidence in the Discipline of the History of Science," in Marta Feher, Olga Kiss, and Laszlo Ropolyi, *Hermeneutics and Science: Proceedings of the First Conference of the International Society for Hermeneutics and Science* (Dordrecht: Kluwer Academic Publishers, 1999), 117–124.

58. Thomas K. Nakayama, "Continuing the Dialogue of Evidence: Disciplining Evidence," *Western Journal of Communication* 59 (Spring 1995): 171–175. That evidence is a matter of debate within this field, see Stuart J. Sigman, "Question: Evidence of What? Answer: Communication," *Western Journal of Communication* 59 (Winter 1995): 79–84.

59. Kenneth D. Mandl, Peter Szolovits, and Isaac S. Kohane, "Public Standards and Patients' Control: How to Keep Electronic Medical Records Accessible but Private," *BMJ* 322 (3 February 2001): 283–287, available at http://www.bmj.com/cgi/content/full/322/7281/283, accessed 5 February 2001.

60. See my "Declarations, Independence, and Text in the Information Age," *First Monday* 4 (June 1999), available at http://www.firstmonday.dk/issues/issue4_6/rjcox/index.html and James M. O'Toole, "The Symbolic Significance of Archives," *American Archivist* 56 (Spring 1993): 234–255.

61. Reported by Peter Kurilecz to the Archives & Archivists Listserv, 30 January 2001, 13:14:11–0500.

62. George Lipsitz, *Time Passages: Collective Memory and American Popular Culture* (Minneapolis: University of Minnesota Press, 1990), 36.

63. *America's Cultural Capital: Recommendations for Structuring the Federal Role* (Washington, D.C.: Center for Arts and Culture, 2001), 2.

64. *America's Cultural Capital* report identifies the National Archives as one of the "federal cultural agencies" (4), but this is only one of the National Archives' roles (or, at least, it should be only one of the roles).

65. Cited from http://www.4literature.net/Washington_Irving/Author_s_Account_of_Himself, accessed 5 February 2001. This was published as *The Sketch Book of Geoffrey Crayon, Gent.* (1819–20).

66. Paddock, "Utilizing E-Mail as Business Records," 64–65.

67. Terry Cook, "Many are Called but Few Are Chosen: Appraisal Guidelines for Sampling and Selecting Case Files," *Archivaria* 32 (Summer 1991): 26.

68. Timothy L. Ericson, "At the 'rim of creative dissatisfaction': Archivists and Acquisition Development," *Archivaria* 33 (Winter 1991–92): 66–77.

69. Gregory J. E. Rawlins, *Moths to the Flame: The Seductions of Computer Technology* (Cambridge: MIT Press, 1996), 21.

70. Judith Shulevitz, "Academic Warfare," *The New York Times Book Review*, 11 February 2001, 35.

71. See Nigel Ford, Dave Miller, Andrew Booth, Alan O'Rourke, Jane Ralph, and Edward Turnock, "Information Retrieval for Evidence-Based Decision Making," *Journal of Documentation* 55 (September 1999), 395.

72. Jane Jacobs, *Systems of Survival: A Dialogue on the Moral Foundations of Commerce and Politics* (New York: Vintage Books, 1992), 41.

8

Archives and the Digital Future

In a self-help book about organizing our lives, the author likens a cluttered desk to the National Archives, playing on the public's perception of archives as places teeming with old paper records.[1] Information technologists appropriate "archives" or "archiving" for backing up or storing digital files, creating another misleading sense of what archives and archivists do.[2] Meanwhile, many archivists and historians, other researchers such as journalists and genealogists, and public interest and government watchdog groups worry that the archives of the future might be shiny, clean, and burdened with few records (just as some worry about the future of similar institutions, such as libraries).[3] The World Wide Web gobbles up everything; you can view it as *anything*—from an organized library to a dump for miscellaneous debris to the mind of God.[4] But we have never seen a library or an archive like this. The growth of the World Wide Web, with millions of websites and an increasing number of e-journals, demonstrates the volatility of the digital era. A web page's life expectancy ranges from forty-four days to two years, yet the increasing number of e-journals has not brought a commitment by their publishers to develop digital preservation approaches. Archivists now are risk managers, not conservative administrators stabilizing and preserving the documentary heritage.[5] The restless activity, committed to persistent and vast change, of the digerati is a far cry from the conserving activity of archivists or their researchers, such as historians.

And archivists and historians have reason to worry. They do not need to predict future losses because we know we have lost much already (sometimes we are even unable to read computer files of a decade ago). As one archivist writes:

> With hardware and software changing and upgrading almost by the minute, how will a scholar in 2099 read an electronic manuscript written in the 1980s on a Macintosh with a Mac platform version of Microsoft Word 2.0? Ninety-nine point nine percent of PC-based users *today* could not open and read that document on their present personal computers.[6]

As a result, some worry that archives will be a place at all, and given the persistent view of the cyber world as an improved version of reality, it is not difficult to imagine why such concerns manifest themselves.[7] An article in *The Guardian* not too long ago reported that a digitized effort to collect data about English life in 1986, celebrating the 900th anniversary of the Domesday Book, was no longer readable. This revelation prompted considerable speculation about the durability of the digital record, with some expressing confidence that the data would be recovered and others stressing the difference between the stability of the old manuscript and that of the fickle digital source.[8] Now we have books such as *Dark Ages II: When the Digital Data Die*,[9] when only a little more than a decade ago some records experts argued that paper was *not* as durable as the digital media.[10] For those of us invested in preserving the documentary heritage, whether as custodians or users, this is not always the happiest of times. Amid such worries, archival stereotypes surface, as when a newspaper article about the Internet Archive suggests that "archive" "conjures up the image of a storeroom of valuable but incomplete, unindexed materials stuffed in boxes."[11] This stereotype is why some self-help books use the archival image negatively. Perhaps some really wish that archives, as they understand them, might disappear, while archivists or historians haven't reached a consensus about what to do in the face of the digital deluge. Views range from the new digital systems' transforming everything to transforming nothing, from their allowing everything to be saved to destroying all.[12]

Some historians may not worry about such matters because, as Michael Stanford notes, "Most historical work . . . is done on an empirical and *ad hoc* basis," even though the historian is aware that not all evidence of the past has survived and that what has survived needs to be analyzed carefully.[13] In fact, archivists have been grappling with the stresses and strains produced by new technologies for a long time. Many archivists recognize that these technologies are evolving at a rapid rate, and we acknowledge that many of our principles and practices date from earlier eras and that all records are the product of technology (whether it be a pencil and paper or a handheld computer) as well as economics, culture, and politics. Twenty years ago, when the nature of electronic records began to cause deep concern, it seemed that these technologies and the records created by and residing in these technologies were being broken apart in unnatural ways, and the first alarms were sounded.[14]

Records and record-keeping systems have always been connected with technology, and the technologies do not have to be very sophisticated (think of credit cards). Pencil, paper, and carbon paper have had substantial impact on how records are created and maintained,[15] suggesting that archivists and historians need to study and understand these record-keeping systems and their implications. Other technologies, such as electronic mail, have posed greater theoretical and technical challenges, most of which have not been resolved by practical solutions and some of which have even led to legal actions testing the assumptions of archival principles, practices, and consequences, including why and for whom such records are saved.[16] What might be different is the degree to which archivists and some historians now worry about the digital technologies and the threats to traditional principles, practices, and mission.[17]

Some historians might not have worried about such matters because they don't fully realize that others have a hand in shaping or determining the records left behind to document events. Historian Michael Stanford notes that even with the massive quantity of surviving documentation, "It frequently comes as an unpleasant surprise to researchers to find how little of it is relevant to their immediate purpose." Stanford and many other historians know that "it is often a matter of chance which documents survive."[18] It could be that many of the users of archives approach the manner in which these records are gathered in much the same fashion as they consider the increasing presence of computers in their life, as another invisible tool or process they need not think much about.

Historians, along with other researchers, mine what is available in archives. Some historians resent the notion that archivists have had a hand in determining what goes into an archive, preferring, one assumes, some sort of metaphysical or magical process whereby no one or no entity is responsible.[19] What these historians and other researchers do not understand about how records come into archives would shock many of them. The divisions between such professionals as archivists, records managers, information resource managers, and others have caused some major difficulties in identifying records from government, corporations, and other organizations, often not providing many opportunities for archivists to have a substantial stake in determining records that should be in archives.[20] Historians and other scholars such as anthropologists and sociologists are writing interesting books with substantial insights into the nature and function of records, but it is the archivist who will have the most profound impact on what survives.[21]

THE LEGACY OF ARCHIVISTS AND ELECTRONIC RECORDS MANAGEMENT

Since the 1960s archivists and records managers have worked with electronic records in an ad hoc manner, often trying to develop practical or stopgap solutions in particular organizational contexts. Over the past decade, archivists have done more systematic research and theoretical or conceptual musing about electronic records management, but they remain somewhat uncertain about what the digital future means. Many archives and historical records repositories remain without the technical or financial resources to cope with digital documents, and they cannot rely on the national and larger repositories to take responsibility for such records. Nearly every aspect of society is either aggressively using or heavily dependent on the new technologies and, we might add, generating more records than ever.

The records are different. The ability to change continuously a document is the computer's strength, but continuous change of records has never been the purpose of archives, nor is it exactly what researchers, especially historians, might desire.[22] The technology's potential for this sort of fluidity is what often generates opposition to it[23] since we must be able to seize and freeze the record. Indeed, the problem with information technologies is not isolated to issues in the archives or history communities but is endemic to all aspects of our modern technology era. Sociologist Manuel Castells argues that the:

> speed of transformation has made it difficult for scholarly research to follow the pace of change with an adequate supply of empirical studies on the whys and wherefores of the Internet-based economy and society. Taking advantage of this relative void of reliable investigation, ideology and gossip have permeated the understanding of this fundamental dimension of our lives, as is often the case in periods of rapid social change.[24]

For historians and other researchers using records, the problem is more profound. Even carefully reasoned efforts to consider the consequences of emerging information technologies, balancing technocrats' claims with long-term views and experiences, tend to miss or dismiss any discussion of whether the digital technologies will enable information and evidence to be preserved.[25] Some argue that our fears about the digital future are no different from the way we have viewed "every new medium . . . , as both the ultimate in mass communication and a threat to world social stability."[26] This possibly explains why some researchers merely use what they can find in the archives and are glad for what exists.

FALSE HOPES?

In this ideology and gossip, borrowing Castells's characterization of matters, is the promise that somehow the information professions are converging, that this convergence will lead to the technical solutions needed, and that the present concerns about the digital future will be resolved in the natural evolution of things. The convergence apologists focus on technology at the expense of other issues, such as disciplinary knowledge, creating an overspecialization with a loss of perspective of the political, financial, legal, and social dimensions surrounding these disciplines.[27] Implicit in this convergence is that we come to know *everything*, certainly not a model I see as being practical.

In this convergence model is the notion that every records professional must be computer literate, but the model ignores the need for
literacy about records and record-keeping systems. In the changing
content of job advertisements for archivists in recent years, little evidence surfaces either of convergence of this profession with closely
related disciplines or of a demand for robust technology literacy.
Many historians worry that archivists are no longer trained as historians, but the greater problem is educating archivists to understand
the records for which they assume responsibility. Computer literacy
means little if it is not applied to organizational and societal contexts
because records technologies can never be separated from what
drives them to be created and used in the first place.[28] Yet we need
to wonder whether archivists, in creating particular courses, workshops, or institutes to solve particular problems, are not restricting
the education of archivists to training (learning short-term skills) or
apprenticeship (learning the particulars of work at a single work-
place). Archivists need to possess knowledge about records, and
this requires scholarship incorporating their own discipline and
including a historical sensibility.

Archivists and their allies need to be realistic. All the technical
expertise in the world won't resolve most of the challenges posed by
the digital stuff because what will be used and what will win out
over competitors depends on a complex set of factors. Judging from
the experiences of the radio, television, and Internet industries, it is
just as likely that archivists will need to hone their abilities as advocates, work with technical experts for standards, learn the needs and
desires of researchers and other groups (like schoolteachers) interested in archival records, and develop workable policies that political powers will be willing to adopt.[29] Archivists are little different
from many others in that when they look out over the technological
future, they sometimes see only unbridled, expensive change and
their own nearly empty coffers. But there could be hope. Virginia
Postrel notes, "Technocrats are 'for the future,' but only if someone
is in charge of making it turn out according to plan. They greet every
new idea with a 'yes, but,' followed by legislation, regulation, and
litigation."[30] Archivists can certainly learn to participate in, and
become experts at, such processes—meaning they can at least operate in the same dimension as the technocrats and produce policies
and procedures protecting the archival heritage. And here they
intersect with historians in that realm called public history, where

historical knowledge is linked to public policy; more often than not these days, archivists see records and their importance debated in the policy forum (whereas in the past archivists were more comfortable in seeing their records discussed at historical and other professional conferences).

The primary attribute still present in archives position advertisements is experience, followed by computer applications knowledge or general computer literacy. Little is in the advertisements about working with records and record-keeping systems and few statements suggest that archivists be experts in record keeping; the references to computers mostly relate to the use of computers in managing archives rather than in working with digitally born records systems. Although society needs records and record-keeping experts—transcending technology, organizational type, or institutional mission—the job advertisements suggest that the archival field has been too static. Given the volatility of digital records, I find this surprising and dismaying.

It is easy to paint bleak futuristic portraits of a society *without* records, primarily because such speculations, no matter how wrong, seem not to be held against those making them. Such dire predictions also make for more dramatic stories by journalists and societal commentators, attracting attention and creating controversy. Making such predictions requires a deterministic view of the technologies, ignoring the impact of multiculturalism, political correctness, civil unrest, and other trends pulling us apart no matter what the supposed communal technologies may be doing for us.[31] These technologies might make us feel involved, but are we really connected? We have been dealing with the World Wide Web for only a decade, so predications about it are premature. And we should note that we are still debating the impact of the printing press on society half a millennium after the advent of printing.[32] Archivists know that record-keeping systems, even those possessing clear societal benefits, often required decades to mature and be accepted, and sometimes they were never fully realized. Today's technologies could enhance the creation, use, and maintenance of record-keeping systems, but despite all the hype about the Information Age, media and public attention seem more fixated on laments about the fate of print and paper than about the challenges of preserving the digital.[33] Obviously, the sensitivity of the historian to the long view should be an essential part of the archivist's arsenal.

Even archivists are not immune from a kind of technological euphoria greeting the users of modern digital technologies. Archivists are creating websites and digitizing holdings and guides to their holdings for the Web as quickly as possible, hoping that the presence of archives on the Web can crystallize the public's understanding of their importance, increase use, target new researcher constituencies, and increase support. But are archivists studying themselves and their users, especially to understand the nature of modern cyberculture and its implications for the record?

One of the attributes archivists and historians both should bring to the present information age is the ability to look at the bigger picture, to understand whether newer records forms are really new or merely extensions of traditional records. In educating future archivists, we are preparing the individuals who will be responsible for the future historical record that historians and other researchers will use. This task raises many questions about what we presently know about maintaining electronic records, the knowledge archivists must possess to administer all records, who archivists are accountable to, and the need for the students to learn not just about the technical issues in electronic records but about the cultural issues and public perceptions that influence how archivists work.

Reality needs to be examined. The digital media can be managed within archival programs, but the technical challenges are often the least daunting of the concerns faced by the archivist. As one Canadian archivist suggests, individual donors might be reluctant to allow the archivist to take their records because so much of a personal or private nature has been captured by their personal computers, with e-mail and financial records.[34] We can allow our minds to drift to corporations, in the wake of recent scandals, and imagine how sensitive they might be to archivists, archives, and researchers. Under these circumstances, technical issues are hardly the most pressing concern.

BACK TO THE RECORD

Records, apart from whatever technologies are used to create and maintain them, are the result of policies, regulations, legal requirements, professional best practices, and traditions (what some term the "warrant" for record keeping). This is true for both personal and organizational records. Although some archivists and researchers might think of any documentary fragment as having potential value, this belief should hardly be the compelling reason for their work. A focus on the reasons records are created shifts archivists' attention from looking through closets for old files to becoming experts on the reasons records should be managed, and it also shifts records managers from running records warehouses to working throughout their institution (and society) for an understanding of the reasons records need to be carefully managed.

Archivists have been sidetracked sometimes by issues of whether records should be managed for cultural or administrative (or other) reasons, which is only an interesting rather than a very crucial issue for debate. The real point is that records are important, necessitate study and understanding, and require sophisticated approaches for their management. A democratic society fails without records documenting the work of government and ensuring the accountability of government to its citizens, even if a few precious symbolic records sit safely on display in the nation's capital. Such a society also fails if it cannot promote the accountability of other crucial organizations, such as corporations, and the evidence is that archivists have not done well convincing capitalists why their archival records are important. We lack adequate business archives, and we notice the severance of corporate records management and archives administration, but many archivists still believe in collecting business records (an impossible task in my opinion) rather than encouraging the creation of institutional archives. A poor foundation for business archives was built long before the challenges of computers, as the recent scandal about the destruction of Enron's records reveals. In a democratic state, it is not just citizens' access to greater amounts of information but to have access to the *right* information that holds government accountable to them.

It is harder, of course, to develop workable solutions for solving the problems or for taking advantage of the new digital documentary universe, primarily because this requires real work and results. Some simply point to the incongruities of the promises and realities of the Information Age, even questioning whether we can term this an age focused on information. We have had a few historical analyses of differing "information" ages,[35] but these have been buried under polemics about the promises and perils of the present information era, many of them maintaining that all anyone needs to be a good citizen is more information.[36] Some historians of and commentators on the modern "information" era note that it is difficult to gain a sense of what the age is about because information is itself so difficult to define.[37] Others worry about the increasing dependency on computers in all aspects of our culture.[38]

If we take the direst perspective, that at present we might be producing *and losing* more information than ever before, it is hard to be so glib in terming this the Information Age. Computer scientist Mark Stefnik mused a few years ago that the "real problem with the information explosion is that it presents us with two dilemmas: being overwhelmed by useless information and having difficulty finding quickly the specific information we need."[39] Then there is our widespread ignorance of the past (although many scholars of public memory argue that the people have a feel for, if not knowledge of, history). The cold technology of electronic bits and bytes, magnetic tapes, and chips and video display terminals might seem to rob us of this ability to sense the past. We have carried about with us, for at least a century, briefcases and bags full of records related to our work, personal lives, and families—all long before dependence on the computer. Although we can romanticize documents such as personal checks as an "unwitting diary,"[40] is it just *more* information that merits calling the present the Information Age?

There might be many positive aspects of the technological challenges of modern documents. If archivists and their researchers can move beyond the fear of the technological threats to records, they might discover new advantages for their work and for understanding the documents they are responsible for. A museum curator, Steven Lubar, argues that electronic records make us more aware of aspects of record keeping we have always been concerned with (similar to the way museum curators have viewed the objects in their care). Now, Lubar says, we can understand that:

> Documents—archives—are sites of cultural production. That means they are centers of power. Archives, and the records of archival use, can tell us about the relationship between makers and users, and the culture that weaves them together. They illuminate social practice. Archives themselves are texts to be interpreted.

Technology, its acquisition and use, *is* about power—and many archivists have traditionally seen themselves as lacking the resources (power) to deal with our present digital technologies. But records, including those accumulated in archives, are also about power:

> Archives reflect and reinforce the power relationships of the institution that organizes them; they represent not just a technological solution, but also an organizational solution. They document and carry out not only knowledge and technique, but also culture and power.[41]

Power and memory have become hallmarks of analysis of our modern society.

A POSTMODERN TWIST?

One might wonder why anyone, even historians, would worry about the loss of records given the prevailing postmodern sensibilities seeming to accept all texts (anything that can be read) as equally valid. One of the frustrating aspects of postmodernism is, of course, how slippery it is to define as it conjures up relativism, the end of history, the equality of all cultural ventures despite merit or significance, and the loss of meaning. The World Wide Web also encourages a focus on trivia and quick results and seems postmodern in its sensibilities, encouraging little more than nostalgia by the public rather than understanding of the past.

In an insightful discussion about the appropriation of the word "archives" by the new information technicians, Lilly Koltun says:

> These digital data banks are not archives that have to do with the past, preserved like memories, succeeding upon done deeds and finished thoughts; these are archives whose future preservation is defined before they come into existence. They are not archives subject to selection, but to creation. Because digital data can be so ephemeral and technologically dependent, they must be saved, if at all, at the moment of creation, or be lost.

Koltun ascribes this difference to the:

> postmodern condition, to chase memory before experience, to focus not on the was, but on the proliferating might be, to rebut teleology, to see life not as pieced and stitched into an ordered, determinable, and

necessary whole, but as unavoidably porous and multiple, subject to particularized, decentred individual perspectives, meshed in continually and rapidly diversifying, never finally coalescing, always contesting discourses.[42]

Some archivists have tried to make digital records be like other records, by printing them onto paper and filing them into archives boxes and stacks (just as they handled fax documents in the 1980s).[43] Now, archivists are gearing up to manage electronic records in electronic form rather than printing them out on paper because there could be loss of evidential status, excessive costs, a weakening of the context of records creation, and improvements in searching for records, even though these digital forms also risk loss through a lack of readability, tampering, and other problems.[44]

Archivists need to help others, including historians, understand the dynamics of the *truth* in records.[45] Electronic record-keeping systems make it easier to dispose of records when they are not wanted, but just what criteria will be used to guide the decisions about disposal? Of course, if *any* records will do, why bother to ask such questions? And, in fact, some wonder if the modern version of information doesn't simply encourage random or fragmentary collecting of stuff, a process not likely to satisfy the scholar studying systematically.[46]

Despite all the theoretical posturing about the nature of historical knowledge or truth, whether we can truly capture a sense of the past or anything approaching the truth about the past, the record still looms large in the path of the historian. A quarter of a century ago oral historian Paul Thompson reminded his colleagues that archives are not "innocent deposits" and that "it is always necessary to consider how a piece of evidence was put together in the first place."[47] Thompson was seeking to legitimize the oral historian and oral source more than to speculate about the ways archives have been formed, but his principle remains crucial (and a suitable phrase for the way archivists perceive appraisal, and, hence, a good title for a book like this). Others have seen that despite seemingly vast chasms between postmodernists and others, there still seems to be a concern to examine evidence even if it goes far beyond archives.[48]

I am not thinking about a fetishistic fascination with old documents, whereby we need to stroke, hug, and bond with original documents (for which we have substantial historical precedent),[49] but I am concerned with the use of records appropriate to the nature and need of the researcher. It might be that we sometimes need originals. One historian says we must come "face to face" with records and "must hold the original document . . . , look at the paper, and smell everything" in order to determine its intent and genuineness.[50] But in the case of digital records, the nature of an original record becomes very problematic. A literary historian believes that literary scholars will come back to archives because they:

> require more than manuscripts; they require notebooks, drafts, revisions, proofs, first editions, presentation and inscribed copies, cancellations of titles, dedications, epigraphs, lines; they want letters, envelopes, postmarks, diaries, clippings books, journals, memoirs, photographs, tapes, dictaphone cylinders (and machines that play them); they require the author's changing choice of paper, the watermarks, addresses, dates; bookplates, variant bindings, every crumbling newspaper file.[51]

What this scholar does not consider, of course, is that the writer of today and certainly of tomorrow might not create many, if any, of these sources. This scholar also ignores that the digital documents and new digital sources might provide deeper understandings into the writing experience. What happens with the supposed emotional power of old documents when we come face to face with old electronic records? Is old now measured in weeks and months? Can the digital record take on symbolic value, albeit a very different one, just as other documents have achieved?

What first attracted me to archives was an interest in history and a fascination with old documents and the material remains of the past. My interests since then have diversified considerably, but I still love to interact with the objects of the past and to visit historic sites. I became fascinated with why certain things survived and others did not, asking questions about why things like records come to be and why some belong in an archives. I wasn't challenged about such matters when I became an archivist in late 1972 because there was little evidence of computers in archives or in producing records that might come into archives. Even when I started teaching in 1988 and became a regular user of e-mail, for most archivists electronic records were a rarity. Within a few years, all this changed for archivists as electronic records and record-keeping systems threatened to absorb all else.

In the present, made more complicated by the way all its technologies can trivialize information, evidence, facts, or truth, we have to ask just what document or record we are seeking to preserve. Many of the information gurus are expanding the concept, reconceptualizing the way we approach the evidence of the past.[52] For those historians who still relish their role as time detectives, the challenges of sorting out the various aspects of documentary remains will be energizing. Historian Richard Evans likes the "basic Rankean spadework of investigating the provenance of documents, of inquiring about the motives of those who wrote them, the circumstances in which they were written, and the ways in which they relate to other documents on the same subject."[53] Others have even predicted the rise of a class of "electronic archaeologists,"[54] but I think we need to be more sensible, even if less romantic, by reequipping archivists to manage electronic records systems by being involved in their design and implementation. Perhaps archivists, aided by historians, will need to build within these new systems the symbolic, intrinsic value they desire.

THE RECORD IS THE REAL THING

Institutional worries about maintaining web pages as a record of the organization or supporting new records or access to other records are certainly something archivists and their colleagues need to work on. Will the World Wide Web obliterate the "record?" Despite Marshall McLuhan, we know that many information technologies exist side by side, and it might be that the Internet will exist concurrently with the traditional book and record, much as the ancient Greeks relied on both orality and writing or moderns depend on radio, television, the newspaper, and the Internet.[55] For a brief while, many archivists thought that the digital records were limited to large business organizations and governments, but personal records are affected by these technologies as well.[56]

The fact is, records are tightly intertwined with organizational structures, records-generating technologies, and a maze of cultural, social, economic, and other aspects of life, requiring archivists and historians not just to focus on quick-fix solutions but to be engaged in scholarship and public relations. Although records within a bureaucracy might be mostly the result of power issues, for the careful archivist or researcher, that factor is only one aspect of understanding how records systems developed and why they need to be evaluated.[57]

EDUCATING REAL ARCHIVISTS
FOR THE REAL WORLD

Many archives and archivists look to graduate education programs with a somewhat unrealistic expectation that their graduates will have all the answers to their technical problems and challenges, ignoring of course that in many cases we can teach only the successful solutions archival programs have instituted thus far. Sometimes archival educators have been unimaginative in how and what they teach. Not more than a decade ago, I did a modest survey of how archival education programs were dealing with the history of record keeping and archival administration. Most were ignoring the topic, for reasons ranging from other priorities in the few courses offered to poor readings on the topic. For a while, historical topics were also crowded out of library and information science programs,[58] programs now the home of the strongest graduate archival education offerings.

One would think that a program asking students to examine the history of records making and administration would mesh nicely with library education because one could focus on the book and information and information systems, but in some of these schools, one has a difficult time finding anything concerning a book. Examining the history of the record can tell us much about the relationship of technologies to records systems and help us to understand whether the radically different, faster-changing technologies of today really will challenge the concept of a record or assign to oblivion the notion of archives. We have lived through the endless wrong predictions of the "paperless" office,[59] but one wonders whether we have learned anything at all about predictions versus reality.

Just a decade ago, it was difficult to find graduate courses on electronic records management in North America, most programs offering instead a potpourri of lectures, readings, and field trips, making one wonder whether individuals entering the field brought much for ensuring a digital future. Relying on only introductory courses, crammed with other important topics and issues, is problematic.

Adding institutes, workshops, and other forms of continuing education offerings might help experienced archivists refresh their skills and knowledge, but just how comprehensive or practical this approach has been is unknown.

Graduate archival education is a relatively recent development in North America, for a long time being a combination of apprenticeship and training, focusing on basic skills and knowledge of history (although what historical knowledge really meant was never very clear). Archivists and others incessantly debated *where* the education of archivists should occur, while we were actually mostly involved in training—imparting basic skills and molding attitudes rather than orienting students to a body of knowledge necessary for practicing.[60]

These debates reduced the attention paid to nurturing archival knowledge. Practice is important, but it is only useful if it is expanded into principles and processes that can be replicated, analyzed, and refined to keep pace with changing record-keeping technologies.[61] And the education of professionals brings an additional problem for archivists because of the lack of dedicated electronic records management programs. Teaching requires you to pull apart practice and to break it down into its most elemental aspects. As one spends years teaching, reading, talking with archivists and other records professionals, and just thinking about what is involved in something as straightforward as archival administration, one's ideas and focus change. My own sense of aspects as fundamental as what a record is and what the mission of the archivist or archives are have been transformed, partly because of the changing technologies.

The primary change has been my growing conviction that archivists must be scholars of record keeping, understanding what a record is, what makes a record an archival record, what the history and organizational context of record-keeping systems has been, and what constitutes the social, cultural, and other importance of such records. And we are seeing better efforts at articulating professional missions, such as this one from the Australian Society of Archivists:

> Archivists ensure that records which have value as authentic evidence of administrative, corporate, cultural and intellectual activity are made, kept and used. The work of archivists is vital for ensuring organizational efficiency and accountability and for supporting understandings of Australian life through the management and retention of its personal, corporate and social memory.[62]

The old debates need to be dismissed and replaced by new debates about the substance of archival knowledge, made more complicated by the numerous discussions by different groups, all with competing interests and agendas, about what they expect from archivists. Corporations, governments, and cultural agencies all seem to have different perspectives about this. The key to understanding records and their information or evidence is dependent not on what some actual or prospective researcher wants, but on the purposes records serve within organizations and for the individuals creating them.

I thought that the strengthening alliance between library and information science schools and the archival profession had the potential to resolve some of the most vexing technical issues in the long-term maintenance of digital objects, but I am no longer sure about this. Although archivists (and some historians) have a greater presence in these schools, I am not sure there has been sufficient cross-fertilization of ideas between archivists and information scientists. We have had predictions about the demise not only of archives but of archivists, and there are historical precedents for dire outcome. More than three centuries ago, a Dutch notary living in New Netherland struggled for existence after the English takeover, taking his own life in 1686.[63] Although I am certainly not suicidal, many archivists and users of archives have despaired about the dramatically different records cultures represented by the new and emerging technologies. We can mull over the advantages of being able to access millions of archival documents over the Web, but this experience is remarkably different than going *into* archives, working *with* archivists, and examining physical documents stored in boxes and folders. Many archivists will now spend more time working with software engineers, technicians, policy personnel, lawyers, and administrators than they will with records!

This is at the heart of what we do now. The Cornell University preservation experts suggest three approaches when considering the challenges of Web preservation: "collaborating with publishers to preserve licensed content, developing policies and guidelines for creating and maintaining Websites, and assuming archival custody for Web resources of interest."[64] These approaches are very different from those of earlier eras, when preservation was generally equated with *physical* custody by an archives. At the heart of all these approaches is the ability of archivists and their colleagues to convey their mission and to be conversant with information scientists and technicians, recognizing that the challenges are difficult, that the solutions require major cooperative efforts extending beyond the archival realm, and, perhaps, that we need to abandon "long-term solutions" in favor of "solutions that will carry us twenty or even just ten years forward, during which time new technologies will surely come to our and our successors' aid."[65]

Even such strategic aims require archivists' and historians' abilities to communicate what they represent. The problems of relating archives to modern information systems are paralleled in linguistics. We know that someone learning a language generally learns a very simplified form at first. Archivists learning about the technical side of computer or information science also will learn a simplified version, one without the intricacies or nuances of those immersed in these schemes, coming across to the experts as possessing only a rudimentary language. We also know that one of the reasons people abandon their traditional language is the desire to fit in with the dominant society and to gain resources that might not otherwise be available to them. Likewise, archivists might be seen as abandoning some of their language and the norms of their work in order to fit in with the dominant Information Age culture, thereby creating some problems with society's understanding of archives. Even the process of preserving languages has a message for us, as those who comment on it often note that doing so will require changes in the global economy and the political balance of power.[66] Archivists, too, must wonder if the hope of preserving the new digital documents won't be seen as requiring them to deal with the political and economic forces of the global technocracy that has a greater investment in making profits from short-term technological advances (ones that are often flawed) than in providing any solutions to the fixity of digital documents.

DIMINISHING THE DIGITAL DOMAIN

The main question about archivists and electronic records might have more to do with appraisal than with the technical aspects of long-term maintenance. The continuing stress on the Information Age has blurred many issues with promises of unlimited memory, but I simply do not believe that the technical feasibility of long-term storage solves anything. We could call this the Memory Age based on the burgeoning scholarship on public memory and the incessant claims made about the possibilities of either saving or losing everything in our computers. Rapidly decreasing costs for computer memory storage and increased capabilities of hardware and software might just neutralize each other, but how and when we figure this out might be a crucial problem.

Archivists need to have strategies for identifying what records should be kept, not only because there are too many records to keep, but because there are too many records to analyze. Archivists must make choices, just as historians and other researchers make choices about what records to examine and to use for evidence. The technical nature of modern organizational record-keeping systems could lead to different ways of keeping and accessing these records, but the digital era is not bringing any magical solutions. Recent reflections on archival appraisal have provided a stronger sense of how appraisal is fraught with controversies and challenges encompassing the social and political issues and agendas of modern society.[67] But the links to the way society works could be tenuous, as many archivists have seemed more committed to collecting everything than to building arguments for institutional archives that can meet the purposes of the records creators and be more relevant to the societal and organizational needs for information, evidence, accountability, and corporate memory.

Collecting everything, neglecting our particular mission, and compounding the problem with separation from records managers and similar professionals has contributed to an unnatural splintering of records' essential elements—their warrant, structure, content, and context—in order to use information instead of what we really need, which is the evidence from the information. Archivists need to cease thinking of records as only grist for the historian's mill and make, instead, new arguments in favor of evidence for the support of the organization's (or individual's) ongoing work. Indeed, attracting creative individuals to the archives and closely related disciplines might be more important than any other activity we can do in ensuring that we have a digital future.[68]

The onslaught of the digital documentary universe must bring with it not merely technical solutions but new appraisal approaches. Electronic record-keeping systems pose new problems for archival appraisal, and a few efforts have stretched the limits of traditional approaches.[69] In my teaching, I stress preparing students for understanding the history of records as well as gaining a foundation in the basic archives and records management functions—appraisal, preservation, reference, arrangement and description, public outreach and programs, and management. Throughout the courses, students are introduced to both traditional paper and electronic records issues, but the need to cover a wide array of professional knowledge and practice does not allow for what anyone could describe as a comprehensive introduction to electronic records management. Basic archival and records management functions are always viewed through the broader perspective of records and record-keeping systems, even though at times this approach seems to breed frustration in students desiring a stress on basic methods and practices and even though it could cause suspicion in prospective employers who expect fresh graduates to know everything.

Information technology courses seem like a good idea for increasing the student's technical knowledge, but there are many questions about what the instructors know about archives and records, the applications of information technology in a record-keeping regime, and the rapidly changing technology itself. Just as important is providing budding archivists with a foundation in managerial skills, enabling them to work with other professionals and individuals in organizations to resolve the complicated technical matters affecting records systems. Future archivists need to be immersed first in records and record-keeping systems, then in the technology supporting the development of the newer electronic record-keeping systems.

Thinking about things in this way does change what archivists have been doing. Archivists don't just acquire and describe records for historians; they seek to understand records and to help society to realize why records are essential. I am not just educating people to work in archives; I am educating professionals who might work in other kinds of institutions and positions and shoulder the responsibility of assisting organizations to comprehend what records and record-keeping systems are about.

CONCLUSION

You might surmise that I believe archivists, historians, and society have a digital future, meaning we will find multiple means of preserving digital records. But you might also surmise that I do not believe this task will be easy. It is also a task in which the best archivists and historians must join together to produce solutions (ones that are not merely technical but also strategic, involving a historical comprehension of records and record-keeping systems and the well-honed ability to appraise the crucial records needing to be maintained).

Historian Joseph Ellis, in his brilliant analysis of the American Revolutionary generation, argues that its:

> vanguard members [Jefferson, Adams, Hamilton, Madison, and so forth] . . . developed a keen sense of their historical significance even while they were still making the history on which their reputations would rest. They began posing for posterity, writing letters to us as much as to one another, especially toward the end of their respective careers. If they sometimes look like marble statues, that is how they wanted to look. . . . If they sometimes behave like actors in a historical drama, that is often how they regarded themselves. In a very real sense, we are complicitous in their achievement, since we are the audience for which they were performing; knowing we would be watching helped to keep them on their best behavior.[70]

If Jefferson and his compatriots were alive today and plotting revolution, they would be using e-mail and the World Wide Web, and the issues Ellis identifies about their concern for posterity would be just as present.[71] In his acknowledgments, Ellis thanks the editors and compilers of the published documentary editions of their papers for the "preservation and publication that, thanks to federal and private funding, permit us to recover the story of America's founding in all its messy grandeur."[72] What Ellis does not acknowledge is that a few years ago there was a horrific battle between archivists and historians/documentary editors over federal funding for these documentary editions versus funding for research for preserving electronic records.[73]

What about the present generation of "Jeffersons" preparing their documents digitally? The insensitivity to such issues by one as smart as Joseph Ellis worries me, but it points out the bigger and more realistic challenge we face. Peter Daly, examining the role of information technology in society, writes about how difficult it is to make forecasts because of the "gravitational pull of the past" and the "incredibly complex crosscurrents of history."[74] Then, Daly gets to the heart of our concern here: "Utopian or grandiose visions not withstanding, there seems to be no such thing as a technological solution to complex social problems. . . ."[75] What we need to do is recognize that the preservation of digital records is a major social problem for our age, not one isolated to archivists or the vendors of hardware and software, or a matter of simple nuts and bolts or, in this case, bits and bytes. We have a challenge requiring archivists and historians to join with others to influence public policy. Otherwise, not only do we lose the documents necessary for understanding our past and our society, but we lose holding government, corporations, and other entities accountable to us in the present. Archives and their digital future depend on what we all do in the most profound way, not merely as a technical issue but as a social problem.

NOTES

1. Stephanie Culp, *Conquering the Paper Pile-Up* (Cincinnati: Writer's Digest Books, 1990), 8.
2. These technologists lack an understanding of archives as records of continuing value to an organization and even of the basic concept of a record itself, making it difficult for archivists to communicate effectively with them, especially in designing and implementing organizations' information systems. I played about with this problem in my "Archives as a Multi-Faceted Term in the Information Professions," *Records and Retrieval Report* 11 (March 1995): 1–15.
3. See, for example, Sallie Tisdale, "Silence, Please: The Public Library as Entertainment Center," *Harper's* 294 (March 1997): 65–68, 70, 72–74, in which the author takes exception to the idea that the wired library is a better version of the historic library, fearing the loss of the cultural role of libraries ("a place where the culture is kept, without judgment or censor, a record of life as it was, is, and may be") (73). Traditional terminology for places like libraries tends to be appropriated by new Information Age advocates or entrepreneurs in ways that make it difficult for us to support public understanding. For example, a study on Information Age metaphors reminds us that the "term *library* connotes an institution for collecting knowledge and keeping it in the public trust," but that the Web has a lot of "transient information." "In this way, much of the network is more like a digital bulletin board than a digital library." Mark Stefik, *Internet Dreams: Archetypes, Myths, and Metaphors* (Cambridge, Mass.: MIT Press, 1996), 5, 11.

4. Gordon Graham, *The Internet: A Philosophical Inquiry* (New York: Routledge, 1999).

5. Anne R. Kenney, Nancy Y. McGovern, Peter Botticelli, Richard Entlich, Carl Lagoze, and Sandra Payette, "Preservation Risk Management for Web Resources," *D-Lib Magazine* 8 (January 2002), available at http://www.dlib.org/dlib/january02/Kenney/01Kenney.html. See also Wallace Koehler, "Digital Libraries and World Wide Web Sites and Page Persistence," *Information Research* 4 (June 1999), available at http://informationr.net/ir/4–4/paper60.html.

6. David S. Zeidberg, "The Archival View of Technology: Resources for the Scholar of the Future," *Library Trends* 47 (Spring 1999): 800.

7. For some discussion of this, see William Knoke, *Bold New World: The Essential Road Map to the Twenty-First Century* (New York: Kodansha International, 1996); M. Christine Boyer, *Cybercities: Visual Perception in the Age of Electronic Communication* (Princeton: Princeton Architectural Press, 1996); Stephen Doheny-Farina, *The Wired Neighborhood* (New Haven: Yale University Press, 1996); Steven Johnson, *Interface Culture: How New Technology Transforms the Way We Create and Communicate* (New York: HarperEdge, 1997); and William J. Mitchell, *City of Bits: Space, Place, and the Infobahn* (Cambridge, Mass.: MIT Press, 1995).

8. Robin McKie and Vanessa Thorpe, "Digital Domesday Book Lasts 15 Years Not 1000," *The Observer*, March 3, 2002, accessed at http://www.observer.co.uk/uk_news/story/0,6903,661093,00.html on March 10, 2002.

9. Bryan Bergeron, *Dark Ages II: When the Digital Data Die* (Upper Saddle River, N.J.: Prentice Hall PTR, 2002).

10. Waegemann asserts, "It must be remembered that information stored on paper is much more vulnerable to loss and destruction than documents stored on microfilm, magnetic media, and optical disks. This is particularly true of the active period when records are used in offices, sent to different departments, and handled by a vast range of people" (3). He argues that paper has a lifetime of fifty years. C. Peter Waegemann, "Storing Paper," *Records & Retrieval Report* 3 (September 1987): 1–12.

11. "Archives Keeps Old News Fresh," *Miami Herald*, January 29, 2002, at http://www.miami.com/herald/content/business/digdocs/029014.htm.

12. See my *First Generation of Electronic Records Archivists in the United States: A Study in Professionalization* (New York: Haworth Press, 1994); "Readings in Archives and Electronic Records: Annotated Bibliography and Analysis of the Literature," in *Electronic Records Management Program Strategies*, ed. Margaret Hedstrom (Pittsburgh: Archives and Museum Informatics, 1993), 99–156; "Re-Defining Electronic Records Management," *Records Management Quarterly* 30 (October 1996): 8–13; and "Searching for Authority: Archivists and Electronic Records in the New World at the Fin-de-Siècle," *First Monday* (January 2000), available at http://www.firstmonday

.dk/issues/issue5_1/cox/index.html, for my changing thoughts about this issue.

13. Michael Stanford, *The Nature of Historical Knowledge* (Cambridge, England: Blackwell, 1986), 21.

14. The 1985 *Report* issued by the Committee on the Records of Government, a nonpartisan group created by the American Council of Learned Societies, the Council on Library Resources, and the Social Science Research Council with funding from the Mellon, Rockefeller, and Sloan foundations and the Council on Library Resources, addressed such matters and did so in a manner suggesting the need for extreme urgency. In the same year an archival educator sounded a pessimistic note when he wrote that archivists needed to focus on electronic records management or be "relegated to antiquarian status—the medieval monks of a post-industrial society"; Frederick J. Stielow, "Continuing Education and Information Management: Or, the Monk's Dilemma," *Provenance* 3 (Spring 1985): 13. The urgency continues. CENSA, the Collaborative Electronic Notebook Systems Association, issued a report at the end of December 1999 entitled *Titanic 2020*, calling for urgent action. The report was available at http://www.censa.org/html/publications/Titanic-2020-Final-Report-01–05–2000.pdf. I have tried to discuss the early efforts in electronic records management in my *First Generation of Electronic Records Archivists in the United States.*

15. See, for example, Henry Petroski, *The Pencil: A History of Design and Circumstance* (New York: Alfred A. Knopf, 1990).

16. Susan S. Lukesh, "E-Mail and Potential Loss to Future Archives and Scholarship or The Dog That Didn't Bark," *First Monday* (September 1999) at http://firstmonday.org/issues/issue4_9/lukesh/index.html. Records professionals have tried to resolve many of these problems by setting policies, but as recent media coverage of the Enron/Arthur Andersen scandal suggests, policies are rarely sufficient in the complex world of large bureaucracies. For an example of setting e-mail policies and the problem of such simple-sounding statements such as "Each organization's e-mail policy will reflect its own culture and the legal and regulatory framework within which it operates," see *Guideline for Managing E-mail* (Prairie Village, Kansas: ARMA International, 2000), 3. The most important case in North America remains the so-called PROFS case; see David A. Wallace, "Electronic Records Management Defined by Court Case and Policy," *Information Management Journal* 35 (January 2001): 4–15.

17. See, for example, the concerns of a manuscript curator, Adrian Cunningham, "The Archival Management of Personal Records in Electronic Form: Some Suggestions," *Archives and Manuscripts* 22 (May 1994): 94–105.

18. Stanford, *Nature of Historical Knowledge*, 67, 68.

19. Raymond Smock, "The Nation's Patrimony Should Not Be Sacrificed to Electronic Records," *Chronicle of Higher Education*, February 14, 1997, is

an angry response by a historian criticizing archivists and their priorities and reflecting, I believe, some of the mistrust and misgivings (as well as misunderstandings) historians have in regard to archivists.

20. See, for example, Robert L. Sanders, "Archivists and Records Managers: Another Marriage in Trouble?" *Records Management Quarterly* 23 (April 1989): 12–14, 16–18, 20; Frank B. Evans, "Archivists and Records Managers: Variations on a Theme," *American Archivist* 30 (January 1967): 45–58; and Tyler O. Walters, "Rediscovering the Theoretical Base of Records Management and Its Implications for Graduate Education: Searching for the New School of Information Studies," *Journal of Education for Library and Information Science* 36 (Spring 1995): 139–154. For a good discussion of the implications of the separation of archivists and records managers for electronic records management, see Dan Zelenyj, "*Archivy Ad Portas*: The Archives-Records Management Paradigm Re-Visited in the Electronic Information Age," *Archivaria* 47 (Spring 1999): 66–84.

21. Some of my favorite writings on records from outside the archives discipline include Jack Goody, *The Logic of Writing and the Organization of Society* (London: Cambridge University Press, 1986); Rosalind Thomas, *Literacy and Orality in Ancient Greece* (Cambridge: Cambridge University Press, 1992); M. T. Clanchy, *From Memory to Written Record: England, 1066–1307* (Cambridge, Mass.: Harvard University Press, 1979); JoAnne Yates, *Control through Communication: The Rise of System in American Management* (Baltimore, Md.: Johns Hopkins University Press, 1989); and James R. Beniger, *The Control Revolution: Technological and Economic Origins of the Information Society* (Cambridge, Mass.: Harvard University Press, 1986). Unfortunately, with some exceptions, the knowledge of archivists is often displayed only within the pages of archival journals, publications not commonly read by historians and other scholars and researchers.

22. Steven Johnson, *Interface Culture: How New Technology Transforms the Way We Create and Communicate* (New York: HarperEdge, 1997), 211.

23. Kirkpatrick Sale, *Rebels against the Future: The Luddites and Their War on the Industrial Revolution; Lessons for the Computer Age* (Reading, Mass.: Addison-Wesley, 1995).

24. Manuel Castells, *The Internet Galaxy: Reflections on the Internet, Business, and Society* (Oxford, England: Oxford University Press, 2001), 3.

25. See Evan I. Schwartz, *The Internet Time Log: Anticipating the Long-Term Consequences of the Information Revolution; A Report of the Tenth Annual Aspen Institute Roundtable on Information Technology* (Queenstown, Md.: The Aspen Institute, 2002).

26. Lilly Koltun, "The Promise and Threat of Digital Options in an Archival Age," *Archivaria* 47 (Spring 1999): 116.

27. For an example of how to see the bigger picture, see Henry Petroski, *The Evolution of Useful Things* (New York: Vintage Books, 1992).

28. Langdon Winner, "Look Out for the Luddite Label," *Technology Review* 100 (November/December 1997): 62.

29. A good reading on this is Bruce M. Owen, *The Internet Challenge to Television* (Cambridge, Mass.: Harvard University Press, 1999).

30. Virginia Postrel, *The Future and Its Enemies: The Growing Conflict over Creativity, Enterprise, and Progress* (New York: Touchstone Books, 1998), 16.

31. A good discussion about the anticommunal tendencies can be found in Cass Sunstein, *Republic.com* (Princeton, N.J.: Princeton University Press, 2001). See also Peter H. Daly, *IT's Place in U.S. History: Information Technology as a Shaper of Society* (Cambridge, Mass.: Harvard University, Center for Information Policy Research, April 2002), available at http://pirp.harvard.edu/pubs_pdf/daly/daly-p02-3.pdf.

32. See, for example, the *American Historical Review* forum on "How Revolutionary Was the Print Revolution?" with exchanges between Elizabeth L. Eisenstein and Adrian Johns in the *American Historical Review* 107 (February 2002): 84–128.

33. Marlene Manoff states:

> It is difficult to conclude that there must be a psychological reason for the intensity of the lament for the fate of the print record and the seeming indifference, or at least, lack of concern, for the electronic one. The difference would seem to be about an emotional investment in print and the print record as well as an attachment to the physical artifact in the face of the proliferation of bits and bytes.

Marlene Manoff, "The Symbolic Meaning of Libraries in a Digital Age," *Libraries and the Academy* 1, no. 4 (2000): 378.

34. Lucia Paquet, "Appraisal, Acquisition and Control of Personal Electronic Records: From Myth to Reality," *Archives and Manuscripts* 28, no. 2 (November 2000): 71–91.

35. Michael E. Hobart and Zachary S. Schiffman, *Information Ages: Literacy, Numeracy, and the Computer Revolution* (Baltimore: Johns Hopkins University Press, 1998).

36. Howard Rheingold, *The Virtual Community: Homesteading on the Electronic Frontier* (New York: HarperPerennial, 1993), is a classic expression of this.

37. Paul Levinson, *The Soft Edge: A Natural History and Future of the Information Revolution* (New York: Routledge, 1997), xi.

38. William Wresch, *Disconnected: Haves and Have-Nots in the Information Age* (New Brunswick, N.J.: Rutgers University Press, 1996); Ivars Peterson, *Fatal Defect: Chasing Killer Computer Bugs* (New York: Vintage Books, 1996).

39. Mark Stefnik, *The Internet Edge: Social, Legal, and Technological Challenges for a Networked World* (Cambridge, Mass.: MIT Press, 1999), 108.

40. This essay can be found in Thomas Mallon's *In Fact: Essays on Writers and Writing* (New York: Pantheon Books, 2001).

41. Steven Lubar, "Information Culture and the Archival Record," *American Archivist* 62 (Spring 1999): 16, 21.

42. Koltun, "Promise and Threat of Digital Options," 119, 120.

43. C. Peter Waegemann, "FAX: Document-Based Communication," *Records & Retrieval Report* 5 (March 1989): 1–14.

44. Justine Heazlewood, Jon Dell'Oro, Leon Harari, Brendan Hills, Nick Leask, Ainslie Sefton, Andrew Waugh, and Ross Wilkinson, "Electronic Records: Problem Solved?" *Archives and Manuscripts* 27 (May 1999): 96–113.

45. If we can have historians struggling with truth—such as in Peter N. Stearns, *Meaning over Memory: Recasting the Teaching of Culture and History* (Chapel Hill: University of North Carolina Press, 1993) and Joyce Appleby, Lynn Hunt, and Margaret Jacob, *Telling the Truth about History* (New York: W.W. Norton and Company, 1994)—why not archivists writing about the nature of truth in records?

46. Michael Heim, *The Metaphysics of Virtual Reality* (New York: Oxford University Press, 1993), 10.

47. Paul Thompson, *The Voice of the Past: Oral History* (Oxford, England: Oxford University Press, 1978), 97.

48. Alan Spitzer, *Historical Truth and Lies about the Past : Reflections on Dewey, Dreyfus, de Man and Reagan* (Chapel Hill: University of North Carolina Press, 1996).

49. We have one study on document fetish by Helen Wood, "The Fetish of the Document in The Liverpool University Centre for Archival Studies," *New Directions in Archival Research*, with an entertaining summary by Cathy Alter, "Eat the Document," in *Timothy McSweeney's More Ephemeral Problems*, posted December 14, 1999, and available at http://www.mcsweeneys.net/1999/12/14document.html. A better view has to do with the public perceptions of archivists, some of which are little more than stereotypes and others that reflect things archivists themselves might do, as suggested by David B. Gracy in his "Archivists, You Are What People Think You Keep," *American Archivist* 52 (Winter 1989): 72–78.

50. Deborah A. Symonds, "Living in the Scottish Record Office," in *Reconstructing History: The Emergence of a New Historical Society*, eds. Elizabeth Fox-Genovese and Elisabeth Lasch-Quinn, (New York: Routledge, 1999), 164–175; 165.

51. Ronald Schuchard, "Excavating the Imagination: Archival Research and the Digital Revolution," *Libraries & Culture* 37 (Winter 2002): 59.

52. John Seely Brown and Paul Duguid, *The Social Life of Information* (Boston: Harvard Business School Press, 2000).

53. Richard J. Evans, *In Defense of History* (New York: W. W. Norton and Co., 1999).

54. Sylvan Katz, "A Cache of Ancient Floppy Discs," *New Scientist* 19 (26 December 1992): 70–71.

55. Rosalind Thomas, in her *Literacy and Orality in Ancient Greece* (Cambridge, England: Cambridge University Press, 1992), provides historic evidence for this.

56. Janine Delaney, "Redefining the Role for Collecting Archives in an Electronic Paradigm," *Archifacts* (2000): 13–24.

57. See Thomas Richards, *The Imperial Archive: Knowledge and the Fantasy of Empire* (London: Verso, 1993).

58. See Rollo G. Silver, "The Training of Rare Book Librarians," *Library Trends* 9 (April 1961): 446–452; Ann Bowden, "Training for Rare Book Librarianship," *Journal of Education for Librarianship* 12 (Spring 1972): 223–31; Roderick Cave, "Historical Bibliographical Work: Its Role in Library Education," *Journal of Education for Librarianship* 21 (Fall 1980): 109–21; and Lawrence J. McCrank, *Education for Rare Book Librarianship: A Reexamination of Trends and Problems*, University of Illinois Graduate School of Library Science Occasional Papers no. 144 (April 1980).

59. Abigail J. Sellen and Richard H. R. Harper, *The Myth of the Paperless Office* (Cambridge, Mass.: MIT, 2001).

60. Some key historical writings about archival education can be seen in Robert M. Warner, "Archival Training in the United States and Canada," *American Archivist* 35 (July/October 1972): 347–358; Frank B. Evans, "The Organization and Status of Archival Training: An Historical Perspective," *Archivum* 34 (1988): 75–91; Richard C. Berner, "Archival Education and Training in the United States, 1937 to Present," *Journal of Education for Librarianship* 22 (Summer/Fall 1981): 3–19; Jacqueline Goggin, " 'That We Shall Truly Deserve the Title of Profession': The Training and Education of Archivists, 1930–1960," *American Archivist* 47 (Summer 1984): 243–254. For examples about the need for history in archival education, see the strident essay by Vernon R. Smith, "Pedagogy and Professionalism: An Evaluation of Trends and Choices Confronting Educators in the Archival Community," *Public Historian* 16 (Summer 1994): 23–43, and the more balanced Lawrence J. McCrank, "History, Archives and Information Science," in *Annual Review of Information Science and Technology* 30 (1995): 281–352, the latter describing a "historical information science" that "lies at the intersection of such methodology with modern information technology applied to historical sources, information systems and processes, and communications" (285).

61. Other educators have written about the importance of principles or theory, such as Terry Eastwood, "Nurturing Archival Education in the University," *American Archivist* 51 (Summer 1988): 228–251.

62. Available at http://www.archivists.org.au.

63. Donna Merwick, *Death of a Notary: Conquest and Change in Colonial New York* (Ithaca, New York: Cornell University Press, 1999).

64. Kenney, et al., "Preservation Risk Management for Web Resources."
65. George Mackenzie, "Searching for Solutions: Electronic Problems Worldwide," *Managing Information* 7 (July/August 2000): 65.
66. John H. McWhorter, *The Power of Babel: A Natural History of Language* (New York: W. H. Freeman, 2001), 270, 272, 276.
67. Hans Booms, "Society and the Formation of a Documentary Heritage," *Archivaria* 24 (Summer 1987): 69–107; Hans Booms, "Uberlieferungsbildung: Keeping Archives as a Social and Political Activity," *Archivaria* 33 (Winter 1991–1992): 25–33; F. Gerald Ham, "The Archival Edge," *American Archivist* 38 (January 1975): 5–13; "Archival Strategies for the Post-Custodial Era," *American Archivist* 44 (Summer 1981): 207–216; and "Archival Choices: Managing the Historical Record in an Age of Abundance," in *Archival Choices: Managing the Historical Record in an Age of Abundance*, ed. Nancy E. Peace (Lexington, Mass.: D. C. Heath, 1984), 11–22.
68. Creativity involves understanding a particular domain and seeing new approaches to it. Howard Gardner, *Creating Minds: An Anatomy of Creativity Seen through the Lives of Freud, Einstein, Picasso, Stravinsky, Eliot, Graham, and Gandhi* (New York: Basic Books, 1993).
69. At a research project at the University of Michigan, records being produced by organizations that were distinguished by their networked and collaborative approaches led to "treating records as part of the technical environment or background in which organizations carry out their activities" and seeing records themselves as "actors within an administrative activity." This leads to a focus on "digital memories . . . as entities that can actively affect the range of actions available to any actor, human or non-human, in the system" and an appraisal approach involving two steps:

First . . . , the archivist seeks to appraise the creators of records by examining the values they place on particular types of records and by observing the pattern of events, that is, the routines, whereby they create records. The archivist then uses the information gained from this investigation to locate existing records as well as information sources that might be captured as records. Second, the archivist appraises actual records according to the four characteristics of infrastructure. . . .

whereby records might be "embedded," "transparent," "conventional," or possess "multiple meanings." Peter Botticelli, "Records Appraisal in Network Organizations," *Archivaria* 49 (Spring 2000): 174, 175, 178–179.
70. Joseph J. Ellis, *Founding Brothers: The Revolutionary Generation* (New York: Vintage Books, 2000), 18.
71. I explored this in my "Declarations, Independence, and Text in the Information Age," *First Monday* 4 (June 1999), available at http://www.firstmonday.dk/issues/issue4_6/rjcox/index.html.
72. Ellis, *Founding Brothers*, xi.

73. See my "Messrs. Washington, Jefferson, and Gates: Quarrelling about the Preservation of the Documentary Heritage of the United States," *First Monday* (August 1997), available at http://www.firstmonday.dk/issues/issue2_8/cox/index.html.

74. Daly, *IT's Place in U.S. History*, 5.

75. Daly, *IT's Place in U.S. History*, 38.

9

Appraisal as an
Act of Memory

Archivists have been wrestling with and arguing about appraisal for a very long time, but they are often transacting this debate within their own disciplinary walls (usually played out in professional journals and conferences). There is, of course, no doubt that the conceptual sense of archival appraisal, as reflected in the professional literature, has become much more sophisticated and important, but one can still wonder about the practical meaning of all this self-reflection and professional musing.

While archivists debate the nature of and various approaches to archival appraisal, often ruminating about the very heart of what archives means, the work archivists do, and what the archival discipline represents, the world is changing. Many historians (and other researchers as well) have adopted new approaches to and new sources for their research, and some have even begun to wonder about the meaning and nature of the archival record. By and large, however, archivists and historians have not engaged in discussion and debate with each other, possibly because the archival community has been in its own professionalization mode and establishing its own distinct identity, knowledge, and practices. When a group emphasizes its own needs and place in the world, it often becomes myopic, and although I would not characterize the archival community in this manner generally (because strengthening itself is also crucial to meeting its responsibilities), I believe that archivists need to expand the knowledge supporting appraisal to encompass a more interdisciplinary realm. Given the importance of records in society and the varying roles of archives as cultural and service functions, any more limited perspective is dangerous, especially in the appraisal function. Archivists who approach appraisal as a function to document something, for example, often ignore or miss the fact that records might be only one aspect of the documentation (other aspects being material culture, landscape, tombs and epitaphs, architecture, place names, movies and television—the list could be extended almost indefinitely).

In many ways, archivists and historians have learned how to live with and without each other, conversing and working with each other when necessary. But something else has occurred affecting this historic if sometimes troubled relationship. Public memory has developed both as a new area of scholarship and as a powerful new social force. Patrick Hutton argues that memory has become the chief historiographical challenge of the past twenty years as historians have tried to shift through the "relationship between memory and history" in such aspects as national identity and the meaning of the atrocities of World War II. Hutton thinks that "history as an art of memory will be remembered as the historiographical signature of our times."[1] Eric Foner stated it best: "To the surprise of historians themselves, in the final years of the twentieth century and opening moments of the twenty-first, history seemed to enter into Americans' public and private consciousness more powerfully then at any time in recent memory."[2] Collective memory is, indeed, a force to be reckoned with; historian David W. Blight senses that historians need to be humble before the power of public memory:

> If history is shared and secular, memory is often treated as a sacred set of absolute meanings and stories, possessed as the heritage or identity of a community. Memory is often owned, history interpreted. Memory is passed down through generations; history is revised. Memory often coalesces in objects, sites, and monuments; history seeks to understand contexts in all their complexity. History asserts the authority of academic training and canons of evidence; memory carries the often more immediate authority of community membership and experience.

Blight sees that public memory is a messy and complicated process: "History and memory are both about the *stories* we tell, but

those stories carry a rich politics born of the streets, of our classrooms, our elections, and the process by which books make it to the
front tables at Barnes and Noble."³ (We might note that, except for
the work of some archivists in documenting such movements or in
trying to convince potential users of archives that there are *many* stories residing within their archives, archival holdings have resided
safely and far from our streets.)

Although public memory studies are only beginning to recognize
the importance of archives as a nexus between some elements of the
public and the broader societal memory, the importance of archives
as a vehicle for public memory is noticeable. About a decade ago, I
reviewed a few major studies of American public memory and both
lamented their poor handling of archives and historical societies and
lauded them for the potential context they provided for understanding archives.⁴ Since then, however, archives seem to be playing a
more prominent role in an increasing number of studies, although
monuments, historic sites, commemorations, festivals, tourism, and
similar societal aspects still attract more attention than archives and
their formation do. Archives seem to capture a primary focus when
they are associated with more typical landmarks in the public's
sense of memory, such as is seen in the archives collecting of the
Australian War Memorial in Canberra after its creation to commemorate the end of World War I.⁵ There are signs, however, of the
expanding of public memory studies to encompass the notion of
archives. In one of the most ambitious efforts to understand how
average Americans interact with the past, countering the notion that
this is a nation not interested in history, Rosenzweig and Thelen find
people volunteering in archives, creating records with cameras, caring for their family papers, using archives and historical society
holdings for genealogical and local history research, and engaging
in a host of other activities giving them a good sense of what
archives are about.⁶ Although sometimes archives are conceptual-
ized more broadly than archivists traditionally ascribe to them in
some memory studies,⁷ we seem to be on the cusp of more deliberate
scholarship that will reexamine the place of archives in modern society. Archivists, if they engage these studies, will benefit in their
work, and they will discover new outlets for their scholarship that
might gain notice in other disciplines and enrich the discussion
about records and archives. ⁸

It is my contention, however, that archivists need to reconsider the implications of public memory for the function and act of archival appraisal leading to the formation of archives and their usefulness in society. Public memory provides a different context for understanding the nature of archives. We can consider, for example, all those archival repositories as being sites for public memory and the very existence of the records accumulation as a beacon for a collective sense of the past. The architectural styles of the archives buildings, the presence of professionals known as archivists, the individuals coming and going to use the records, and the records themselves all contribute to a public memory role for archives and archivists. But public memory, as we look more closely at its meaning, also suggests a different way to perceive the most crucial of archival functions, the identification of what records should reside within the archives or be designated as archival in value. Although archivists have debated appraisal theory and methodology, archival values and criteria, and whether this function is more art than science, it is possible that public memory has loomed up to make all of this discussion nearly meaningless. Whatever comes into archives and however it gets there might be beside the point because archives are a symbolic way station on the road to a collective memory.

Public memory suggests that whatever comes into an archives, by whatever route, is important for society's collective sense of its past. Archives in this sense are testimony to the loss, imagined and real, of societal memory. Irish historian Ian McBride, drawing on the work of his French colleague Pierre Nora, contends that the "relentless packaging of history serves as an index of our memory loss. Thus, the proliferation of archives, the heritage craze, the popularity of genealogical research and the obsession with anniversaries are all ways of compensating for the loss of an organic relationship with the past."[9] In this sense, public memory not only affects the nature and utility of archival repositories, but the process of memorialization becomes a societal and scholarly characteristic that should seek to understand or scrutinize archives, their creation, transformations, and uses. If we study the origins of archives—institutional and personal, government and private—we can discern that in many instances they came about in order to provide social cohesion, enhance identity, resist oblivion, influence historical interpretation, and the like. The formation of the first state government archives in the United States occurred in the American South as part of the former Confederacy's effort to commemorate the passing of the "Lost

Cause" generation, and the role of archives had as much to do with mythology as it did with evidence.

Considering public memory also removes archivists from an academic exercise that seems to have characterized most of the discussion about archival appraisal within the archives profession. Alexander Stille recently wrote that "If the humanities departments at our universities [in the United States] function as our collective historical memory, then it would be hard not to conclude that we are putting few of our resources into that part of life."[10] Yet collective memory is not isolated in academe but seems to be moving away from it as the public displays interest in history in a multiplicity of unorthodox and sometimes quite grotesque ways. Historians and others have become interested in the disparity between knowledge of the past and public fascination and even obsession with it, leading historians and other scholars to try to study public memory as a means of understanding their own lot in life. We can look at archives, in their gathered state, as systematic reflections of an individual, organization, government, or society, or we can consider them as a mess. Haitian historian Michel-Rolph Trouillot has written about the "silences" in society's historical knowledge, implying that they are the result of power and that this relationship extends back to both the creation of records and the establishment and development of archives.[11] The more widely held notion of archives and history is that it is a "flea market, a jumble shop,"[12] where people can sort through records as if they were in their basements or attics, discovering all sorts of interesting and quaint stuff. Suspended over both views (and others, perhaps), and connecting them, is the substance of what we now consider to be public memory. The large number of volunteers and amateurs who strive to create and service archives is testimony to the fact that archives are not the province of a profession or elite but perform a more pervasive function in society. Thinking about public memory and its connection to archives helps us to reconsider what archives and archivists are all about.

WHAT IS PUBLIC MEMORY?

We need to define what we are discussing as public memory. Although there is increasing concern about the methodological rigor of memory studies,[13] there are enough cogent studies to posit a working definition. Barbie Zelizer, a professor of communications and the author of two books on public memory, describes public memory using eight dominant attributes she finds considered in recent public memory scholarship. In general, Zelizer argues, "Collective memory suggests a deepening of the historical consciousness that becomes wedged in-between the official markings of the past and ourselves in the present." The predominant characteristics start with the sense that public memory is "processional," where it is "constantly unfolding, changing, and transforming." Public memory is also "unpredictable," in that "memories pop up precisely where they are least expected." Public memory also "has had little to do with the passage of time in its expected form," with transformations occurring outside of a logical sense of time. Public memory is further defined by a relationship to "space," by links through "monuments, artifacts, even texts, which themselves bear a definitive relationship to space." Public memory is also "partial," consisting of "memories [that] are often pieced together like a mosaic," unfolding in bits and pieces. Public memory is "usable," and "evaluated for the ways in which it helps us to make connections—to each other over time and space, and to ourselves." Public memory is also both "particularistic and universal," meaning that the "same memory can act as a particular representation of the past for certain groups while taking on a universal significance for others." Finally, public memory has "texture," meaning that it is "embodied in different cultural forms," such as "objects," "narratives," and "even the routines by which we structure our day."[14] In these characteristics, the fluidity of public memory is most noticeable, especially in contrast to how some archivists seem to feel about appraisal—that it is a one-time, monumental function; once records are in the archives, they are meant to stay there, no matter whether they are used or not. It is an idea that does not reside well within the confines of public memory (and it might not make much sense from an administrative perspective).

A more useful, friendly sense of public memory can be found in the work of historian John Lukacs. Lukacs gives us a good sense of the relationship between history and public memory when he writes:

There is the past; there is the remembered past; there is the recorded past. The past is very large, and it gets larger every minute: we do not and cannot know all of it. Its remnant evidences help: but they, too, are protean and cannot be collected and recorded in their entirety. Thus history is more than the recorded past; it consists of the recorded and the recordable and the remembered past. The past in our minds *is* memory.[15]

This view provides an insight into both the strengths and the weaknesses of archives, as well as the archival function of appraisal that by necessity must start with the entire universe of documentation. Lukacs deals more directly with the place of records when he notes:

> For history is, and always was something more than a study of records; and just as actuality must, by necessity, include at least a recognition of the element of potentiality, if history is the memory of mankind (which it is), then it is something more than the recorded past; it must include something of the remembered past, too.[16]

It is precisely because of this relationship between memory and records that so much of historical research will occur outside of the archives. It is also why many archivists remain puzzled by the failure of their efforts to lure historical scholars into their research rooms; those scholars are out studying signage, landscape, magazine advertisements, MTV, movies, and Madonna—all legitimate documents as far as they are concerned.

Sociologist Barry Schwartz also provides a useful definition of collective memory: "Collective memory refers simultaneously to what is in the minds of individuals and to emergent conceptions of the past crystallized into symbolic structures." Collective memory includes individual memories but also what is in museums, libraries, archives, and other repositories. Schwartz believes that "collective memory is based on two sources of belief about the past—*history* and *commemoration*. Collective memory is a representation of the past embodied in *both* historical evidence and commemorative symbolism." Among other things, collective memory "embodies a *template* that organizes and animates behavior and a *frame* within which people locate and find memory for the present experience. Collective memory affects social reality by *reflecting, shaping,* and *framing* it."[17] The clear inclusion of archives within the frame of public memory suggests that we will see more studies about archives in this light. Archivists, in my opinion, might be surprised to see how those on the outside consider the formation of their holdings. Although archivists seem to have developed schools of thought (in the positive mode) and factions (in the negative) within their ranks about appraisal, it could be that those studying public memory will reorder these groups or dismiss them altogether, generating their own intellectual genealogies and attitudes about whether appraisal has worked or is a legitimate element of a real discipline. Given that archivists appraise records generally to be used by those outside their own field, how others see archivists will be important in their continuing contract with society.

MEMORY IN THE RECORD

Archivists have had considerable speculation about the record, as well as substantial debate, some of it possibly quite confusing to the outside world (if the outside world even knows of it). Evidence, information, and content are usually crucial elements of the record, but memory is, of course, also closely associated with the creation of a record. Alexandra Johnson, who teaches writing, including journal writing, notes that the "driest factual record often evokes a history far longer than the life it chronicles—memories of war, the Holocaust, transplanted cultures." She reminds us of the millions of people keeping personal journals of some kind, and she thinks of a journal as unlocking or recreating the "archive of memory." Johnson sees that "writing from the cool recesses of memory was how to begin journals." As she suggests, "From journals we reconstruct the world, transforming it through memory and imagination."[18] This sounds like a therapeutic process, and Johnson intends it to be just that, but it would be a mistake if we dismiss such notions so readily. Some records, as transactions of even the most mundane activities, will later cause a remembrance—of either the creation of the record or the actual transaction. Journals obviously are intended to be the kind of memory device Johnson describes, but so are minutes, correspondence, and receipts. The question is when, or if, a particular record will need to be reused. Archivists and records managers want to ensure that records are created and administered in such a fashion that they can be utilized as needed for a great variety of legal, administrative, fiscal, and research uses. Public or collective memory will have an impact on the when and if of eventual use or nonuse (as accumulated archives, used or not, still may play a role in how a society remembers).

Although memory might be a relatively new topic for scholarly scrutiny, there is ample evidence that many individuals have been very cognizant of its importance, especially in the creation and use of their records. In the early days of the American Revolution, John Adams wrote to himself about how he bought a "Folio Book" for recording the "great Events" he was involved in. Joseph Ellis reminds us how the leaders of the Revolution wrote not just to each other but with an eye to posterity and how they would be remembered. Ellis also describes Adams, in his retirement, focusing "within himself," the "interior architecture of his own remembrances, the construction of an Adams version of American history, a spacious room of his own within the American pantheon."[19] Clearly, we can find many other examples of such self-reflective musings on how the creation of records serves a memory function. Writer Ian Frazier sorted through his family's papers searching for the meaning of his parents' lives "because the stuff they saved implied that there must have been a reason for saving it."[20] Louise Steinman's discovery of her late father's letters, carefully filed and numbered by her mother, written when he was a soldier in the Pacific theater of World War II, starts her on a journey of remembrance enabling her to gain deeper understanding about her parents.[21] Writer Mary Gordon starts on a journey to discover more about her deceased father that ultimately takes her into archives. Her trip there, triggering and correcting her memories, causes her to speculate on the meaning of memory: "All of us in the archives are acknowledging the insufficiency of memory. The falseness of the myth of continuity. The loss of living speech. Our own inability to live with the blanks. To live in the enveloping whiteness of imagination and of love."[22]

Examining public memory and documents (and I use this term deliberately as being broader than the concept of record) also raises interesting questions about the reliability of many of the sources pointed to as authentic proof of a particular event and its interpretation. Jeremy Popkin's reading of the use of memoirs of the Holocaust generates interesting questions and possibilities as well as troubling issues for the archivist. Although these memoirs provide first-hand accounts, they can be unreliable (because of memory issues) and more easily open to fabrication, as was the case in the

mid-1990s when Bruno Grosjean published under the pseudonym
Binjamin Wilkomirski his experiences in the Nazi concentration
camps. The irony here is that, according to Popkin, some believe that
if this "memoir":

> successfully communicates the horror of the Holocaust experience, it
> may be "authentic" even if the details it relates happened, not to its
> author, but to other victims. The fact that authentic child survivors of
> the Holocaust embraced Wilkomirski as their spokesperson could be
> interpreted in this sense.

Popkin sees these memoirs as being "part of a larger human effort to
transmit the truth of the human past, an effort in which first-person
literature joins hands with both fiction and history."[23]

The reemergence of diplomatics, with its emphasis on the trustworthiness of records and their content, came about mostly because
of the challenges posed by digital systems.[24] A perhaps greater challenge may be the constant ebb and flow of public memory that may
provide the context for how society and its organizations care about
their records. Indeed, the movement within organizations to try to
institute knowledge management, capturing their intellectual capital, which is largely seen to reside in the minds of corporate employees and to be teased out by consultants and new professionals, also
generally seems to bypass the information and evidence captured
by records.[25] Nevertheless, there is a symbolic value often associated
with corporate archives, as many consist not of comprehensive
archives but more of memory rooms where documents and objects
imbued with (or assigned) symbolic value—the original charter of
incorporation, the shovel used to toss the first earth in the construction of the corporate headquarters, the corporate seal—are displayed (rather than used).

If archives have been the substance of historical research, archives
in their broadest sense—encompassing everything that constitutes
the remnants of the past (including debris)—is the stuff of public
memory. But in this broader view, we see the challenge to archives
and archivists in the future. Barbie Zelizer, for example, sees that
"collective memory is both more mobile and mutable than history,"
that it is a "kind of history-in-motion which moves at a different
pace and rate than traditional history." Zelizer continues:

> This means that while traditional scholarship on memory presumed
> that memories were at some point authentic, credible accountings of

events of the past, we do not regard this as necessarily the case. In distancing themselves from personal recall, collective memories help us fabricate, rearrange, or omit details from the past as we thought we knew it. Issues of historical accuracy and authenticity are pushed aside to accommodate other issues, such as those surrounding the establishment of social identity, authority, solidarity, political affiliation.

In an interesting play on the kind of terminology that archivists use, Zelizer asks, "But what has [collective memory study] demonstrated about the ability of collective memory to act as a finding aid to the past?" Zelizer says that the answer is "still not evident. For collective memory studies are still in the dressing room, waiting to be brought onto the front racks and display windows of academic thought."[26] Scholars of memory, and scholars in general, bring skepticism to the table where the records sit for them to examine. Jacques Le Goff, for example, states, the "document is not objective, innocent raw material, but expresses past society's power over memory and over the future: the document is what remains."[27] And, of course, scholars of public memory have expanded the documents far beyond what are found in archival repositories.

CHANGING AND DIVERSE MEMORIES

Archivists, when considering appraisal (especially in this new digital era), mostly have worried about when in the life cycle of the record to perform this function. Most of the speculations about this have come about because of growing use of digital technologies for creating and maintaining records, transforming the length of time that we can afford to allow to pass before appraising. In the past, archivists seemed to be just as content to discover a previously unknown cache of records in a closet or basement corner, and then to deal with them as best as they could (often with the advantage of considerable hindsight). But the notion of a public memory also suggests the ability of society to be constantly forming and reforming the manner in which we view a record or artifact—making one wonder, if memory is a criterion for appraisal, just how many times an appraisal decision would change over a few decades.

One also can speculate just how willing archivists have been to recognize the complexities of society when they conduct appraisal.

Many hold to the idea that they are appraising for scholarly historians, but as the public memory scholarship suggests, the aims, methodologies, and sources of academic history are quite diverse in their own right. Expand the audience to the public, which in fact consists of many actual and potential publics, and the challenges facing the appraisal task become even more monumental in scope and responsibility. Otis Graham, scanning the emerging scholarship on public memory, believes that a critical aspect of this scholarship is the discovery that there are many "sub-publics" bringing "different memories into museums, historic sites, classrooms, and couches in front of TV sets." Graham sees that the various subgroups "expect, want, and respond warmly or coolly to different historical themes and events. Their minds are inhabited by different historical memories, variously acquired through experience, folklore, media, family stories, earlier education."[28] Discerning the varying interests in and perspective of the past of different segments of society is the hallmark of the new scholarship on public memory. David Glassberg notes that historians have long been interested in memory although the difference in recent scholarship is the "approach." "Whereas earlier studies primarily sought to characterize a single group or institution's beliefs about its past, the new studies primarily seek to understand the interrelationships between different versions of history in the public."[29] If we believe that appraisal is a function meeting the needs of specific constituencies archivists serve, and if we adopt use of archives as a measure of how successful archivists are in making appraisal decisions, then archivists face two dangers: the possibility of attempting to achieve far too many objectives to have any chance of success and the possibility that what archivists believe will meet these objectives is very far from what various sectors of the public want. Complicating matters even more, archivists bring all their own perspectives to the task. This is the reason some believe that archivists' previous appraisal decisions should be left alone (ignoring, of course, that many of these decisions are as affected by politics, resource development, public relations, and accident as by clear and rational approaches and professional agendas).

Archivists might be confused about the notion of memory these days because so much of their emphasis is on the issues of memory associated with the computer. The great attraction of the computer is the decreasing costs of its memory storage. Some argue that everything now can be saved because this memory is, in fact, so inexpensive and so easily within reach of most organizations and a large portion of the population (at least in the Western nations). But the computer as a means of social memory is very limited. Philosopher Edward Casey makes a distinction between computers and human memory: Computers:

> *cannot remember*; what they can do is to record, store, and retrieve information—which is only part of what human beings do when they enter into a memorious state. . . . Computers can only collect and order the reduced residues, the artfully formatted traces, of what in the end must be reclaimed by human beings in order to count as human memories.[30]

But, of course, many archivists and records managers think of their function as little more than to record, store, and retrieve information. This view is far too limited. Their accumulated assemblage of generations of records represents something more than information. The archives provide societal identity, reassurances that the past is real, evidence that is more than mere information, and the source of accountability of individuals and organizations, public officials and business and community leaders. This is especially hard as computer memory is really very different from any other form of memory. In a study about nostalgia, Svetlana Boym states:

> Computer memory is independent of affect and the vicissitudes of time, politics and history; it has no patina of history, and everything has the same digital texture. On the blue screen two scenarios of memory are possible: a total recall of undigested information bytes or an equally total amnesia that could occur in a heartbeat with a sudden technical failure.[31]

Archivists need to remind the creators and users of hardware and software not only that "archives" are different from mere system backups and that there is a distinction between "records" and "documents," but that computer memory is very different from individual, corporate, and societal memory.

Ruminating on the computer as reflective of our modern era makes us reconsider the metaphors for our age. As Douwe Draaisma reminds us, we have produced many metaphors for memory, of which "storage spaces," such as libraries and archives, is one. Draaisma also reminds us that:

Metaphors as literary-scientific constructs are also reflections of an age, a culture, an ambience. Metaphors express the activities and preoccupations of their authors. Without intending to, metaphors capture an intellectual climate and themselves function as a form of memory.

What we might wonder about now is whether archives are the primary metaphor for the memory of our age, or whether it is a metaphor for earlier periods and is now being replaced by the computer.[32] The modern impulse to create archives, similar to the impulse to create instant memorials, suggests that some aspect of the relevance of archives is still operational, although in ways that might be different from the archivists who staff the repositories. In America, the long-standing notion is that the mere act of assembling collections will attract researchers, perhaps with a little publicity now mostly aided by the existence of the World Wide Web. These archives, many underutilized by researchers, might be more valuable or meaningful as acts of memorialization, reassuring society or an organization that it is tracking its past but not requiring anyone necessarily to study the past through its records.

Archivists do not need to engage in the debates of historians and philosophers about the meaning of the past or the implications of public memory to detect these nuances and notions. They can detect them in our consumer-oriented society as well. One of the commentators on the chaos after the September 11, 2001, terrorist attacks examined the impact of the more vulgar aspects of Western consumerism on our relationships with the Arab world. Charles Paul Freund notes how the world is filled with many "disposable" artifacts that many see as having no value or that represent the worst of a culture. But Freund finds meaning in them and notes how their meaning often changes. He comments that the:

> generation that in the 1950s was dismissed as Elvis-loving, hot-rod-building, gum-chewing, hog-riding, leather-wearing, juvenile delinquent barbarians eventually achieved a mature respectability in which the artifacts of their vulgarity became sought-after nostalgia, and even a beloved part of the common cultural heritage. In less than two decades, the menacing hoods of *Blackboard Jungle* became the lovable leads in *Grease*. By then, however, that same generation had become, in its turn, concerned about the disruptive social effects of rap music and violent electronic gaming.[33]

As archivists we can imagine that viewing records about the 1950s *in* the 1950s will produce a different result from examining these records twenty, thirty, or forty years later. Society's shifting ideas about the past are one reason for this. Archival appraisal is, then, always to some extent an artifact of its times, and the documentation we should have of the appraisal process could be very useful in helping both users of archives and archivists themselves to comprehend the effects of appraisal decisions. As I have argued elsewhere, in the future archivists at work and their archives as place and institution may be studied as much as their holdings (see the previous chapter).

The constantly shifting notions of public memory have come much closer to home, however. Over the past year and a half, Nicholson Baker's caustic and critical analysis of libraries' preservation of paper has garnered overwhelmingly positive reviews, from both within and without the library profession, and built up the notion that everything has value and most if not all must be preserved.[34] Some of this idea comes close to the role of both the library and archives as a source or sustainer of public memory. Tara Brabazon, in praising Baker's efforts to make libraries rethink their views, argues that a:

> good library is determined as much by what it excludes as what is incorporated into its collection. The history of a library is always a narrative of the knowledge that transcends it. Libraries must direct beyond their collection, linking past, present, and future. The point of a library is to make available the sights, sounds, and textures of an earlier age, for the purposes of the current reader. . . . Yet they are not archives, which preserve a corporate or societal memory frequently focused on a very precise period, topic, or organization. Libraries provide a record of a far wider information landscape. They hold not only content, but provide a context for information. While libraries are not archives, if the material is not preserved, then it cannot be read.[35]

Baker does not understand the differences between libraries and archives or, for that matter, the archival mission of libraries, but that is not the point here. The point is that Baker's romanticizing of the original artifact is very much in harmony with the kinds of issues scholars of public memory are investigating and recognizing as crucial to the notion of a societal memory.

THE RECORD AND PUBLIC DEBATE

The notion of public memory resident in archives, both the records and the repositories, is nowhere more evident than in the continuing controversies making the news about libraries, museums, historic sites, and public commemorations, many of which bring increased attention to the nature and meaning of historic records. Edward Linenthal's examination of the effort to build the Holocaust Museum in Washington, D.C., is a study of the controversy, debate, false starts, second-guessing, personality clashes, conflicting agendas, politicization, and other challenges of gathering the appropriate evidence to present in a meaningful way to the museum's visitors. As Linenthal writes:

> The act of collection itself—quite apart from the results—was a vibrant form of memory work. The design team acted as archaeologists of the Holocaust, digging into the attics of homes, weighing the impact of the physical remnants of a camp, in order to make the Holocaust "real" through physical contact. The signing of agreements and the physical exchange of artifacts themselves became acts of Holocaust commemoration.[36]

Given the Holocaust deniers, the continuing passing of those who remember these horrific events, the ever-prevalent anti-Semitism, and even trials about the nature of evidence related to the Holocaust, it is not surprising that this museum faced so many challenges and controversies. Journalists often contribute to the nature of public memory by covering stories (often concerning libraries and archives) that do not challenge our understanding of the past but merely affirm some continuing notions held by the public. This kind of coverage is why archives and archivists are so often treated in a stereotypical fashion when public controversies involving archives happen (journalists easily grasp onto the stereotypes as a means of explaining the nature of the controversy, something that never places archives and archivists in a positive light).[37]

Interesting cases continue to appear that demonstrate the powerful implications of public memory for archives. The acrimonious debate about the exhibition marking the fiftieth anniversary of the end of World War II at the Smithsonian reveals, according to Elizabeth Yakel, that "combining memory, good historiography, and professional museum practice is not easy." Yakel notes that the "exhibition demonstrates what can happen when organizations ignore social, political, and cultural factors in the environment." One of Yakel's points most relevant to this discussion is her observation that the Smithsonian's shift in collection management policies was noted on the outside of the museum, although in this instance doing this did not win friends for the museum and the exhibit designers:

> Instead of collecting everything, items were selected more judiciously and with different criteria. Here, archivists and librarians should note that internal collection development and management decisions can be noted externally. However valid the decision to change collection development practices . . . is, alienating an institution's major constituency should not be done lightly and cannot be done without consequences.[38]

We can push this exhibition and the nature of both public memory and records even further. Philip Nobile, one of the essayists in the first book chronicling the debate and including the contested exhibit script, wrote:

> Since the Sixties, a steady stream of diaries, memoirs, interviews and declassified documents has moved revisionism solidly into the mainstream. Among academic historians, conventional wisdom holds that dropping the bomb was probably a strategic blunder and a moral disaster.[39]

In this volume, Nobile and Barton Bernstein provide numerous examples of new documentary evidence challenging the older accounts of the reasons for the atomic bombings. Their book affirms the importance of records for accountability, evidence, and memory, no matter what one might personally believe about the justification for dropping the atomic bomb.

There is a marked contrast between what archives and museums, historic sites, and libraries face in our controversial and contentious society. David Glassberg makes an interesting observation archivists need to think about:

> Since it is nearly impossible to reach a consensus on the public interpretation of a historical event that anyone still cares about, public his-

torical representations such as an exhibit, war memorial, or commemorative ceremony are often deliberately ambiguous to satisfy competing factions.[40]

But archives cannot generally be ambiguous in that the records they will appraise and acquire usually have decided and diverse points of view. If historians can study the changing interpretations of the past in museums and historic sites because of shifting contexts imposed by the interpretations of visitors, archivists have a much more difficult task in that they must be aware of their own views' impact on what they appraise as archival and therefore be more deliberate in recording their principles, practices, and preconceptions. Dianne Britton, in her presidential address to the National Council on Public History, grasped for an activist posture for public historians, saying they should try to find a "balance between memory and professional historical interpretation" while being "cognizant of the diversity of views that audiences bring to interpretations of the past if their constituencies are to be served effectively."[41] While Britton probably meant to include archivists with public historians, her description was more of public historians working on exhibitions and publications in museums and libraries. Again, the task facing archivists is even more difficult because they are involved in making the decisions leading to forming the collection of archival sources historians and other researchers use.

Many archivists seem to focus so much on the public *good* of saving and assembling historical records that they forget the many elements in society who would resist such efforts as challenging common perceptions and values. One commentator, in one of the more cynical views of public memory, sees that "public memory, like personal memory, is highly selective. We prefer myths that exalt rather than facts that might demean. We like good wars, inspiring stories, and happy endings."[42] Records are created, after all, by every kind of person and organization of every political, religious, and other perspective and of every kind of organization and individual who might be characterized as either good or evil. Because the symbolic process in forming archives constitutes a kind of memorialization activity, documenting groups and individuals counter to the public norms can be seen to be a negative thing. One historian argues that:

popular nationalistic history writing solidifies into a canon which maintains an indefinite shelf-life. . . . Much as community remembrancing resists revisions and has a pious sense of the enduring validity of its established truths, so too its standard texts are recycled continuously.[43]

Archives can either support or oppose that canon, although sometimes it is possible that many members of the community might accept the general remembrancing function of archives without ever looking into the contents of the repository. And there are pressures on many of these publicly funded cultural institutions like archives, libraries, and museums to assume a different role. A commentator on the situation in Ireland suggests that the "keeping alive of memory, then, when placed in the hands of the state, or bodies responsible to the state, or even in purely commercial hands, reflect[s] current political preoccupations." In Northern Ireland, he says, schools and museums should be "oases of calm."[44]

REMEMBERING APPRAISAL FOR THE FUTURE

Over a half-century ago, in 1946, a fifty-foot *tsunami* slammed into the town of Waipi'o in Hawaii, destroying every building, but sparing the lives of all the residents. The survivors, years later, had no evidence of their former lives. Much the same has occurred with appraisal; as we go back to examine how archival holdings were formed, we often discover that we have no precise evidence of how appraisal decisions or acquisitions were made. M. T. Clanchy, writing about medieval literacy and record keeping, made an aside that "archivists still serve a similar function to [the ancient] remembrancers, since they are the keepers of a society's collective record of its past." I suggest that archivists *all* must be the keepers of the past, in terms of ensuring that records with all their values for memory, evidence, and accountability are protected, defended, and fought for as strenuously as we are all able. And keeping the past includes documenting ourselves and our work so that the researchers in archives can better understand what they are examining and so that archivists themselves are accountable to the creators and users of records and all of society that depends on these records for many purposes. Through the years, I have witnessed different archival repositories handling appraisal documentation in very different ways. I have seen some institutions prepare very elaborate appraisal reports, reflecting a scholarship that would help colleagues and archives users understand just what the records now residing in the archives really represent from the documentary universe. I also have seen quite the opposite: only a bare-bones records retention schedule or an entry into some sort of accession or registration log but little reflecting the decision-making process supporting appraisal. (Indeed, it has sometimes appeared as if no appraisal has actually taken place unless the simple act of receiving material into stacks could be construed as appraisal.) If archives and archivists do not leave behind a clear sense of what they are striving to accomplish in the appraisal realm, it is quite likely that public memory will provide its own understanding of what has transpired. Clear and precise documentation of the appraisal responsibility should prevent the memorialization process from resulting in complete fantasy.

An example, present and ongoing, might provide an idea of how careful archivists' work must be. Immediately after the terrorist attacks on the World Trade Center and the Pentagon on September 11, 2001, memorials and related efforts were begun by archivists and others intent on documenting the events. Virtual memorials utilized websites and allowed individuals to post their thoughts about the events or about people who had lost their lives.[45] Other projects, involving the collecting of more traditional archival resources, such as audio and audiovisual recordings, also quickly emerged.[46] The New York State Historical Records Advisory Board also quickly mobilized itself to help coordinate the World Trade Center Documentation Task Force—a group:

> coordinating information and initiating collaborative efforts to document the many aspects of this tragedy including the role of: state government, local government, organizations such as hospitals, schools, mental health organizations, religious groups, and others involved in this event and its aftermath.[47]

Many interesting connections between the notion of public memory and archival appraisal are being played out in these (and other) efforts to document and contend with the aftermath of the September 11 tragedy. On one level, we know that terrorist groups often target sites of particular cultural or symbolic value. One exploration into the nature of modern terrorism argues:

> oppressed people in many countries view the U.S. government as the incarnation of evil and greed. . . . [Terrorist organizations] do not narrow their sights to military installations or even to heavily populated areas; they may be targeting any community, institution, or structure in the United States or any symbol of American interest abroad.[48]

The World Trade Center, as a target, fulfilled many of these roles, as both an international commercial center and a symbol of globalism, American power, and Western-style capitalism.[49] M. Christine Boyer captures some of the symbolic power of the World Trade Center in her meditation on the power of the skyline of a modern city:

> The skyline is most powerfully a celebration of work and the competition that it entails. Horror and suffering lie in the opposite: in the unmaking of the artifact, in its ruin and wounds. In the skyscraper's demise, its image will henceforth be associated with expressions of death. Projected onto the human body, its memory-image is one of mournfulness and pain.[50]

This is partially why there has been so much debate about how the World Trade Center site should be handled. One commentator, Roger Rosenblatt, urged that a library be put on the site (or at least part of the site) "since the whole purpose of a library is to keep the dead alive. Memory is what we have of one another when we no longer have one another, which may be said of words as well."[51]

The archives projects being undertaken in relationship to the events of September 11 are a curious mix of archival appraisal and public memory, and they reveal the strengths and weaknesses of the relationship between the two. Archivists and other records professionals, along with museum curators, historians, and others, should be responding to the destruction because we now know that a lot of archival records and museum objects were lost in the destruction of the World Trade Center and the Pentagon.[52] Responding to the lost and damaged objects and records is one thing, but seeking to document September 11 is quite another. Although the issue of *The Economist* appearing immediately after the disasters featured a dramatic photograph of the collapse of the World Trade Center with a banner headline reading "The Day the World Changed" compared the attacks to the 1941 attack on Pearl Harbor, and stated, "This week has changed America, and with it the world, once again,"[53] it is still way too soon to know how these events will really stack up in the timeline of world history. Efforts to gather up archival documentation and to establish archival repositories dedicated to the events of September 11 may assemble materials that need to be reappraised several decades from now as the true importance of that day emerges. We now seem to be indulging in the memorial function of archival records and repositories (as no doubt we should). What archivists need to be careful about is what they convey to the public and policymakers about archives and their purposes. After all, the most crucial records of these events will be found in government archives, and archivists will need to fight not merely for their preservation but for their release; archival records are valuable for many more purposes than memory, and these other uses—especially accountability and openness—are sometimes more fragile than we care to recognize.[54]

We can gain a sense of the challenge in mixing memory and the archival impulse by looking at a similar event and response, the 1995 Oklahoma City bombing. In early 2001, the Oklahoma City National Memorial Center was dedicated and opened. Edward Linenthal notes:

> With the opening of the Memorial Center, memorial expression was *anchored* in a specific site (clearly delineated sacred space *embodied* by family member and survivor docents, *expressed* in the Memorial Center's exhibition, *preserved* in massive archival collections, and *disseminated* through the activities of the institute and the educational imperative of the foundation to engage in public education about the impact of violence, the human face of government, and the necessity of nonviolent means of social change as an integral element of civil society.[55]

Linenthal studies the response because of his interest that "memorialization had become a significant form of cultural expression." Linenthal was especially intrigued by the "contemporary American memorial culture . . . characterized by the democratization of memorials and memorial processes, the compression of time between event and memorial planning, and the rise of activist memorial environments."[56] In fact, with both the Oklahoma City and the September 11 events, the majority of archival activities, especially identifying and acquiring documents, were dreamed up and carried out by groups and individuals other than archivists. What should give archivists pause for thought is that the primary or initial impulse for the Oklahoma City memorial was that the bombing there represented the worst "single act of domestic terrorism in American history"[57] at the time (a "distinction" that held for only six years). Building archives so quickly after an event seems to guarantee the full documentation of that event but it might also be very premature as the sense of the event's significance could change dramatically in a relatively short time.

CONCLUSION

Archivists, wrangling about how to approach appraisal, also need to reconsider just what it represents in the broader societal context. The vicissitudes of public memory may force archivists to reimagine appraisal, not as a one-time act in regard to a specific group of records, but as a continuous process. This change in approach will not be easy for many reasons. For one, it works against the conservative nature and function of archives. Eric Ormsby, reflecting on the many claims for the computer's role in academic libraries, notes, "Libraries have been unusually hesitant to change, and with justice: an institution and a profession whose sacred duty it has always been to safeguard and make available the records of our past should be conservative, indeed, should be exceedingly cautious, about change."[58] Archivists might say something very much like this. But the bigger problem is that *everyone* is involved in appraisal, or at least they think they are. The public confuses archives with the stuff left behind at the sites of the World Trade Center, the Alfred P. Murrah Federal Building, and even the Vietnam Memorial. Archivists need to be able to explain the distinctive nature of archival records and the manner in which they are formed via clear appraisal strategies and methodologies, or they need to acknowledge that their repositories are merely miscellaneous accretions of records operating mostly as signposts of public memory in their own right.

NOTES

1. Patrick Hutton, "Recent Scholarship on Memory and History," *History Teacher* 33 (August 2000): 545.

2. Eric Foner, *Who Owns History? Rethinking the Past in a Changing World* (New York: Hill and Wang, 2002), ix.

3. David W. Blight, "Historians and Memory," *Common-Place* 2 (April 2002), available at http://www.common-place.org/vol-02/no-03/author/. For the idea about the differences between historical memory and public or collective memory, the latter dependent on the role of the individual responding to the past, see Susan A. Crane, "Writing the Individual Back into Collective Memory," *American Historical Review* 102 (December 1997): 1372–1385.

4. Richard J. Cox, "The Concept of Public Memory and Its Impact on Archival Public Programming," *Archivaria* 36 (Autumn 1993): 122–135.

5. Alistair Thomson, *Anzac Memories: Living with the Legend* (Melbourne: Oxford University Press, 1994).

6. Roy Rosenzweig and David Thelen, *The Presence of the Past: Popular Uses of History in American Life* (New York: Columbia University Press, 1998).

7. An example is Thomas Richards, *The Imperial Archive: Knowledge and the Fantasy of Empire* (London: Verso, 1993).

8. See, for example, Brian Brothman, "The Past that Archives Keep: Memory, History, and the Preservation of Archival Records," *Archivaria* 52 (Fall 2001): 48–80. Brothman's perspective is, however, very different from mine, at least in what I am trying to discuss here. Brothman stresses the scholarship about public memory and its implications for archives—such as recognizing that "records are cognitive artifacts as much as evidential artifacts" (79), while I am stressing that the notion of public memory, seen as how society remembers, challenges archivists' assumptions about appraisal and their role in society. Brothman's argument is interesting, and his call for scholarship about memory by archivists is worth consideration, but it is merely a different viewpoint from what I am considering here.

9. Ian McBride, "Memory and National Identity in Modern Ireland," in McBride, ed., *History and Memory in Modern Ireland* (Cambridge, England: Cambridge University Press, 2001), 11.

10. Alexander Stille, *The Future of the Past* (New York: Farrar, Straus, and Giroux, 2002), 336.

11. Michel-Rolph Trouillot, *Silencing the Past: Power and the Production of History* (Boston: Beacon Press, 1995).

12. Howard Mansfield, *In the Memory House* (Golden, Colorado: Fulcrum, 1993), 12.

13. See, for example, Alon Confino, "Collective Memory and Cultural History: Problems of Method," *American Historical Review* 102 (December 1997): 1386–1403. See also Wolf Kansteiner, "Finding Meaning in Memory: A Methodological Critique of Collective Memory Studies," *History and Theory* 41 (May 2002): 179–197, and Jeffrey K. Olick and Joyce Robbins, "Social

Memory Studies: From 'Collective Memory' to the Historical Sociology of Mnemonic Practices," *Annual Reviews in Sociology* 24 (1998): 105–140.

14. Barbie Zelizer, "Reading the Past against the Grain: The Shape of Memory Studies," *Critical Studies in Mass Communication* 12 (June 1995): 218, 221, 222, 223, 224, 226, 230, and 232.

15. John Lukacs, *At the End of an Age* (New Haven: Yale University Press, 2002), 52.

16. Lukacs, *At the End of an Age*, 62.

17. Barry Schwartz, *Abraham Lincoln and the Forge of National Memory* (Chicago: University of Chicago Press, 2000), 8, 9, 18.

18. Alexandra Johnson, *Leaving a Trace: On Keeping a Journal; The Art of Transforming a Life into Stories* (Boston: Little, Brown, 2001), 11, 65, 68, and 194.

19. Joseph J. Ellis, *Founding Brothers: The Revolutionary Generation* (New York: Vintage Books, 2000), 3, 18, 23.

20. Ian Frazier, *Family* (New York: HarperPerennial, 1995), 39.

21. Louise Steinman, *The Souvenir: A Daughter Discovers Her Father's War* (Chapel Hill, N.C.: Algonquin Books of Chapel Hill, 2001).

22. Mary Gordon, *The Shadow Man: A Daughter's Search for Her Father* (New York: Vintage Books, 1996), 164.

23. Jeremy D. Popkin, "First-Person Narrative and the Memory of the Holocaust," *Ideas* 9 (Spring 2002): 20.

24. Luciana Duranti, "Concepts and Principles for the Management of Electronic Records, or Records Management Theory Is Archival Diplomatics," *Records Management Journal* 9 (December 1999): 153–175.

25. One of the pioneering primers on this subject is Thomas A. Stewart, *Intellectual Capital: The New Wealth of Organizations* (New York: Currency-Doubleday, 1997).

26. Zelizer, "Reading the Past against the Grain," 217, 218.

27. Jacques Le Goff, *History and Memory*, trans. Steven Rendall and Elizabeth Claman (New York: Columbia University Press, 1992), xvii.

28. Otis L. Graham, Jr., "No Tabula Rasa—Varieties of Public Memories and Mindsets," *Public Historian* 17 (Winter 1995): 13.

29. Historians are now studying autobiographical memory and reminiscences, images constituting political culture (including archives and museums), images in commercial mass media and tourist attractions, and place as purveyor of memory. David Glassberg, "Public History and the Study of Memory," *Public Historian* 18 (Spring 1996): 9.

30. Edward S. Casey, *Remembering: A Phenomenological Study*, 2nd ed. (Bloomington: Indiana University Press, 2000), 2.

31. Svetlana Boym, *The Future of Nostalgia* (New York: Basic Books, 2001), 347.

32. Draaisma considers writing, phonographs, photographs, the com-

puter, and other metaphors, but never does the notion of archives appear, although we get close with the notion of a treasure chest or warehouse (although archivists do not think kindly of the description of their repositories as warehouses). Douwe Draaisma, *Metaphors of Memory: A History of Ideas about the Mind* (Cambridge, England: Cambridge University Press, 2000), 4.

33. Charles Paul Freund, "In Praise of Vulgarity: How Commercial Culture Liberates Islam—and the West," *Reason* (March 2002), 35.

34. Nicholson Baker, *Double Fold: Libraries and the Assault on Paper* (New York: Random House, 2001); Richard J. Cox, *Vandals in the Stacks? A Response to Nicholson Baker's Assault on Libraries* (Westport, Conn.: Greenwood Press, 2002).

35. Tara Brabazon, "Double Fold or Double Take? Book Memory and the Administration of Knowledge," *Libri* 52, no. 1 (2002): 33.

36. Edward T. Linenthal, *Preserving Memory: The Struggle to Create America's Holocaust Museum* (New York: Viking, 1995), 164.

37. Jill A. Edy, "Journalistic Uses of Collective Memory," *Journal of Communication* 49 (Spring 1999): 71–85.

38. Elizabeth Yakel, "Museums, Management, Media, and Memory: Lessons from the *Enola Gay* Exhibition," *Libraries & Culture* 35 (Spring 2000): 298, 299, and 300.

39. Philip Nobile, ed., *Judgment at the Smithsonian* (New York: Marlowe and Co., 1995), xix.

40. Glassberg (see note 29), "Public History and the Study of Memory," 13–14.

41. Diane F. Britton, "Public History and Public Memory," *Public Historian* 19 (Summer 1997): 22.

42. Scott L. Bills, "Public Memory, Commemoration, and the 'Regime of Truth,'" *Peace & Change* 23 (April 1998): 185.

43. Josep Leerssen, "Monument and Trauma: Varieties of Remembrance," in McBride, *History and Memory in Modern Ireland*, 219–220.

44. D. George Boyce, "'No Lack of Ghosts': Memory, Commemoration, and the State in Ireland," in McBride, *History and Memory in Modern Ireland*, 268–269.

45. Efforts to "memorialize" the tragedies emerged quickly and can be seen in websites. The World Trade Center and Pentagon Disaster Information and Memorial (http://www.pentagondisaster.com) includes everything from music and poetry to information about how to help the victims to background information on terrorism and related topics. The World Trade Center/Pentagon Internet Memorial Site (http://www.worldtrade centermemorial.com) is focused on memorializing the destruction of the World Trade Center and those killed. See also the "September 11 Web Archive" at http://150.156.112.3/main.plx, with the "aim . . . to preserve

the Web expressions of individual people, groups, the press and institutions from around the world, in the aftermath of the attacks in the U.S. on September 11, 2001." The creators of this website "hope [that] the archive provides resources for many kinds of reflection on the meanings of these events."

46. The Library of Congress also established the "September, 11, 2001 Documentary Project" at http://lcweb.loc.gov/folklife/nineeleven/nineelevenhome.html. This project is described as follows: "The American Folklife Center at the Library of Congress is calling upon folklorists and other ethnographers across the nation to document on recordings the thoughts and feelings expressed by average citizens following the tragic events of September 11, 2001. These recordings and other documentation materials will become part of the Center's Archive of Folk Culture, where they will be preserved and made available to future generations. The Center will collect and preserve the audio-taped interviews and supporting materials that present the personal experience stories of average Americans in the wake of the terrorist attack. In addition, the Center will collect photographic documentation of the memorial tributes that have sprung up near the Pentagon and at the site of the World Trade Center disaster. These temporary memorials include posters, photographs, flowers, flags, and other memorabilia through which those connected to the disaster victims and others express their grief and sympathy."

47. A description of the work of this group can be found at http://www.nyshrab.org/WTC/projects.html#Planning.

48. Glenn E. Schweitzer, with Carole Dorsch Schweitzer, *A Faceless Enemy: The Origins of Modern Terrorism* (Cambridge, Mass.: Perseus, 2002), 299.

49. For an interesting discussion of the symbolic nature of the World Trade Center, see Angus Kress Gillespie, *Twin Towers: The Life of New York City's World Trade Center* (New Brunswick, N.J.: Rutgers University Press, 1999), containing some eerie descriptions based on the reasons for the 1993 terrorist attack on the structures.

50. M. Christine Boyer, "Meditations on a Wounded Skyline and Its Stratigraphies of Pain," in Michael Sorkin and Sharon Zukin, eds., *After the World Trade Center: Re-thinking New York City* (New York: Routledge, 2002), 110.

51. Roger Rosenblatt, "Ground Zero: Build a Monument of Words," *Time*, May 25, 2002, available at http://www.time.com/time/nation/printout/0,8816,249998,00.html.

52. See Heritage Preservation, *Cataclysm and Challenge: Impact of September 11, 2001 on Our Nation's Cultural Heritage* (Washington, D.C.: Heritage Preservation, Inc., 2002) n.p.

53. "The Day the World Changed," *The Economist* (September 15–21, 2001), 13.

54. See Athan G. Theoharis, ed., *A Culture of Secrecy: The Government versus the People's Right to Know* (Lawrence: University Press of Kansas, 1998), and Richard J. Cox and David A. Wallace, eds., *Archives and the Public Good: Accountability and Records in Modern Society* (Westport, Conn.: Greenwood Press, 2002).

55. Edward T. Linenthal, *The Unfinished Bombing: Oklahoma City in American Memory* (New York: Oxford University Press, 2001), 233.

56. Linenthal, *Unfinished Bombing*, 4.

57. Linenthal, *Unfinished Bombing*, 2.

58. Eric Ormsby, "The Survival of Culture, II: The Battle of the Book," *The New Criterion* 20 (October 2001): 13.

10

Archival Appraisal Alchemy

THINKING ABOUT TURDS AND STICKS

The ancient study of alchemy was the quest to turn lead into gold, to discover the philosopher's stone, which would transform base material into precious metal. During the Renaissance, it was as noble a science as any other, and some of that age's greatest minds were devoted to it or, at least, did not dismiss the notion. A curious mix of science and magic, alchemy seems to be a good image for what archivists and manuscript curators (and from here on, when I write "archivist," I include all those responsible for managing the documentary heritage, regardless of institutional affiliation, public or private) have been doing with appraisal and the collecting of documents. Faced with a nearly limitless documentary universe, archivists have been devising appraisal methods and theories meant to make that universe more manageable (and in this effort, of course, I include myself). The scientific aspect of archival appraisal alchemy might be that the struggles with the appraisal responsibility have led to more precise notions of studying and understanding records and record-keeping systems, especially as a substantial chunk of that documentary universe has become digital (or threatens to become so). The magical portion might be the persistent incantation of keywords, such as "evidence" and "information," to justify or explain a process that is really quite messy and generally not handled very systematically (and some critics of my own work might argue that I should be included in this category as well).

Alchemy does not appear, it seems, to be considerably different from what many archivists have been doing when they appraise or acquire records (even if the acquisition of records involves no more than accepting anything offered or buckling under political pressure to accept certain records). Another magical aspect of archival appraisal might be the transformation of a record, no matter how carefully appraisal is conducted, when it enters into an archival repository, and this transformation is an inherent aspect of the collecting function as well. In a recent review of scholarly studies of collecting, Peter Monaghan commenced, "Captain James Cook, as he sailed about the Pacific in the late 1700s, was so eager a collector that mocking Tongans offered him rocks and twigs. One local wit even tried to sell him a turd on a stick."[1] We might ask what it is that archivists have been trying to buy in both their musings about appraisal as reflected in their professional literature and their practice as they examine records offered to them or seek out records they believe should be in their repositories. The explosion of popular interest in collectibles seems to run parallel in our modern society to the interests, controversies, and activities of our traditional cultural repositories of museums, libraries, and archives.[2] How many archives have both turds and sticks (literally and figuratively)?

Despite the better titles for this chapter that could come from considering archival appraisal and collecting in this manner, the vision of someone or some institution wistfully acquiring the turd or the stick is not that far from what we get into when mulling over this archival function and responsibility. Something strange can transform even the most seemingly useless records when they are sent to the archives and historical manuscripts repository. In a class session, I tried to get my students to visualize this by walking out into the hallway with a simple piece of paper (it could have been a 3.5" disk or a CD) and then walking back into the room with the paper, asking them to think of the classroom as the archival repository and the hallway as everything outside of the repository. I then asked the students to tell me what was *different* about the paper, what had changed if anything had. The difference was that in the hallway the paper was simply a document, but in the classroom it had become an *archival* document. I then asked the students to visualize the doorway as being where the process of appraisal would occur and asked them to consider the implications for the document's transformation if the appraisal process were nonexistent or highly flawed or the best and most intelligent process achievable. Essentially, there were few differences with the document; once in the archives it was an archival record, added to the steadily growing backlog of processing projects.

Considering this change in a document raises many questions, of course. The most obvious one relates to the power invested in the archivist to *make* archival records, a power that most archivists don't believe they have or don't think about and an influence that some archival thinkers, especially those in the neo-Jenkinsonian school, want to discount.[3] Is a record "archival" merely because it is in an archives, or is an archival record something that exists on its own because of its special attributes, values, and uses? There does seem to be some sense of an alchemy event because an ordinary or even seemingly useless record does seem different when it resides in the archives. The transformative process of turning ordinary records into archives shows up a little more clearly in spectacular events such as the looting of archives, museums, and libraries in order to build new collections, subjugate a people, or even finance a war. Although we have gained a stronger sensitivity in the past decade or so to the ethical and moral issues involved in such areas as the cultural assets of native peoples, conquered nations in the World War II era, and the victims of genocide and racial hatred, archivists still have more thinking to do when it comes to acquiring the work of collectors and dealers, not all of whom have been very scrupulous.[4]

Although all this might suggest that no one should worry in a serious fashion about the appraisal process, or what happens to documents as they are placed in the repository, I am concerned that archivists might have been trying to accomplish too much and trying to serve too many groups, interests, and purposes in their appraisal work. The result is a mix of valuable and useless archival records with records of unknown value. Another result is a very confused idea of archives on the part of the public and policymakers and, sometimes, even archivists themselves. The sometimes confusing fictional treatment of archivists, one that often irritates us, could be merely the logical result of public uncertainties about the nature of archives and archivists.[5] For many in the public, archivists are descendants of musty antiquarians.

I am using alchemy, then, for a variety of obvious reasons. I have long thought that many archives are full of dross because of poor or nonexistent appraisal policies and processes, and I have written much over the past decade about rethinking archival appraisal because of such problems.[6] On the other hand, I have been curious about my sense that somewhat undisciplined collecting often seems to generate modest concern within the archival field (at least by its practitioners) and by those who use or value archives. Some attribute the problem of poor or uneven archival holdings to a weak knowledge about how records are used, while record-keeping theorizing continues to muddle things, an argument that does not seem to be very credible (given archivists' tremendous and decades-long emphasis on use); use as an affirmation of successful appraisal adds to appraisal's already heavy burden of responsibilities.[7] One recent critique of the flawed stress on use acknowledges that most government archives have not and will not be used but criticizes the new stress on the records continuum, evidential concepts, and a new form of functional appraisal (ignoring the possibility that overburdened appraisal methods and practices themselves may be identifying too many or the wrong records).[8] And, as will become obvious in my following comments, I am not sure that something magical doesn't happen to documentary texts entering and residing in an archives. Indeed, some archivists might cling to the public's vague perception of archives and their formation as a way of enhancing the aura of their profession, as if they possess esoteric knowledge that separates them from the public and other professionals). Moreover, the incessant focus of many archivists on basic manuals and decision templates that produce a final (hopefully easy) appraisal decision all also suggest a kind of quest for the magic of an alchemist. And finally, the traditional allusions to archival science, building on the late Renaissance notion of diplomatics and the Progressive Era's fixation with discovering universal laws by which to reform society and humankind (the era in which both the modern professions and sciences were organized), also seem to suggest a kind of pseudoscience that alchemy represented.

WHAT DOES IT MATTER?
ARCHIVES ARE ARCHIVES

Like the ancient alchemist's quest to turn mundane material into valuable assets, however, there is a lot to respect and admire in the archivist who seeks a science of record keeping and longs for universal and overarching principles to ensure that the most crucially important and useful records are identified and preserved. The business of archival appraisal might be so complicated and so flawed that there is plenty of room for all perspectives, although the limited resources for administering the documentary heritage provide reason enough to worry. The researcher who comes to the archives might be just as grateful for the records saved by accident as for those preserved via careful scrutiny and decisionmaking. Researchers might want to know about how the records came to the archives because this might tell them something about the nature of the records and the evidence and information contained in them. At the least, archivists need to work to document how they appraise and to make that documentation available to those who use or support the importance of archival records. I do not believe, however, that explaining some sort of magical transformation of ordinary documents into precious archival records will carry much weight with many. They will be believers or nonbelievers before they arrive at the archivist's door.

Other magic seems to be at work these days. With the transformation of records and information systems into digital modes, the persistence of paper at the same time, the endless media coverage of records issues and controversies, and a diversifying constituency of researchers, it seems to be a good time to reconsider just what archivists are trying to accomplish and actually succeeding at when they do appraisal. At the most general level, we can attribute some of the interest in original texts and objects to a reaction to the coldness of digital stuff (akin to the renewed interest in handwritten letters, diary writing, and scrapbooking). All the news about accounting scandals and document shredding or orders forbidding shredding also instill in the public's sensibilities the notion that records destruction is illegal and just plain bad. This implication influences the public's reactions to decisions by archivists, museum curators, librarians, and historic preservationists to preserve and, by implication, to destroy as well, especially in the reformatting of documents for reasons of accessibility and maintenance of some aspect of the content.

This business of destruction is a hard one since the public and many users of archives have the sense that no destruction occurs under the auspices of archivists. Yet every appraisal decision leads to the destruction of some records, either deliberately or as a consequence of a decision to focus attention and resources elsewhere. Even a decision to acquire records leads to a degree of destruction as the records are removed from their context of creation and use to the different environment of the archives (a loss that archival description tries to compensate for). Then there are the more basic archival questions and concerns. Do the scale and nature of the documentary universe and the various appraisal approaches developed by archivists lead to archival holdings that make any sense at all for potential researchers, documenting the past, holding certain individuals and organizations accountable, and enriching public understanding of both archives and societal memory? Or is it time to begin to rethink what archival appraisal represents and how it is done?

Not only is the documentary universe immense and complex, but the notion of the users of archives has expanded considerably as well. The range of educational and disciplinary backgrounds and purposes of researchers in archives has become so large as to belittle the notion that use is a defining purpose or measure of appraisal. Regardless of what kinds of institutions archivists work in and for, they will be confronted with hard decisions about selecting some records to be preserved, and they will need to justify their decisions with some sort of political purpose, values criteria, or conceptual framework. One question is which of these appraisal approaches apply and when. Does one approach override others? Can an archivist be aware of and sensitive to the use of records for protecting rights, serving particular constituencies, speaking for multiple segments of society, and a host of other functions—all at the same time and in the same decision? The alchemy of appraisal suggests that this is the case, but I believe it is time archivists were more forthright about the limitations of their appraisal work and results. They can garner both understanding and support if they present how and why they appraise and the strengths and weaknesses of their methods.

WHAT DO ARCHIVISTS NEED TO COMMUNICATE ABOUT APPRAISAL AND COLLECTING?

There is ample opportunity for communicating something about archival appraisal to our modern society. People collect and save lots of stuff. So do repositories like museums, libraries, and archives. Saving usually starts with the process of collecting or acquiring. We can assign, rather easily, anthropomorphic characteristics to these institutions until it is possible to see a public repository as merely an extension of a great collector, tortured by his or her nightmare of not having a complete collection, perplexed by the possibility of missing the "best" examples of a form or type, or embarrassed when a competing collector snaps up a juicy item. Some object to psychoanalyzing these repositories,[9] yet so many are the result of a pioneer collector that the two are often blurred into an incoherent mess of aims, passions, quests, and torments, handcuffing the institution's future.[10] Keener insights (or at least more focused ones) into what an archives should hold, for example, generally have come long after the origins of the archives, and the process of deaccessioning what we can see as dross throws some into conniptions. If archivists don't more rationally reconsider what they are doing in the way of collecting by transforming it into appraising (with more substantial methods, stronger aims, discernible benchmarks, and evaluative tools), archivists (along with museum curators and librarians) will confuse themselves as well as society.

The situation is already somewhat confusing. The ever shifting array of historical records repositories—private historical societies, public historical societies, government archives, corporate archives, university archives and special collections, institutional archives, theme or topically focused archives—all suggest the richness, challenges, and needs posed by the documentary universe. To the layperson, however, there are both immense differences within the community of archives and confusing similarities between libraries, museums, and archives. Have these archival repositories proliferated primarily because of recognition by society that the archival record is important or because archivists and others sense that earlier efforts have not succeeded? Or is the landscape of archival and historical records programs the result of a scale of the documentary universe that makes it impossible for existing repositories to cope? Either way, archivists are supporting additional efforts as part of a continuing quest for ways of preserving the documentary heritage. It is why archivists also seem to be searching for new and improved means to appraise and acquire records. Archival appraisal alchemy looms ahead.

TROUBLE AHEAD

Everywhere we look, we can find examples of warnings about both unbridled acquisition and injudicious decisions to stop acquiring or to start deaccessioning. Recently a museum director, contemplating the many challenges and paradoxes of museums, sounded this alarm: "Most of our great museums, having started with a single driving idea and purpose, have allowed their strengths to be diluted through growth and proliferation of efforts until they risk being overwhelmed."[11] This individual was referring, of course, to the numbers of objects with potential to be collected, preserved, interpreted, and exhibited and to the increasingly diverse audiences to be served. Archives and archivists face the same challenges, including the postmodern broadening of the concept of record and archives.[12] If the mission is too broad or too incoherently defined, archives can come to be seen as little different from unopened attics, flea markets, or antique stores with very elastic notions of antique, and in such views the powerful message that archives bring to society might be lost. I wonder, for example, if the public understands the difference between autograph collecting, whereby an individual strives to acquire the signatures of the famous and infamous for a range of personal and pecuniary reasons, and acquiring by archival repositories to accomplish a worthy aim—documenting an institution or some aspect of society, acquiring the raw materials for a particular group of researchers served by the archives, or protecting the evidence and information intended to keep someone or something accountable (and we could enumerate other purposes as well). The differences are certainly blurred when many archives also acquire the collections of autograph collectors. In addition, a considerable part of autograph collecting revolves around financial value, a value that archivists are interested in only when it comes to matters like security, insurance, exhibitions and loans, and access policies.[13]

The more recent troubles of cultural institutions like historical societies and museums have come despite the wealth represented by their holdings, one of the great ironies of our modern age and the process of appraising and acquiring documentary materials. One of the aspects of the alchemy archivists sometimes seem to expect is the ability to acquire in almost unlimited fashion with the expectation that somehow, some way, the financial and other resources necessary to manage or preserve the records will be found. As some have experienced, the public often does welcome the news that many archives, museums, and libraries holding historic documents are not financially secure.[14] There are limits and even dangers in what we do in the appraisal responsibility because acquiring records through poor decisions will transform those records into archives that are difficult to get rid of at a later time and that squeeze out more important records that ought to be preserved.

The reality of archival limitations is harsh. The bigger challenge has little to do with scholarly, philosophical, or even the most mundane practical issues represented by lots of stuff needing to be examined and sifted by archivists. The bigger challenge has to do with societal attitudes about saving stuff, some of it dressed up in scholarly jargon. Nicholson Baker created a storm with his essays and then book-length diatribe (*Double Fold*) about library preservation. Reviewers in mass media outlets lavished praise on the book, reveling in Baker's conspiratorial tone and highly quotable critical assessments. Some, like myself, provided less adoring reviews.[15] More recently, G. Thomas Tanselle, a scholar of the history of printing, for example, took after me because I suggested that Baker was arguing to save *everything*. Tanselle countered that Baker was not saying this, and then in a comical and convoluted assessment noted that all originals have value and deserve to be saved and that to think otherwise is to be *arrogant*. Wading in against me, Tanselle states:

> Archivists, indeed, often express the view that they have a duty to society, and to the future, to weed out insignificant material. The arrogance of this position is astounding. There is no way for anyone to know just which artifacts someone else, now or in the future, will find of significance; and there have been innumerable instances of materials that were ignored at one time but highly prized as another for the new insights they offer.[16]

Selection is bad because everything has value, we cannot predict use, and it implies the destruction of those documents and artifacts not saved. Of course, Tanselle never tells us how everything can be saved, but insists he is not advocating saving everything. What is amusing about the antipathy to selection is that every document is, in its own right, a representation of selection processes. Maps, to take just one example, are:

thematic: selecting and highlighting specific phenomena, consciously removing others, ignoring yet more and rendering some choices incapable of adoption by virtue of prior decisions about scale and frame. Such choices and the presences and absences they create are profoundly significant both in the making and the meaning of maps.[17]

If archivists can recognize that context, structure, and content are essential to a record—and, in fact, inherently important in every kind of document—it should not be that difficult to acknowledge that every record is also a tangle of selection decisions from the point of creation and the design of the generating systems to the final disposition. Selection is a key activity of life.

One can question who is being arrogant, but the real issue is that this is the environment in which archivists have found themselves forced to labor. The struggle with archival appraisal is that people do not want to let things go, that they worry about what might have value in the future, and that it is easy to be persuaded either to do nothing or to try to do everything in the appraising—selecting— acquiring function that is at the heart of the archival enterprise. The incessant interest in all things associated with the past, whether leading to simplistic or sophisticated comprehension of that past, is another powerful force working against the notion of analysis and selection.[18] We are back to turds and sticks. And, perhaps, I should have considered a different title for this chapter—"Archival Appraisal Arrogance."

In reacting to the kinds of criticisms offered by a Baker or a Tanselle, we can take realistic, but extreme, views. Archivists can dismiss their criticisms outright as the commentary of the uninformed, or we can respond in order to engage in public debate, or we can work on honing our own knowledge about what archives mean and what archivists must know and do. For example, Tanselle sees anything like archival appraisal as representing arrogance. Tanselle's strengths rest in his scholarship—his considerable work on the book as artifact and his understanding of its history, commercial fortunes, and societal importance. Yet those who study the record and record-keeping systems do not conclude that all must be saved. Archivist Terry Cook embraces some aspects of postmodernism because it provides a means for the archivists to understand records and record-keeping systems as things that are "constructed products," and this insight shows archivists that their process of appraisal needs to be understood as contributing to this societal construction. For Cook, appraisal in this postmodern meaning becomes a process "based on the contextual narrativity found within the records-creation process rather than on anticipated uses of the records' subject content." And for Cook this adds more to the appraisal task: "Appraisal would attend as carefully to the marginalized and even silenced voices as it now does to the powerful voices found in official institutional records."[19] Although I am not as sanguine about the usefulness of postmodern scholarship, I do concur with Cook that the essence of appraisal is understanding records and record-keeping systems. South African historian Greg Cuthbertson draws on postmodernism and postcolonial theory in a similarly useful way by stressing, for example, that we should be "concerned with process and production rather than with content. The context becomes more important than the text. We dare not forget that documents have been removed from their original locations to the space of the archive, which itself has another context."[20] (I also note that Cook's reflections produce more purposes for archival appraisal, reminding us of the complexities of appraising records or, as Tanselle and others believe, rolling dice with the future.)

THE EVOLUTION OF ARCHIVAL APPRAISAL

Archival appraisal has not always been viewed as something that was particularly troublesome or challenging. Nothing approaching what we could term an archival or historical manuscripts repository worried about a function such as appraisal until well into the middle of the twentieth century. The private and public historical societies saw their objective as acquiring anything, and, indeed, in the days of primitive firefighting and security, such a goal seems noble and rational. Preservation was equated, mostly, with collecting and housing, although ultimately the business of acquiring caught up with, passed by, and then overwhelmed these traditional historical manuscripts repositories.[21] National and local pride, a celebratory notion of promoting the present by demonstrating the blessings of history, the antiquarian's delight in the aged and crumbling document, and an eclectic passion for anything seeming to provide a pathway into the past were among the prime motivators in the acquisitions by historical societies. Certainly, when all else fails, acquiring records seems to be the safest route for most archives to take in order to perform their missions; while collecting can be explained or criticized from a multiplicity of angles, we must recognize that collecting, whether with sophisticated criteria or none at all, is a predominant and traditional form of archival appraisal. There remain archivists who believe that others, records creators or individual collectors, should make the decisions about what should reside in archives, but even their end result is collecting colored by motivations that may not be far different from those of the nineteenth-century societies. Indeed, some archivists today acknowledge that virtually anything can have value to someone at some time in the future.

Before things got too complicated, despite the continuing lament about the growing quantity of records to deal with, the notion of appraisal got codified and, in another sense, simplified. In the American context, it was the work of the staff of the National Archives, mostly explained or codified by T. R. Schellenberg, that produced the first framework for appraisal, giving us the notion of primary/secondary and evidential/informational values.[22] Whether this framework was used in a systematic fashion is hard to determine because the documentation of appraisal decisions is uneven and in many archival repositories nearly nonexistent. However the paradigm was used, it became a powerful explanation for what archivists do. To this day, most American archivists speak in Schellenbergian terms about appraisal. We could adopt a postmodern explanation, as does historian Cuthbertson when he writes:

> Museums both created and reflected the prevailing imperial beliefs of the nineteenth century, and curators in an age of positivism had none of the uncertainties of our own times. They had confidence in their classification and organization of collections, which they regarded as scientifically arranged and presented, and therefore authentic and objective.[23]

Perhaps the archivists of the thirties and forties were operating in the same mindset. However, I believe this might be nothing more than overinterpretation. In fact, adopting the language of evidence and information as used by Schellenberg seems often to cover many bases and purposes, explaining why I often resort to the same language in this chapter. Indeed, we can see a kind of appraisal alchemy at work here in the chanting of the evidential/informational nodes. I worry, for example, when I use these terms, whether people understand them in the manner in which I intend or if they interpret them as a handy paradigm to cover the variety of reasons for which records might and ought to be saved.

It is unfair, for sure, to criticize Schellenberg or the National Archives more than half a century later (although it is also ridiculous to suggest, as some have, that Schellenberg or Jenkinson or any other archival scholar has neatly summarized all there is to know about archives and records management).[24] The root problem in all this has been that most contemporary archivists seem intent on finding a simple, straightforward model for making all appraisal decisions. One desired aspect of the alchemy is appraisal approaches, and preferably a single grand scheme, to take care of records in all media. Traditional paper systems, laden with office memos and canceled checks, need to be dealt with at the same time as increasingly complex digital systems, creating and holding things that stretch the definition of a record. Indeed, every time a system needs to be migrated to new hardware and software, the records might need to be reappraised, transforming the appraisal process into one that is nearly continuous; I have argued in other venues that archives need to become a process, not just a place.

Appraising digital systems has created problems for many archivists, primarily because they have operated with an eye on the cultural or symbolic value of archives but also because it is not as easy to mouth the evidential or informational concepts for these records systems as it is for paper-based systems. Where are such values in the bits and bytes of a geographic information system or an electronic spreadsheet? Although some can take solace in the idea that the cultural symbolism of an archives rests with its building and accumulated holdings, there are problems even with this view. A number of archivists are identifying their aim to be more a regulatory one, in which records systems with archival importance are identified but are administered within the offices of the records creators via rules and policies set by the archival agency. The goal of accumulation may be antiquated, except when the records systems are threatened by the demise of an office or a functional responsibility. This threat might explain some of the tensions between manuscript curators, archivists, records managers, and knowledge managers as society shifts gears into a digital era;[25] in one sense, there is a spectrum here from collectors and accumulators to those mining all information and evidence sources for particular uses in support of their organizations, or from those stressing the artifact to those managing content. (I continue to lament the various schisms within the records professions because they weaken all aspects of the importance of records and especially the responsibility for selection.)

There is little doubt that the archival facilities being constructed today, with provision for digital media, suggest through their architectural styles and locations something very different from their predecessors. We have seen a shift from Neoclassical styles, with their suggestion of stability, history, and permanence, to postmodernist steel and glass skeletons that suggest a shopping mall and certainly appear less permanent. An essay in the *Washington Post* tried to relate the glass and steel structure of the new National Archives building to its preservation function, a kind of emergency room for archival documents:

> The National Archives at College Park radiates a sense of intrigue normally lacking in our houses of government affairs. It is sleek—all planes and angles, except for a foyer that comes sweeping out across the courtyard. The bright steel-and-glass facade reflects a grove of protective trees. Armed guards watch the doors. One might say the place looks dangerous.[26]

The shifting architectural styles of archives buildings and their symbolic importance might not be unrelated to how and why archivists approach appraisal. That the notions proposed by Schellenberg and affirmed by subsequent archival commentators such as Maynard Brichford and Gerry Ham,[27] with some revisions and revamping, remained in effect for more than half a century flies in the face of an ever changing sense of the past, historical research, and the nature and use of historical documentation. The public seems determined to believe in its heroes and icons no matter what evidence is mounted to challenge that heroism. Some have argued that only those in power and who wish to retain that power create records, presenting a lopsided view of the past.[28] Some of this cynicism comes from good old-fashioned conspiracy theorizing, but some emanates from scholars who have created detailed and sometimes mind-boggling approaches to deconstructing documents and who also have expanded the sense of documents to include oral tradition, material culture, landscape and place, movies and television, and a host of other sources. Archives as a term now have a more complex and richer sense, and this makes the business of appraisal more complex and more challenging. Searching for one model or one-formula-fits-all appraisal method seems doomed to failure.

As the archival profession has matured and knowledge of the challenges presented by the documentary universe has increased, we have witnessed the appearance of many new concepts with promise for aiding or guiding archival appraisal. Documentation strategies, functional analysis, macroappraisal, the rebirth of diplomatics, the record-keeping warrant, and a variety of other techniques have been discussed, used, abused, and in some cases shelved.[29] These new or reworked appraisal concepts stemmed from a growing sense, in the 1970s and 1980s, that archivists were acquiring the wrong records or that they had no prevailing models for what they were trying to achieve in the appraisal function.[30] We even entertained the concept of reappraisal to help archivists determine whether past appraisal decisions had merit.[31] Over time, archivists have promoted cooperation, institutional collection analysis, and other ways of seeing beyond the walls of their own repositories in order to contend with the problems and promises of modern records systems.[32] More sophisticated notions of the collections policy and other long-valued concepts all suggest that archivists are at least grappling intellectually with the promises, perils, and pitfalls of archival appraisal.[33] All their efforts share one characteristic—a search for a broad approach to archival appraisal because of the realization that the documentary universe, growing in size and complexity, is outpacing the effectiveness of traditional methods.[34] Moreover, they all suggest the reality that appraisal is a very subjective process, fraught with the possibility of mistakes and certainly limited by the fact that we cannot predict what will be used or of use in the future. This reality has led to some interesting and heated debates as well.[35] Even the records manager, armed with his or her schedule based on laws and accounting requirements, has to admit that these legal and best practice principles are also flawed because they are the products of ever changing societal interests. Whether any of these principles have become practical, daily aids to the appraisal process is uncertain because we have little research (except for a few rare exceptions)[36] that analyzes what archivists do or do not do appraisal-wise in their repositories.

The increasing richness of writing (and some research) about archival appraisal, especially since the mid-1980s, is counter to the fact that many archivists seem to ignore or express frustration with their professional literature. Most of the Internet discussion lists devoted to archival topics seem to avoid references to publications. When archivists do discuss publishing, they are referring to basic manuals, again reflecting the quest for rules, benchmarks, and procedures, which do not always support a complicated process like appraisal (an area that might be more susceptible to detailed case studies). A number of archivists have taken the view that appraisal is a craft to be learned on the job and that experience is far more important than the theoretical literature about appraisal methods. Although it is certainly true that much can be learned about appraisal by doing it, one wonders what archival institutions are doing that offers an educational framework or that sustains and builds on the knowledge supporting appraisal. One wonders as well why more case studies have not been published, either in the professional literature or on websites associated with archival programs, capturing what is being learned by appraising certain kinds of records. In recent months, for example, I had a conversation with an archivist working with electronic records in a repository that refused to state the criteria it uses to select what electronic systems and data files will be maintained as part of the archives. In my own experience, I have heard archivists who confuse appraisal with fiscal accounting merely restate Schellenberg's parameters without any specifics or acknowledge that they do not have the time to do any substantial analysis as part of appraisal.[37] No wonder we cannot explain the process of forming archival holdings to the public, policymakers, and scholars who use archives.

EDUCATING FOR APPRAISAL

Like the ancient alchemists, the pioneering archivists working in appraisal learned their craft as apprentices. The heyday of the formation of American and English archival theory, extending from World War I through World War II, occurred when there were no archival education programs of any serious nature or substance. In North America, as single courses and occasional workshops expanded to multiweek institutes and then to multicourse programs in history departments and library and information science schools, appraisal remained on the back burner, far behind arrangement and description and the reference functions. By the late 1980s, we began to see full courses on archival appraisal, but it is fair to say that even at the present, archival appraisal is downplayed in favor of descriptive and reference activities. The lack of formal education in appraisal forces practitioners to learn it on the job, but we really do not know how this happens. My experience in having students interview archivists about appraisal work and collection policies suggests that it is a professional function that is still not done well (or, at the least, one that is done very unevenly). A sense emerges that archival appraisal is too time consuming amid the throng of other responsibilities, and the pressure is on to find a magic formula for doing appraisal quickly and efficiently or to use Schellenbergian language as if it were a magical incantation to justify what has been done.

That archival appraisal, the most intellectual aspect of archival work, has not become the linchpin of all education programs in the field should not be surprising—but it is revealing about the problems associated with this archival function. Educators face some interesting challenges in preparing individuals to be archivists. On the one hand, most of the expansion of graduate archival education has taken place in professional schools, which emphasize skills, techniques, and methods rather than reflection on the work of archivists and the knowledge they need in order to function. On the other hand, the field itself seems to add pressure for programs to turn out practitioners, ready to go at the outset of their careers knowing everything or having answers for every problem or challenge. I have had numerous discussions with archivists who wonder whether in my course on archival appraisal the students actually do any appraisal, betraying the field's continuing preoccupation with the practicum or fieldwork as the essential aspect of education. Most education programs continue to stress the arrangement and description aspect of archival work both because the educators recognize that prospective employers still mostly hire entry-level archivists to do this kind of work and because arrangement and description remain the predominant need of institutions willing to host student interns. The fixation with processing backlogs is ironic given that some of these backlogs possibly reflect poor appraisal decisions and because appraisal, done well, can speed up the processing work itself.

THE CENTRAL PLACE OF APPRAISAL

I am sure many archivists would argue, vociferously, about my statement that archival appraisal is the core intellectual responsibility of the archivist. Most would contend that descriptive work is the core function, and even the older European tradition of diplomatics supports this concept. I wonder if we haven't lost our way somewhere in the past twenty or so years of increasingly more thorough descriptive standards and techniques. Despite all these elaborate standards, archivists still seem prone to write descriptions based on the content of records and a laborious reading of them. The question is, however, whether this depth is even possible (how do you read thousands, hundreds of thousands, and more documents?) or desirable. Does the content of documents, no matter how important, constitute the most important or crucial aspect of what people need records for? In some cases this is certainly the case, but not in all or perhaps even most cases. The descriptive information that is really needed is the form, function, warrant, origins, and other aspects of the records and the system supporting them, and most of this information does not necessitate a traditional reading of the records but rather an analysis of the kind required in conducting appraisal. It has always amazed me how often archivists either provide incredible detail about the scope of their processing backlogs but nothing about the appraisal of the records that form these mounds or, worse, admit they do not have or follow any appraisal guidelines or standards.

For me, this is both the Achilles' heel of archival descriptive work and the potential partial solution to better administering this work. How can we complain about archival processing backlogs if significant portions of what are in the archives have not really been appraised? If an appraisal process is followed that relates closely to what has been called macroappraisal, then I submit that most of what should constitute the key parts of the descriptive apparatus should be in place long before the records are either accessioned or examined for additional descriptive work. A proper appraisal process should amass a substantial amount of information providing both better data for final descriptions and most of the same information that would eventually come to light if an archives had a good descriptive process in place. Even if the set of records comes from a private collector, the description of the records should focus as much on the aims, means, and nature of the collecting process as on the content and nature of the documents assembled. Archivists have an opportunity to both draw on and contribute to the abundance of scholarship on collecting. They can contribute through finding aids, websites, and journals of disciplines interested in both collecting and records (such as history, librarianship, anthropology, sociology, and psychology).

The impatience with the inquiry and research required for appraisal is predictable given the nature of our archival programs and our society. There is no reason to believe that any archival programs are not short of staff, space, and funds. This circumstance impacts appraisal in many ways, even occasionally leading to a moratorium on acquisition but more often than not resulting in snap or defensive decisions to take records rather than risk their loss; the sense is that a leisurely analysis will not work because there are many other things to do and too few resources to do them. There is a problem with making such decisions. A decision that is not carefully considered results in acquisitions that will be difficult, either legally or politically, to be rid of at a future date—that magical transformation business again. When a private collector decides to be rid of an unwanted item, the collector has only to sell or trade it—a far cry from the situation at a public repository, where an item has become an archival record and legal and ethical issues entangle its deaccessioning. There are vast gaps between archival appraisal and collecting.

The collapse of a sense of time in modern society has made both individuals and institutions worry about what they do and how long it takes. Work and home have been blurred, the computer has us connected to our work around the clock, and we microanalyze the time to do even the most routine task. I also sense this obsession in the work expected of archivists. In the past, an archivist might take years to evaluate records *after* they were created (sometimes accidentally discovering them long after their creation), but now with modern digital systems, archivists seem to need to make appraisal decisions *before* the records are created. Archivists can be forgiven for their frustration about shortages of time; it is a modern preoccupation. It also is another goad for formulaic solutions. Archivists sometimes wish to decide quickly whether a document should be acquired. The reality is, however, that archivists need, first, to have a clear plan or agenda for appraisal and, second, to do careful analysis of the records, their origins, their functions, and their importance for purposes such as accountability, evidence, information, research, and symbolic or cultural value. All of the latter can require immense resources, especially time.

Another aspect of the appraisal alchemy is the belief, usually unspoken, that archives can sweep up all these records, in multiple media, and that they will be protected, managed, preserved, and used. Archivists know, however, that the conservation needs of the archival holdings far exceed the resources available for this purpose, especially with the addition of digital media with its greater needs for technical expertise. The net effect is that we need to view archival appraisal as a kind of continuous, not one-time, process. There are no magic formulae nor will the records pulled into an archives in a haphazard or emergency way necessarily transmute into real archives with real uses. And even if the worst or most inane materials ultimately gain respectability and use, one must still wonder whether valuable records were ignored or lost as attention was diverted to lesser stuff. Accumulated piles of documents, texts, and information of whatever quality are a symbolic nod to the power of those who control writing, literacy, and information.[38] Because the process of bringing records into archives transforms them into archives, it is crucial for archivists to develop processes ensuring that the crucially important records get there and that society understands why records are important to it and its citizens.

WHERE DO ARCHIVISTS GO FROM HERE?

We have a wide array of intriguing and useful approaches to appraisal and face constantly changing records technologies and warrants governing records systems. Some of the technologies, laws, policies, and other external aspects of these systems already strain the operating assumptions many archivists have about their mission and responsibilities. It is one thing to cheerfully and easily say we are in the business of identifying, preserving, and making available for use the records of enduring or continuing value. However, each of the components of this usefully articulated professional mission is fraught with nuances, questions, challenges, and problems. Moreover, and most importantly, each aspect of this mission may not be clearly understood by the public and policymakers, the people archivists ultimately are responsible to in their work. As for the research users of archives, their lack of understanding might be even greater. Historians, often heralded as the most important of the research constituencies of archives, often expect that the shaping of the documentary heritage has had little to do with archivists (and is more the result of human frailties, accidents, circumstances, and the powerful who control corporations and governments and create the majority of the records). There are, however, other scholarly and important users of archives—sociologists, journalists, political scientists, anthropologists, and the like—and we have little information about what they know of the formation of archives.

We need public scholarship that explains, warts and all, the way archives' holdings are formed. This can be accomplished by exhibitions at archives although exhibitions will reach only those individuals coming into archives, but it is important that we begin to support scholarship that reaches the public and policymakers. We have had and will continue to have opportunities to explain ourselves. I do not believe the publicity generated by Nicholson Baker's *Double Fold* is a unique or isolated occasion. Enron/Arthur Andersen, Executive Order 13223, Mayor Rudolph Giuliani's records, and other cases grabbing the attention of reporters and columnists all provide opportunities for archivists to discuss how and why archives are formed and are important. Deliberations in Florida about whether to preserve the contested ballots and other voting records associated with the controversial 2000 presidential election, normally disposed of after twenty-two months, is yet another example of an opportunity to explain what archives represent.[39] Public understanding of archives is especially important as archivists face a swarm of ordeals: some major reappraising and deaccessioning decisions necessitated by poor past appraisal decisions, the limitations of our space and other resources, and the increasingly challenging documentary universe. Many archivists have been dismayed by the confused and negative media attacks on efforts to dispose of archival holdings, and our only effective comeback is a clear appeal convincing the public that not everything should or can be saved. Making this case will not be easy. In the public's mind, archives are little different from flea markets, antique stores, or the warehouses Baker applauds in his critique. At the least, archivists need to explain that appraisal is not the process of assigning financial value to old records, akin to what happens on *Antiques Road-*

show. Archivists also need to discuss the meaning of archives in modern society. Archivists have pointed to use studies as a way of describing themselves and their success,[40] but comment cards at the controversial *Enola Gay* exhibition at the Smithsonian revealed that many museum visitors were confused about the museum's very different roles of celebrating the American past and educating visitors about it.[41] At present, museums seem to be drawing more fire than archives in these issues of public sentiment about politics and the past. However, what archivists appraise will make up the evidence for studying the past, so archives can expect their share of closer scrutiny. Imparting an understanding of archives in society will prepare archivists for these public jousts. It will also assist archivists to think about the constituencies they are serving when they appraise. In some cases, archivists need to admit that their accumulation of records may be more important as a cultural symbol than as sources for research. The closest archivists have gotten to this idea is accepting the fact that some records might have intrinsic value and deserve to be maintained primarily for exhibitions and publicity purposes. In this contentious and often conflicted society likely to question or protest decisions about its past, archivists also will recognize that there is no single or simple formula for appraisal. Public understanding is especially critical because engaging writers and scholars such as Nicholson Baker and Thomas Tanselle argue so cleverly against the kinds of selection decisions made by archivists, preservation administrators, librarians, and museum curators.

To continue the education of the public, each appraisal decision must include information enabling others to understand how and why the decision was made. These reports need to be included in the finding aids prepared by archivists. It is interesting that the archivist's emphasis on finding aids over the past half century— from manuscript registers and archival inventories to the U.S. MARC Archives and Manuscripts Control format to the Encoded Archival Description—has not included these reports. The reasons for this omission are not clear. Perhaps it is the result of uneven and sketchy information about the decisions or the result of a concern for privacy about the acquisition process. More likely, the reasons emanate from archivists' sense that researchers are not interested in such matters but prefer to focus on getting information and evidence from the records themselves (unfortunately, the small number of user studies have not provided sufficient depth about such use).[42] Jacques Le Goff, reflecting on modern historical scholarship, notes that considerable attention is now being given to the silences in documentation. He advocates that historians must ask "about the holes and blank spots in history, the things it has forgotten. We have to inventory the archives of silence, and write history on the basis of documents and the absence of documents."[43] Archivists need to ensure that one of the silences is not about how archival collections have been and are being formed.

As new types of record-keeping systems emerge that might transform the appraisal process into a continuous process, it is likely that archivists will want more input from researchers and others when making reappraisal decisions. And, given the symbolic or cultural aspect of archives, it might be that researchers will be just as interested in the process of the formation of archives as they will in the information or evidence found in them. We know that records systems reflect the needs and intents of individuals and institutions in ways that can be deciphered. Equally important, the researcher will want to know why certain records are still in existence and what has been lost. Others outside the archives field but working with similar aims of preserving information documents have commented on changes in their work in a similar way. In an essay about coping with the growing number of e-journals and e-publications, Julia Martin and David Coleman argue that we need to take up a:

> metaphoric conceptualization of the archive as a living ecosystem, where information and its delivery systems are recognized as dynamic, highly changeable, and inhabited by humans. If we want to keep data alive, strategies involving all players in the ecosystem—publishers, librarians, archivists, information consumers, and authors—are vital.

They continue,

> Data grows, lives, and dies, as do delivery systems. As never before, the task of keeping data alive requires frequent adaptations to and perpetual evolution of the archival system. To keep pace with technological flux, an ongoing process of selection—of media platforms, of preservation structures, of migratory patterns—is necessary to avoid data extinction. In these various ways, an ecological force is at work. In fact, several ecological themes are already at play in electronic archives. These include the encouragement of symbiotic relationships,

the use of anti-extinction preservation and migratory schemes, and the deliberate adoption of cloning/breeding campaigns.[44]

Archives are, of course, partly a means of remembering (as well as understanding) the past. One historian has questioned whether we have too much memory and whether this memory is a drag on our ability to consider the future. Charles Maier senses that

> modern American politics . . . has become a competition for enshrining grievances. Every group claims its share of public honor and public funds by pressing disabilities and injustices. National public life becomes the settlement of a collective malpractice suit in which all citizens are patients and physicians simultaneously.[45]

Many of these groups, of course, want an archives as part of their claim on society. Many also would desire to ensure that some documentary presence of its role in society is being protected. Yet these groups also might differ over what records are saved or how they might be interpreted by others (suggesting that they want control over access and use of the records). Appraisal, placed in this context, will require archivists to explain themselves. It will also require archivists to recognize a fuller range of implications and purposes of appraisal.

One aspect of such study of archival appraisal is a fuller appreciation of the power archivists actually hold in society because of their shaping of the documentary heritage. The question of the objectivity and objectives of the archivist in carrying out appraisal has been debated within the discipline to a certain extent, with some objecting strenuously to the notion that archivists have a role in shaping anything. Although I am not an advocate of the archivist's shaping anything in a deliberate fashion, I realize there is power or authority associated with the process of saving records in an archives. Archivists have been loath to discuss any sense of power, even when considering their own societal status and credentials, but scholarship about public memory and postmodernist studies about texts or documents has witnessed the power associated with the formation of both records and public memory.[46] It is important that archivists have some power because the emergent records systems utilizing digital technologies require archivists to associate themselves with corporate and government entities that are building the information networks. The power of records does not reside only in the cultural, symbolic, or scholarly uses of archives but also includes the importance of records in legal, evidence, and accountability issues. Many archivists see problems with the latter because they see records managers using these principles and ignoring the archival components of records programs. The separation between records managers and archivists is now more than half a century old. The collapse of Enron and the complicity of the accounting firm Arthur Andersen in its fiscal mismanagement will change forever just how records managers conduct their work and justify their existence. Archivists do need to recognize the power of records for holding people, governments, corporations, and other institutions accountable to society.[47] As I was writing this chapter, news coverage appeared about the opening of records related to Mexico's "dirty war." The article reported, "As journalists, scholars and prosecutors pore over the archives—more than 80 million index cards and 30,000 photographs—the emerging information about the government's abuses has sparked a national catharsis as well as investigations of former presidents and cabinet ministers."[48] "Catharsis" and "investigations" suggest that archivists need to be especially careful when they appraise records. Accountability, societal and organizational memory, evidence, and the law need to be on their front burners just as much as informational value, symbolic and cultural attributes, and the scholarly potential of the records. The real archival appraisal alchemy might be in just how effectively archivists can sort through these purposes and processes to develop the most suitable appraisal criteria at particular times and for particular types of records, document appraisal effectively, and explain archival appraisal to the people and institutions needing to understand its importance.

As an educator, it is natural for me to also consider the changes needed in the education of archivists and the place of appraisal in this education. As I have written elsewhere, I believe that the focal point of education is studying records and record-keeping systems, not just the history, theory, or principles associated with archival knowledge and practice, and the archival educator must therefore be multidisciplinary in outlook.[49] It worries me that a generation or more of graduate archival education was devoted to archival arrangement and description and the creation of finding aids, as if this is the crux of what archivists know and do. Appraisal, with its need to understand records and record-keeping systems and the demand to make decisions that force archivists to think about their purpose and societal role, is the better focus for graduate education. Appraisal is more conceptual, theoretical, intellectual, and broad than all of the other functions combined. In fact, if archivists do not accept appraisal and the other aspects of the epistemological parameters of archival work as the foundation for archival education, it is possible that the strides made in this education in the past twenty years will be lost. The practical bent of many education programs seems to suggest that archival education will have a niche in the universities where utilitarian knowledge predominates, but this emphasis on practical skills could lead to a failure to construct a research knowledge, public scholarship, and challenging and credible curriculum with recognized scholars (recognized beyond the narrow confines of archives programs and the discipline itself) that are the hallmarks of university education and most professional education within the university.[50]

The mere acquiring of records and forming archival collections, no matter what the means, is not enough to support the importance of records in our society. Admittedly, a lot of fascinating and important stuff is in our archives, and perhaps it seems to be a fruitless exercise to worry about how it got there. I would have to agree that the most important task is to look ahead. In looking down the road, however, it seems to me archivists will need to explain themselves and their holdings in more coherent ways than ever before. Resources do not seem to be growing, and many interests are competing for what resources there are. Archivists need to sort through all their various appraisal methodologies and concepts and identify those that are most effective for supporting the importance of records in our modern society.[51]

Whether by education or experience, archivists have acquired substantial knowledge of appraising records, not all of which is captured in their professional literature or reflected in their public profile. They need to be more public in their discussions about the selection and preservation of records and more forceful in engaging those critics who question the fundamentals and aims of the appraisal function. Although acknowledging that archives are a powerful source of cultural and symbolic value (which explains both why they need greater support and why they are targeted for destruction by terrorists), archivists also need to demonstrate that they are not magicians performing tricks or oracles with foreknowledge of what should be saved. Rather, archivists are the guardians of an important societal responsibility, protecting our documentary heritage, holding our officials and institutions accountable, and allowing scholars and others to connect with a past that is the doorway for self-understanding.

CONCLUSION: MORE ARCHIVAL ALCHEMY? MAYBE

Some might believe that I have contributed to the archival alchemy as well, by offering support for the archival documentation strategy, pushing more rigorous research and education as crucial pillars for archival work, arguing for evidence as a better focus for archival appraisal, and pushing for a new kind of archival professionalism less concerned with credentials and more concerned with knowledge. I am probably partially guilty of such a charge; at least I feel the need to confess that I, too, have searched for better ways of performing most archival functions and responsibilities. In theory, we might have too many objectives, in practice most archivists might really only be appropriating the language of appraisal, but our greatest challenge is in explaining ourselves to the public and winning its support.

Appraisal is hard, careers are short, and there are too many turds and sticks.

NOTES

1. Peter Monaghan, "Collected Wisdom," *Chronicle of Higher Education*, June 28, 2002, A17.

2. Read, for example, Susan Sheehan and Howard Means, *The Banana Sculptor, the Purple Lady, and the All-Night Swimmer: Hobbies, Collecting, and Other Passionate Pursuits* (New York: Simon and Schuster, 2002), and try to imagine what the differences might be between collecting by an individual as a hobby and supposedly more professional collecting by repositories like museums, archives, and libraries.

3. See, especially, Luciana Duranti, "The Concept of Appraisal and Archival Theory," *American Archivist* 57 (Spring 1994): 328–344.

4. James M. O'Toole, "The Symbolic Significance of Archives," *American*

Archivist 56 (Spring 1993): 234–255, provides some background on this kind of value associated with archives. A good introduction to the theft and looting during World War II of museum, library, and archival collections is Elizabeth Simpson, ed., *The Spoils of War: World War II and Its Aftermath; The Loss, Reappearance, and Recovery of Cultural Property* (New York: Harry N. Abrams, 1997). For an excellent analysis of the manner of collecting that was conducted within the Nazi regime, see Jonathan Petropoulos, *Art as Politics in the Third Reich* (Chapel Hill: University of North Carolina Press, 1996), and *The Faustian Bargain: The Art World in Nazi Germany* (New York: Oxford University Press, 2000).

5. See, for example, Martha Cooley, *The Archivist: A Novel* (Boston: Little, Brown, 1998).

6. My first professional essay was a story of the pursuit and purchase of the personal papers of Maryland's proprietary family by the Maryland Historical Society in the nineteenth century, published as the "A History of the Calvert Papers, MS. 174," *Maryland Historical Magazine* 68 (Fall 1973): 309–22. Most of my early writing on appraisal was historical, such as the histories of the formation of the Maryland Hall of Records and the development of archival programs in Alabama or the work of individual collectors, published as "A Century of Frustration: The Movement for the Founding of the State Archives in Maryland, 1811–1935," *Maryland Historical Magazine* 78 (Summer 1983): 106–117; "Alabama's Archival Heritage, 1850–1985," *Alabama Review* 40 (October 1987): 284–307; and "The Origins of American Religious Archives: Ethan Allen, Pioneer Church Historian and Archivist of Maryland," *Journal of the Canadian Church Historical Society* 29 (October 1987): 48–63. In the mid-1980s I became interested in the concept of documentation strategies, influenced by Helen Samuels and Larry Hackman, and wrote a series of articles about this methodology, "The Archivist's 'First Responsibility': A Research Agenda for the Identification and Selection of Records of Enduring Value" (written with Helen W. Samuels), *American Archivist* 51 (Winter/Spring 1988): 28–42; "Selecting Historical Records for Microfilming: Some Suggested Procedures for Repositories," *Library & Archival Security* 9, no. 2, (1989): 21–41; "A Documentation Strategy Case Study: Western New York," *American Archivist* 52 (Spring 1989): 192–200; "The Documentation Strategy and Archival Appraisal Principles: A Different Perspective," *Archivaria* 38 (Fall 1994): 11–36; "The Archival Documentation Strategy: A Brief Intellectual History, 1984–1994 and Practical Description," *Janus,* 1995, no. 2: 76–93; and "The Archival Documentation Strategy and Its Implications for the Appraisal of Architectural Records," *American Archivist* 59 (Spring 1996): 144–154. In the past half decade or so, I have shifted to critiquing the notion of collecting and appraisal methodology, somewhat prompted by my concerns with the implications of electronic records and the schism between archivists and records managers,

resulting in essays such as "The Archivist and Collecting: A Review Essay," *American Archivist* 59 (Fall 1996): 496–512; "Archival Anchorites: Building Public Memory in the Era of the Culture Wars," *Multicultural Review* 7 (June 1998): 52–60; "Records Management Scheduling and Archival Appraisal," *Records and Information Management Report* 14 (April 1998): 1–16; and "The Traditional Archival and Historical Records Program in the Digital Age: A Cautionary Tale," *Records and Information Management Report* 17 (May 2001): 1–16 (included in this book). More recently the acclaim for Nicholson Baker's book about library preservation of books and newspapers has led to articles about the need for clarifying the mission of archivists and the role of appraisal and selection in preservation, including essays such as "The Great Newspaper Caper: Backlash in the Digital Age," *First Monday* 5 (December 4, 2000), available at http://firstmonday.org/issues/issue5_12/cox/ (reprinted in *Collection Building*). In the past two years I have found myself asked to give presentations at a number of conferences on appraisal issues, and some of these papers have been published, such as this chapter; "Evidence and Archives," *Records and Information Management Report* 17 (November 2001): 1–14; "The End of Collecting: Towards a New Purpose for Archival Appraisal," *Archival Science* 2 (2002): 287–309; and "Archives and the Digital Future," *Journal of the Irish Society of Archivists*, forthcoming—all included in this book.

7. One of the most direct connections between use and appraisal is Terry Eastwood, "Toward a Social Theory of Appraisal," in Barbara L. Craig, ed., *The Archival Imagination: Essays in Honour of Hugh A. Taylor* (Ottawa: Association of Canadian Archivists, 1992), 71–89.

8. See, for example, Paul Macpherson, "Theory, Standards and Implicit Assumptions: Public Access to Post-current Government Records," *Archives and Manuscripts* 30, no. 1 (2002): 6–17.

9. Indeed, we can go to extremes when we apply psychological perspectives to the business of collecting. An English professor of psychology writes, "Psychologists have identified healthy and unhealthy responses to the influx of paper. The healthy response is supposedly to file, act or toss, while the unhealthy response is supposedly to pile, copy and store." He continues:

> Pathological hoarding has been associated with an obsessive/compulsive personality syndrome. Hoarders, according to the theory, are likely to be very concerned with cleanliness, time-keeping and order. Freudians argue that these attitudes start very early—at the potty training age, in fact. Further difficulties at this time can lead to opposite behaviors—both rather abnormal. Thus the obsessional hoarder and miser as well as the compulsive spendthrift may have had a traumatic power conflict over the potty (Adrian Furnham, "Freud and the Office Hoarder," *Financial Times*, July 4, 2002, available at http://www.emailthis.clickability.com/et/emailThis?clickMap = viewThis&etMailToID = 169471649&pt = Y; accessed July 6, 2002).

For a more insightful assessment of the psychology of collecting, see Werner Muensterberger, *Collecting: An Unruly Passion; Psychological Perspectives* (Princeton, N.J.: Princeton University Press, 1994).

10. Something of the origins of great institutional collections in the efforts of individual, private collectors can be seen in Nicholas A. Basbanes, *A Gentle Madness: Bibliophiles, Bibliomanes, and the Eternal Passion for Books* (New York: Henry Holt, 1995).

11. Keith S. Thomson, *Treasures on Earth: Museums, Collections, and Paradoxes* (London: Faber and Faber, 2002), 106.

12. For interesting thoughts on this, see Sarah Tyacke, "Archives in a Wider World: The Culture and Politics of Archives," *Archivaria* 52 (Fall 2001): 1–25.

13. An understanding of autograph collecting can be gained from Kenneth W. Rendell, *History Comes to Life: Collecting Historical Letters and Documents* (Norman: University of Oklahoma Press, 1995), and Charles Hamilton, *Collecting Autographs and Manuscripts* (Norman: University of Oklahoma Press, 1961, 1970). Of course, many archivists have commented on the financial implications of appraisal as part of the managing of this process; it figures prominently in the "black box" schematic for appraisal suggested in *Archival Appraisal* by Frank Boles in association with Julia Marks Young (New York: Neal-Schuman Publishers, 1991).

14. Walter Muir Whitehill, *Independent Historical Societies: An Enquiry into Their Research and Publication Functions and Their Financial Future* (Boston: Boston Athenaeum, 1962); Charles Phillips and Patricia Hogan, *The Wages of History: The AASLH Employment Trends and Salary Survey* (Nashville: American Association for State and Local History, 1984); and *A Culture at Risk: Who Cares for America's Heritage?* (Nashville: American Association for State and Local History, 1984).

15. Nicholson Baker, *Double Fold: Libraries and the Assault on Paper* (New York: Random House, 2001); Richard J. Cox, *Vandals in the Stacks? A Response to Nicholson Baker's Assault on Libraries* (Westport, Conn.: Greenwood Press, 2002).

16. G. Thomas Tanselle, "The Librarians' Double-Cross," *Raritan* 21 (Spring 2002): 258.

17. Denis Cosgrove, ed., *Mappings* (London: Reaktion Books, 1999), 11.

18. Roy Rosenzweig and David Thelen, *The Presence of the Past: Popular Uses of History in American Life* (New York: Columbia University Press, 1998).

19. Terry Cook, "Fashionable Nonsense or Professional Rebirth: Postmodernism and the Practice of Archives," *Archivaria* 52 (Fall 2001): 30.

20. Greg Cuthbertson, "Postmodernising History and the Archives: Some Challenges for Recording the Past," *South African Archival Journal* 39 (1997): 10.

21. As can be seen in the excellent case studies by Sally F. Griffith, *Serving History in a Changing World: The Historical Society of Pennsylvania in the Twentieth Century* (Philadelphia: Historical Society of Pennsylvania, 2001), and Kevin M. Guthrie, *The New-York Historical Society: Lessons from One Nonprofit's Long Struggle for Survival* (San Francisco: Jossey-Bass, 1996). Something of the larger historical context of these institutions can be seen in such studies as David D. Van Tassel, *Recording America's Past: An Interpretation of the Development of Historical Societies in America 1607–1884* (Chicago: University of Chicago Press, 1960); George H. Callcott, *History in the United States 1800–1860: Its Practice and Purpose* (Baltimore: Johns Hopkins University Press, 1970); H. G. Jones, *For History's Sake: The Preservation and Publication of North Carolina History 1663–1903* (Chapel Hill: University of North Carolina Press, 1966); and H. G. Jones, ed., *Historical Consciousness in the Early Republic: The Origins of State Historical Societies, Museums, and Collections, 1791–1861* (Chapel Hill: North Caroliniana Society, Inc., and North Carolina Collection, 1995).

22. T. R. Schellenberg, "The Appraisal of Modern Public Records," *National Archives Bulletin* 8 (Washington, D.C.: National Archives and Records Service, 1956).

23. Cuthbertson, "Postmodernising History and the Archives," 8.

24. Linda Henry, "Schellenberg in Cyberspace," *American Archivist* 61 (Fall 1998): 309–327. Despite the sometimes vigorous defense of Schellenberg's principles, especially related to his schema for appraisal, the U.S. National Archives has consistently been criticized about many of its functions concerning appraisal responsibilities. For example, the most recent report about NARA's electronic records management focused as much on appraisal and scheduling matters as on technical ones; see General Accounting Office, *Information Management: Challenges in Managing and Preserving Electronic Records*, GAO-02-586 (Washington, D.C.: General Accounting Office, June 2002).

25. This kind of tension was first exhibited in Australia; see, for example, Adrian Cunningham, "Beyond the Pale? The 'Flinty' Relationship between Archivists Who Collect the Private Records of Individuals and the Rest of the Archival Profession," *Archives and Manuscripts* 24 (May 1996): 20–26.

26. Bret Schulte, "The ER for the Nation's History: Archivists Give Paper New Life," *Washington Post*, July 4, 2002, C4.

27. Maynard J. Brichford, *Archives & Manuscripts: Appraisal & Accessioning* (Chicago: Society of American Archivists, 1977), and F. Gerald Ham, *Selecting and Appraising Archives and Manuscripts* (Chicago: Society of American Archivists, 1992).

28. Ironically, this sense has most forcefully emerged in relationship to the control of the records of former New York City Mayor Rudolph W. Giuliani and access to the records of former Presidential administrations (the

Giuliani rationale for the administration of his records echoes the sentiments used by Franklin Delano Roosevelt in his creation of the first presidential library). For a good discussion of the Giuliani case and its
connections to the presidential records, see Celestine Bohlen, "Whose History Is It, Anyway? The Public's or the Officials'?" *New York Times*, February
24, 2002, 3. In a later editorial about the Giuliani case, the *Times* opined,
"Mr. Giuliani says he only wanted to help archivists by letting his people
do the hard work. But even with assurances that documents will not be
destroyed, questions about the credibility and completeness of his records
will always remain" ("Chasing the Giuliani Papers," *New York Times*, June
25, 2002). The case also has made more difficult the efforts by archivists, or
whoever hires and directs them, to conduct appraisal and destroy some of
these records. The explanation by Giuliani spokespeople, that they are dealing with the records in this fashion because the New York municipal
archives takes too long to process such records, is particularly ludicrous in
that Giuliani never expressed any concerns about providing better support
for the public archives when he was mayor and responsible for the archives;
see Saul S. Cohen's letter to the editor, *New York Times*, July 2, 2002.

29. A sense of the nature of the new approaches can be found in Hans
Booms, "Society and the Formation of a Documentary Heritage," *Archivaria*
24 (Summer 1987): 69–107; Catherine Bailey, "From the Top Down: The
Practice of Macro-Appraisal," *Archivaria* 43 (Spring 1997): 89–128; Richard
Brown, "Macro-Appraisal Theory and the Context of the Public Records
Creator," *Archivaria* 40 (Fall 1995): 121–172, and "Records Acquisition Strategy and Its Theoretical Foundation: The Case for a Concept of Archival Hermeneutics," *Archivaria* 33 (Winter 1991–92): 34–56; Wendy Duff,
"Harnessing the Power of Warrant," *American Archivist* 61 (Spring 1998):
88–122; and Luciana Duranti, *Diplomatics* (Metuchen, N.J.: Scarecrow Press,
1998).

30. F. Gerald Ham was the first to sound the alarm about this in "The
Archival Edge," *American Archivist* 38 (January 1975): 5–13, and he continued expressing his concerns a decade later with his "Archival Choices:
Managing the Historical Record in an Age of Abundance," *American Archivist* 47 (Winter 1984): 11–22.

31. Leonard Rapport, "No Grandfather Clause: Reappraising Accessioned Records," *American Archivist* 44 (Spring 1981): 143–150, and Karen
Benedict, "Invitation to a Bonfire: Reappraisal and Deaccessioning of
Records as Collection Management Tools in an Archives—A Reply to Leonard Rapport," *American Archivist* 47 (Winter 1984): 43–49.

32. Richard A. Cameron, Timothy Ericson, and Anne R. Kenney, "Archival Cooperation: A Critical Look at Statewide Archival Networks," *American Archivist* 46 (Fall 1983): 414–432; David J. Klaassen, "The Archival
Intersection: Cooperation between Collecting Repositories and Nonprofit

Organizations," *Midwestern Archivist* 15, no. 1 (1990): 25–38; Judith E. Endelman, "Looking Backward to Plan for the Future: Collection Analysis for Manuscript Repositories," *American Archivist* 50 (Summer 1987): 340–55; and Christine Weideman, "A New Map for Field Work: Impact of Collections Analysis on the Bentley Historical Library," *American Archivist* 54 (Winter 1991): 54–60.

33. Faye Phillips, "Developing Collecting Policies for Manuscript Collections," *American Archivist* 47 (Winter 1984): 30–42, and Timothy L. Ericson, "At the 'rim of creative dissatisfaction': Archivists and Acquisition Development," *Archivaria* 33 (Winter 1991–92): 66–77.

34. David Bearman, *Archival Methods* (Pittsburgh: Archives and Museum Informatics, 1989), revealed the problems with archivists' trying to examine all the records with their standard approaches to appraisal and other archival functions. Some archivists still insisted that these approaches worked well enough; see, for example, Max J. Evans, "The Visible Hand: Creating a Practical Mechanism for Cooperative Appraisal," *Midwestern Archivist* 11, no. 1 (1986): 7–13.

35. Luciana Duranti, "The Concept of Appraisal and Archival Theory," *American Archivist* 57 (Spring 1994): 328–344, and Frank Boles and Mark A. Greene, "Et Tu Schellenberg? Thoughts on the Dagger of American Appraisal Theory," *American Archivist* 59 (Summer 1996): 298–310, provide an example. Others are Terry Cook, " 'Another Brick in the Wall': Terry Eastwood's Masonry and Archival Walls, History and Archival Appraisal," *Archivaria* 37 (Spring 1994): 96–103, and Terry Eastwood, "Nailing a Little Jelly to the Wall of Archival Studies," *Archivaria* 35 (Spring 1993): 232–252.

36. Such as the Boles-Young study published a decade ago as *Archival Appraisal* and the Anne Gilliland-Swetland dissertation, "Development of an Expert Assistant for Archival Appraisal Of Electronic Communications: An Exploratory Study" (Ph.D. diss., University of Michigan, 1995). We can also add Wendy Duff's dissertation, summarized in her "Harnessing the Power of Warrant," *American Archivist* 61 (Spring 1998): 88–105.

37. One of the major criticisms of the archival documentation strategy seemed to be that archivists were too busy doing other things to work on what they viewed as elaborate and time-consuming appraisal processes. See the complaint by Terry Abraham, "Collection Policy or Documentation Strategy: Theory and Practice," *American Archivist* 54 (Winter 1991): 45–52; "Documentation Strategies: A Decade (or More) Later," at http://www.uidaho.edu/special-collections/docstr10.htm; and the analysis by Jennifer A. Marshall, "Documentation Strategies in the Twenty-First Century?: Rethinking Institutional Priorities and Professional Limitations," *Archival Issues* 23:1(1998): 59–74.

38. See, for example, Thomas Richards, *The Imperial Archive: Knowledge and the Fantasy of Empire* (London: Verso, 1993).

39. The Florida Division of Library and Information Services has been trying to decide whether these records should be maintained, especially after a task force established by the Florida Elections Supervision Association failed to make recommendations. State Archivist Jim Berberich led the Florida state archives in sending the following position statement to the state elections supervisor:

> In considering the ultimate disposition of the ballots and related records from the 2000 election in Florida, the Division of Library and Information Services has determined that the proper decision requires a balance between the potential historical significance of these ballots and the cost of their preservation that only the Florida legislature can strike effectively. Thus while the general records schedule GS-3 under federal law would permit the destruction of any or all of these ballots after September 2002, the Division has voluntarily extended the retention period for these ballots until July 1, 2003. This extension will permit the Florida legislature to pass the necessary legislation to effectuate its wishes regarding the preservation of these ballots beyond July 1, 2003.

A report will be sent to the state legislature by November 2002, and the legislature will make the ultimate decision. Given the high profile of this case, it seems that it represents an exciting opportunity to explain how appraisal works in a way that will get coverage. See "Preserving the Stuff of History: What about the Florida Ballots?" *NCC Washington Update*, vol. 6, no. 44, December 15, 2000; "Florida Ballot Controversy Update," *NCC Washington Update*, vol. 7, no. 19, May 11, 2001; and "Florida Ballot Controversy—Future of Ballots Still in Limbo," *NCC Washington Update*, Vol. 8, no. 26, June 27, 2002.

40. See, especially, Mark Greene, "The Surest Proof: A Utilitarian Approach to Appraisal," *Archivaria* 45 (Spring 1998): 127–169.

41. Tasslyn Frame, "'Our Nation's Attic?': Making American National Identity at the Smithsonian Institution," *Material History Review* 50 (Autumn 1999): 57–66.

42. Paul Conway showed archivists how and why to do user studies in his "Facts and Frameworks: An Approach to Studying the Users of Archives," *American Archivist* 49 (Fall 1986): 393–407.

43. Jacques Le Goff, *History and Memory*, trans. Steven Rendall and Elizabeth Claman (New York: Columbia University Press, 1992), 12.

44. Julia Martin and David Coleman, "The Archive as an Ecosystem," *Journal of Electronic Publishing* 7 (April 2002), available at http://www.press.umich.edu/jep/07-03/martin.html. Others within the archival field have commented on changing notions of what constitutes the sense of a permanent record in a similar way; see James M. O'Toole, "On the Idea of Permanence," *American Archivist* 52 (Winter 1989): 10–25.

45. Charles S. Maier, "A Surfeit of Memory? Reflections on History, Melancholy, and Denial," *History and Memory* 5, no. 2 (1993): 147.

46. For public memory, see Michael H. Frisch, "The Memory of History," *Radical History Review* 25 (1981): 9–23.

47. Richard J. Cox and David Wallace, eds., *Archives and the Public Good: Accountability and Records in Modern Society* (Westport, Conn.: Greenwood Press, 2002), and Sue McKemmish and Frank Upward, eds., *Archival Documents: Providing Accountability through Recordkeeping* (Melbourne, Australia: Ancora Press, 1993) are good places to start.

48. Ginger Thompson, "Files Bare Dark Secrets of Mexico's Dirty War," *New York Times* July 6, 2002, A3.

49. See my recent books, *Closing an Era: Historical Perspectives on Modern Archives and Records Management* (Westport, Conn.: Greenwood Press, 2000) and *Managing Records as Evidence and Information* (Westport, Conn.: Quorum Books, 2001).

50. More traditional fields, such as the classics, have suffered from the eroding of higher education and misguided academic discourse; see Victor Davis Hanson and John Heath, *Who Killed Homer? The Demise of Classical Education and the Recovery of Greek Wisdom* (New York: Free Press, 1998).

51. Mark A. Greene and Todd J. Daniels-Howell, "Documentation with an Attitude: A Pragmatist's Guide to the Selection and Acquisition of Modern Business Records," in *The Records of American Business*, ed. James M. O'Toole (Chicago: Society of American Archivists, 1997), 161–229, pulls together and critiques a number of existing appraisal methods in order to develop a more systematic approach for documenting American business.

Index

About the Author

Richard J. Cox is Professor in Library and Information Science in the School of Information Sciences at the University of Pittsburgh, and is responsible for the archives concentration in the Master's in Library Science degree and the Ph.D. degree. Dr. Cox served as editor of the *American Archivist* from 1991 through 1995, and he is presently editor of the *Records and Information Management Report* as well as serving as the Society of American Archivists Publications Editor. He has written extensively on archival and records management topics and has published eight books in this area: *American Archival Analysis: The Recent Development of the Archival Profession in the United States* (1990), winner of the Waldo Gifford Leland Award given by the Society of American Archivists; *Managing Institutional Archives: Foundational Principles and Practices* (1992); *The First Generation of Electronic Records Archivists in the United States: A Study in Professionalization* (1994); *Documenting Localities* (1996); *Closing an Era: Historical Perspectives on Modern Archives and Records Management* (2000); *Managing Records as Evidence and Information* (2001), winner of the Waldo Gifford Leland Award in 2002; coeditor, *Archives and the Public Good: Records and Accountability in Modern Society* (2002); and *Vandals in the Stacks? A Response to Nicholson Baker's Assault on Libraries* (2002). He is currently working on additional books on the concept of information documents, the impact of electrostatic copying on the modern office, and principled records management (addressing ethical and legal issues).